CUBA

*in the 21st Century:
Realities and Perspectives*

CUBA

in the 21st Century:
Realities and Perspectives

Coordinators:
José Bell Lara
Richard A. Dello Buono

Traduction:
Richard A. Dello Buono

EDITORIAL JOSÉ MARTÍ

Edition: Mayda Argüelles Mauri and Josefina Ezpeleta Laplace
Design: Enrique Mayol Amador
Desktop publishing: Liuba Paramónova

ISBN 959-09-0298-7

INSTITUTO CUBANO DEL LIBRO
Editorial JOSÉ MARTÍ
Publicaciones en Lenguas Extranjeras
Calzada No. 259 entre J e I, Vedado,
Ciudad de La Habana, Cuba
e-mail:editjosemarti@ceniai.inf.cu

Dedicated to the memory of Marina Majoli.
A woman radiant with humanity
and solidarity...
a consummate revolutionary.

CONTENTS

INTRODUCTION

The final decade of the 20th century first began to unfold in a manner that seemed destined to put an end to Cuba's revolutionary aspirations. As the new century arrived, however, the Cuban Revolution remained firmly intact. Today, Cuban Socialism continues to present a reality that must be reckoned with.

The debacle of Eastern Socialism and the disappearance of the Soviet Union signified for Cuba the termination of a comprehensive system of trade relations associated with the former Socialist Bloc (CMEA). This effectively cut Cuba off from the economic system which had long the island a rather favorable insertion in the international sphere of commerce. This previous system of commercial integration contained a mechanism by which Cuba enjoyed preferential prices for sugar, the principal export of the island, alongside of ample access to credits and development financing. It was this kind of integration that had nurtured the creation of mutually compatible production plans as well as a whole set of commitments that had permitted Cuba to plan its economic development with a high level of security. When all of these highly structured relations later evaporated, they did so in a very rapid period of time and without any form of compensation whatsoever.

Such were the circumstances in which Cuba found itself in the 1990s. It was a time in which the U.S. blockade became tightened under the optimistic premise that the moment had finally arrived for a complete economic asphyxiation of the Cuban Revolution. A variety of errors and accumulated shortcomings within the Cuban development model itself, tendencies which had been in place up through the end of the 1980s, all served to further exacerbated the crisis of Cuban development experienced in the 1990s.

In this context, the end of the Cold War signified for Cuba a frigid peace, one far colder than for any other country in the world. The Gross Domestic Product fell by one-third during the first half of the 1990s, both per capita and in absolute terms, while industrial production declined by four-fifths and foreign trade by 75%. While such figures clearly reflect an economic crisis of immense proportions, they fail to adequately express the total magnitude of a downturn that most closely resembled the effects of a cataclysmic natural catastrophe or the aftermath of a devastating war. The Cubans baptized the economic emergency with the name "Special Period in Time of Peace," six words that added up to the biggest crisis experienced in the entire history of the Revolution.

Despite the enormity of the crisis, it ultimately did *not* translate into a social collapse as many had predicted. On the contrary, it was squarely confronted by the Cuban people. In a relatively short period of time, the process of economic recovery had begun alongside of a new reinsertion of the economy into the global market. This reintegration into the international sphere was definitely carried out under complex and frequently difficult circumstances. Most notably, the socialist system was maintained throughout this recovery process, providing the means both for sustaining the nation and the social gains won by the Revolution. To the amazement of many, all of the predictions and proclamations concerning the impending end of the Cuban experiment fell one by one by the wayside.

How was all of this possible given the extraordinary impact of the economic crisis?

What factors can explain how Cuba managed to avoid falling into a generalized social collapse?

How could Cuba overcome the economic crisis and maintain its commitment to the socialist project?

What kinds of factors can explain why the majority of the Cuban population continues to defend Socialism as their life option?

The answers to these and similar questions need to be placed in the context of what the historical as well as present-day conditions of the Revolution meant for the Cuban people. Without pretending to exhaust this topic, we can just begin to mention here a few elements that can help us shed some light on some of the questions cited above.

It was a little over a century ago that the Republic of Cuba was proclaimed on May 20, 1902 following four years of U.S. military occupation. The Cuban Republic was finally a reality and yet its constitution contained an appendix consisting of an amendment passed by the U.S. Congress and signed by President McKinley in March of 1901. This article attached to the Cuban Constitution, the so-called Platt Amendment, was imposed upon the island under U.S. military occupation as a pre-condition for its independence, this in the aftermath of the U.S. intervention in Cuba's war for independence. It specifically conveyed to the United States the right to intervene in Cuban affairs at any time it deemed necessary to safeguard its interests in the region.

The United States became transformed by virtue of the Platt Amendment into the grand overseer of Cuban affairs. Indeed, the U.S. Ambassador to Cuba was *de facto* the second most important political figure of the country and at times was even more important than the Cuban president as various ex-ambassadors of that period delighted to point out. Although the Platt Amendment was formally abolished in 1934, the structural situation remained essentially the same throughout the rest of the pre-Revolution period. All of this provoked a tremendous sense of frustration in popular sentiments throughout the island, fueling a protracted struggle to complete the yet unrealized project of genuine independence.

Up until January 1st of 1959, Cuba had experienced the 20th century under the yoke of U.S. interests whose widespread presence in the political and economic spheres was always decisive in Cuban affairs. The revolutionary victory headed by Fidel Castro put an end to this foreign domination, initiating a process of social and economic transformation which exhibited a strong sense of social justice, all under heavy U.S. opposition. Cuba had finally asserted its real sovereignty and the people began to recognize themselves as free and independent actors for the first time in the island's history.

Following passage of the Agrarian Reform Law of 1959, a myopic Eisenhower administration gave the green light to various actions designed to overthrow the Cuban Revolution. This attempt at destabilization culminated with Operation Pluto where the organization, logistical preparation and training of a mercenary brigade was carried out, spearheading a mission to establish a beachhead on the island that could subsequently facilitate an all out U.S. intervention. As it is well known, the operation was defeated in less than seventy-two hours at the Bay of Pigs. Since then, ten different U.S. presidents have systematically pursued policies aimed at destroying the Cuban Revolution. In this, virtually no instrument of intervention has been left untried and among them all, the U.S. economic blockade over the island has constituted the most visible component.

Beginning with the Moncada Program of the pre-victory 1950s, the Cuban Revolution clearly represented a radical project of reforms with a popular and anti-imperialist orientation. Given the geopolitical conditions of the era, Cuba's early revolutionary years experienced a relentless and threat-ridden opposition on the part of U.S. imperialism. The implementation of a revolutionary program in this context was not a passive process but rather a tenacious process of struggle, taking on all aspects of social life. Success depended upon building the broadest possible base of participation on the part of the Cuban people at every step along the way. Notable examples include the Agrarian Reform and the transformation of Cuba's large landed estates into state farms; the introduction of massive educational programs, beginning with the Literacy Campaign; the creation of people's militias in which hundreds of thousands of Cubans voluntarily participated in the nation's defense; the nationalization of the U.S. monopolies as well as of the largest national companies while simultaneously training thousands of administrators to maintain their productive operations; and last but not least, the creation of popular mass organizations such as the Committees for the Defense of the Revolution.

Throughout the process, there was the ever-present ultimatum: waiver and return to a neocolonial status—or continue on the path of revolutionary transformation and guarantee the defense of the national social project. In the latter option that always proved to be the popular favorite, Socialism provided both the means for preserving the new reality created by the Revolution and the blueprint for making future advances.

From that point forward, Socialism became identified in Cuba with a profound transformation of the country in all societal spheres. In the economic order, Cuba notably expanded its industrial capacity, developed technologically innovative branches such as in biotechnology and the pharmaceutical industry, and went about accumulating a tremendous productive base and unprecedented level of human capital. The economic transformations which were eventually achieved resulted from a constant process of sustained investment.

Between 1959 and 1989, national investment amounted to 63,250 millions of pesos (during which time the peso was equal to the U.S. dollar), thus creating more than a thousand new industries. The average rate of economic growth reached 4.3% across this extended period, representing an average per capita growth of 2.8%, while the nation's capacity to produce steel grew by 14 times over, cement by 6 times, nickel by 4 times, fertilizers by 10 times, refined petroleum by 4 times and textiles by 7 times.

At the culmination of this period, the principal quality of life indicators for the Cuban people showed levels similar to those of the world's most advanced societies. Life expectancy, infant mortality, percentage of health-personnel assisted births, the number of physicians per inhabitant, mortality indicators, and the rates of illiteracy and schooling were all comparable to those of the developed world.

In summary, it is not possible to understand either the Cuba that confronted its greatest crisis in the 1990s or the Cuba of today without first understanding that there is a legacy of the Revolution that permeates all spheres of social and economic life. That legacy is identified with Socialism, not just a promising rhetoric but rather a whole set of social and economic achievements that were in turn only made possible through high levels of popular participation.

In essence, the defense of the social achievements made earlier by the Revolution provided the basis for resistance and struggle all across the island. But if this past legacy provides the reason why there was no crisis in the Cuban socialist paradigm, the way in which Cuba confronted the crisis can provide the explanation of why the majority of Cuban people today continue to adhere to the model. Since the larger share of the burden was assumed by the Cuban state, applying a compensatory social policy that effectively neutralized the most negative effects of the Special Period, the crisis did not result in the closing of a single school or a single hospital. Free education and health care remained in full force while the food shortages and effects of paralyzed factories and social services were mitigated by the compensatory social policies designed to provide a minimally acceptable nutritional level for the entire population. Similar policies of social security offered formulas so as to defend the income of those workers most affected by stalled or greatly reduced production.

There is no denying that Cuba is a country which continues to face numerous economic difficulties. It nevertheless remains a society in which access to basic social services is guaranteed, a society free of discrimination where people are not abandoned to hunger or to beg, or to find refuge in the scourges of drug abuse, gambling and child labor. This is not just a material fact but also a moral fact. It can be seen in the values of the Revolution as most fully expressed in a society characterized by solidarity, one where the moral per capita is not measured by consumer goods but rather by human dignity. In the final analysis, the Revolution with all of its peculiarities and errors have given the average Cuban a fuller and more secure life than that which was possible in the pre-Revolution era. For this reason, the impressive social accumulation that has resulted provides an explanation of the persistence of Cuban Socialism.

Nor would it be possible to ignore the role played by Fidel Castro. Ernesto "Che" Guevara once qualified Fidel as a guiding force and summarized the fundamental elements of the important role his leadership has played:

> . . . his ability to assimilate knowledge and experience in order to understand a situation in its entirety without losing sight of the details, his unbounded faith in the future, and the breadth of his vision to foresee events and anticipate them in action, always seeing farther and more accurately than his *compañeros*. With these great cardinal qualities, his capacity to unite, resisting the divisions that weaken; his ability to lead the whole people in action; his infinite love for the people; his faith in the future and with his capacity to foresee it, Fidel Castro has done more than anyone else in Cuba to create from nothing the present formidable apparatus of the Cuban Revolution.*

*. Ernesto Che Guevara, "Cuba: Historical Exception or Vanguard in the Anticolonial Struggle?," in *Che Guevara Reader*, ed. David Deutschmann, 2nd expanded ed. (Melbourne, New York: Ocean Press, 2003), 131.

The only thing we can add to Che's estimation is that in the extraordinary circumstances of the final years of the 20th century, only a leader like Fidel Castro could have so successfully led the struggle of the Cuban people in preserving its social project. An extraordinary creativity in political leadership, at once audacious yet cautious not to lose touch with reality, was necessary for the defense of the historical gains of the Revolution, the search for a short term reinsertion into the international economic order, and for implementing political and economic changes adequate for maintaining an internal consensus. The favorable results could be observed in the strong and stable state that welcomed in the 21st century, one backed by organized participation and a popular hegemonic consensus that permits Cuba to defend its sovereignty, national security, and the economic interests of a people imbued with great expectations for the future.

The works that make up this book set out to analyze the principal elements of a complex process and the resulting dynamics that condition present-day Cuba. Some of these academic contributions consider the most important measures taken during the 1990s while others focus more upon present realities and the strains involved with coming to grips with the complex and multi-dimensional reality of Cuba in the 21st century. We have followed up the collection with a brief analysis at the end that extends some of the essential elements put forth by the contributors insofar as they shed light upon Cuba's present realities and future prospects. If this book in its totality contributes to a better understanding of the complex processes currently unfolding in Cuba, we will have accomplished our primary objective.

JOSÉ BELL LARA
RICHARD A. DELLO BUONO

Cuba: Underdevelopment, Socialism and Strategies of Development

DELIA LUISA LÓPEZ GARCÍA

DELIA LUISA LÓPEZ GARCÍA

Ph.D. in Economic Sciences. A specialist in the study of social class dynamics and economic strategies throughout the Latin American continent. She is a senior researcher in the FLACSO-Cuba Program and coordinator of the Cathedra Ernesto Che Guevara.

Background

The state of the Cuban economy following the revolutionary triumph of January 1959 could be defined in just a couple of words: *an economy in crisis*. Its monocrop and monoexport character reflected a historical pattern of massive sugar production, comprising close to 80% of exports and 30% - 40% of the national rent. Moreover, the island's foreign trade was dominated by the United States. Around 75% of Cuba's total imports came from the United States while 66% of Cuban exports were destined for the U.S. market. The penetration of U.S. capital in the principle sectors of the Cuban economy was very profound. The United States was in possession of 50% of sugar production, enormous agricultural estates and cattle ranches, mining operations, the country's largest industrial factories and the public services of electricity and telephone communications. It is estimated that leading up to 1958, U.S. investments in Cuba hovered at around U.S.$ 1.001 billion.

Despite constituting the foundation of national wealth, the sugar sector was in stagnation since 1925 as a result of various structural obstacles, notably including: a system of land tenure consisting of large estates; preferential trade treaties with the United States in effect since 1903, assigning U.S. products a minimum 20% tariff advantage; and in short, the total dependency of the Cuban economy upon the United States, enforced by U.S. imperialism since the beginning of the 20th century. Together, these factors ensured the perpetuation of social and political control that tied the ruling class to a solidly established regime of subordination to the United States. The estate owners, the sugar bourgeoisie, and the commercial bourgeoisie that controlled sugar imports together constituted the most retrograde social forces of the country. They maintained a tightly interwoven relationship with those sectors of U.S. finance capital invested in Cuba.

The combined rate of unemployment and underemployment was high, with an annual average of around 738,000 Cubans out of 2,204,000, hovering around one-third of the total workforce. The minimum wage was at 75 pesos for the years 1956-57, but more than half of the employed workforce earned less than that amount. The distribution of income was highly unequal as can be seen in the figures for 1953 where the poorest 40% of the population received 6.5% of the national income while the 10% richest sector received 38.8% of income.[1]

In 1953, almost a quarter of the island's inhabitants were illiterate. During that same year, only 45.2% of the primary school age population was attending school and the rates of attendance for middle and high school were at 8.7% and 4% respectively.[2] The segment of the population over 15 years of age had an average educational level of below the third grade.

The public health care system was mostly concentrated in the nation's capital and in the main cities of the island: 65% of all physicians resided and 62% of hospital bed capacity was located in Havana (where only 22% of the Cuban population lived back in the 1950s).[3]

The total number of physicians amounted to 6250 which together with 250 oral health physicians, 394 nurses and 478 medical technicians, comprised the principle human resources of Cuban health services in 1958.[4] There existed 98 public hospitals (only one of them in a rural area) and the state public health budget amounted to 18 million pesos for the fiscal year 1956-57, that is to say, 5.3% of total state expenditures.[5] At the national level, there was 1 physician for every 1067 inhabitants, although in rural areas, the figure was 1 physician for every 2378 people while in urban areas, the ration was 1 physician for every 361 inhabitants.[6]

These conditions constituted the causal factors for the typical sort of health indicators of underdevelopment that Cuba exhibited during that era:[7]

Life expectancy from birth	62 years (in 1950)
Rate of infant mortality	40 per 1000 live births (in 1958)
Maternal mortality	118.2 per 10,000 live births (in 1960)

To the above must be added the state of moral decomposition, political and administrative corruption, and the existence of anti-democratic governments that practiced a systematic violation of the most elemental rights and liberties of the people. Indeed, there was a near total absence of national sovereignty and self-determination. Given that situation, the war of liberation not only signified the struggle against tyranny but also that "the people became educated in the process to remain forever vigilant against any return to that ignominious past."[8]

The First Decade of the Cuban Revolution: 1959-70

The triumph of January 1st of 1959 initiated a period of profound social upheaval for Cuban society. The revolutionary vanguard managed to bring about the complete collapse of the neocolonial bourgeois state and a definitive dissolution of the repressive professional apparatus utilized by the ruling class for maintaining their control over the island in the service of U.S. imperialism. The substitution of the old army by the Rebel Army constituted the initial guarantee of national sovereignty won through struggle and permitted the consolidation of subsequent revolutionary achievements.[9]

The dismantling of the prior existing judicial establishment, infamous for being one of the most corrupt in Latin America, was accomplished with the immediate creation of Revolutionary Tribunals for trial and sentencing of war criminals. At the same time, the Revolutionary Government promulgated various laws to benefit the popular sectors with the overall objective of redistributing national income. These enacted measures included the following:

- An increase in the minimum wage of the lowest income earning sectors (of particular importance for the sugar sector).
- The reinstatement of work for all those workers who had lost their jobs for political or trade union-related disputes.
- The reduction of rents by 50% (which would now amount to up to 15% of the family budget in families earning between 1000-3000 pesos per year).
- Electricity rates were lowered by 30%.
- The price of medicines was reduced by 15%-20%.
- The price of home cooking gas was lowered from between 11% and 15%.

In May of 1959, the Agrarian Reform Law was enacted. This constituted the first and most important measure aimed at fundamentally transforming the country's economic structure. Its immediate application, both in the letter and spirit of the law, was aimed at the expropriation of the largest estate holders, national and foreign, and yielded a distribution of land to over 100,000 campesinos across the island. This resulted in a simultaneous restructuring of the nation's largest agricultural and livestock operations.

As soon as this process of transformation got underway, imperialism and the ruling oligarchy reacted with a campaign of aggression, beginning with political pressures via diplomatic notes from Washington and quickly escalating up to and including the economic and political blockade, followed soon after by military aggression. A treacherous campaign of propaganda was unleashed both inside and outside the country with the aim of discrediting the Revolutionary Government and of weakening popular support for the Revolution. The mass response to the threats could be seen in the immediate formation of the National Revolutionary Militias, made up of workers, campesinos, students, and the larger population in general. This was followed with the creation of the Committees for the Defense of the Revolution (CDRs) in 1960. With this,

21

the basic task of defending the revolutionary process became converted into the responsibility of every Cuban amidst an upsurge in mass revolutionary consciousness.

During its first year and a half, the Revolution fulfilled the fundamental economic and social demands that had been proclaimed in the Moncada economic program. The idea of putting the country on the path of economic development was articulated by the revolutionary leadership from the very beginning. The programmatic content of *History Will Absolve Me*[10] had keenly established that the final objective of the struggle went far beyond the mere overthrow of the tyrannical dictatorship. In order to achieve those revolutionary aims, five new laws were proclaimed that together moved to "immediately undertake the country's industrialization, mobilizing all the inactive capital—currently estimated at some 1.5 billion pesos. . . ."[11]

During the course of 1959 and part of 1960, a considerable lack of definition existed with respect to solving the nation's pressing problems. This was due to the scant possibility that existed for elaborating long term projects and designing coherent strategies of economic development amidst an acute internal class struggle and intensifying external pressures. The possibility of utilizing private national capital in the service of encouraging growth in specific sectors of the Cuban economy was fully explored during this period as the Cuban state meanwhile sought to control the key sectors of the economy in the form of state property. To support this arrangement, the Central Planning Board (JUCEPLAN) was created in March of 1960 with the mandate of promoting an integration of private capital and state productive activities in the service of economic development, something which at that time was considered synonymous with industrialization.

Over the course of those first two years, historic highs were reached in terms of consumption within the popular sectors. This was essentially due to the redistributory measures applied by the Revolutionary Government, aimed towards increasing the income of the majority of the population and the gradual elimination of unemployment. In that favorable context, the policy of industrial growth was promoted with the participation of private capital. The slogan "Consume Cuban Products!" embodied the demands of the traditional, non-sugar national industrialists.[12]

This notwithstanding, the accelerated social transformation that revolutionary Cuban society was experiencing in its race towards total decolonization displayed a markedly anti-imperialist character from the onset. Without this clarity, the most elemental tasks of social transformation would have been im-

22

possible to consolidate. The class fraction composed of small- and medium-sized non-sugar, industrial producers, a minority group within the Cuban ruling class, proved unable to fully embrace the range of opportunity that the Revolutionary Government offered it. Their own distorted genesis and feeble process of growth had led the country's economy into stagnation, particularly in the absence of protection on the part of heavily intervened governments. All of this revealed a fundamental incapacity to incorporate themselves into the new conditions of the country's economic development. Instead, they opted for the counterrevolutionary path charted by the oligarchy in alliance with imperialism, thus condemning them to disappear as a social fraction just a short time later.

Towards the first half of the 1960s, the Cuban bourgeoisie defected en masse from the revolutionary process. Their desertion was manifested in multiple forms and with an essential content, namely, to cause maximum destruction to the national economy. In this regard, they acted in concert with imperialism in an attempt to provoke the economic collapse of the country.

On January 26, 1960, a year which became dubbed nationwide as one of definitive advance for the Revolution, Commander Ernesto "Che" Guevara affirmed:

> And there remains as one final point in this outline of our history of economic development for this year, an issue somewhat distant from the central theme that concerns us. The problem of foreign economic aggression that you all know quite well for being in close contact with all of the banks and all of the foreign commercial agents that operate in and outside of the country. You all know by now that credits are being restricted and that the conditions are being prepared for trying to produce an economic crisis in the country, both by sabotaging production as well as by sabotaging the raw materials that come in from abroad, some so important as petroleum, as well as credits.[13]

In effect, the social process that led to the nationalization of the basic means of production was being circumscribed in the violent context of class struggle and the harassment and aggression waged by the enemy both within and outside the country.

The Revolutionary Government, in trying to alleviate the tense crisis regarding the balance of payments, set about acquiring a 300 thousand ton purchase of oil from what was then the Soviet Union, this as a logical counterpart to the recent Russian purchase of Cuban sugar. The oil refineries, still the property of U.S. monopolies, refused to process Soviet crude while at the same time driving down their petroleum reserves in a move clearly designed to paralyze the overall economy. The rapid response of the Revolutionary Government proved decisive as the state directly intervened by nationalizing the refineries. This marked the beginning of a tit for tat process of blow and counter blow as the conflict between imperialism and the Cuban Revolution quickly evolved.

It cannot be affirmed, lest we fall into a grievous misinterpretation of the revolutionary process and of the ideology that led it to triumph, that the revolutionary advances of 1960 were merely the result of the countermeasures of the Cuban state in response to imperialist aggression. The most fundamental question was whether the Revolution, once having fulfilled the strategic economic goals put forth in the Moncada economic program, should aspire to a more profound process of social transformation. Indeed, if this much higher and more difficult objective was even possible to put forth by a small and backward country just ninety miles off the coast of the most powerful imperialist nation on Earth. The dilemma was resolved in the affirmative by the revolutionary vanguard[14] that culminated its resolve during the August-October period of 1960 with the nationalization of the island's largest companies, both Cuban and foreign, thereby leaving the basic means of production in the hands of the Cuban people.

During this red hot moment of internal class struggle amidst an intensifying imperialist harassment, it was essential to initiate a reorganization of the state apparatus so as to ensure an adequate administration of the recently nationalized companies. In February of 1961, JUCEPLAN was restructured so as to render it capable of taking on the tasks of planning the Cuban economy, the majority of which now rested in the hands of the state. The organic laws for both the National Bank of Cuba and the Ministry of Foreign Trade were promulgated, providing them with the faculties for exercising their functions within a socialist organization of the economy. Distinct sectors of the economy were then grouped together, unified as productive enterprises, and placed under the management of various, newly-created ministries.

To preside over all of these changes, an economic strategy was essential. The conception that predominated at that time was one oriented towards eradicating the historical difficulties of an underdeveloped country, namely, the elimination of a monocrop economy through the diversification of agricultural production and the development of national industry. For that to be carried out, it was deemed necessary to place the management of the economy under the mechanism of an overarching plan of development. The plan of the national economy based on the sketched strategy began to be written, immersed in a process of general reorientation of the foreign trade towards the socialist countries.

As the enormous accumulation of difficulties in carrying out that process became increasingly evident, it was necessary to take additional and serious steps towards the aim of putting the country's industrialization on a more solid footing. On February 23, 1961, Che Guevara was appointed Minister of Industries, heading up an agency that was created to implement all such necessary steps. From that point forward, with the department level experience of industrialization gained through his work with the INRA (National Institute of Agrarian Reform), Che was fully positioned to put forward his conceptions concerning the direction of the Cuban economic process, notably, in the accelerated transformation of our underdeveloped economy towards a definitively socialist destiny.

It would be useful to remember that at that moment in history, the accumulating difficulties confronted by the Revolution in its first three years of existence were in no small measure due to external factors. In the first place, the economic and political blockade enacted by the United States and followed by a large part of its Atlantic allies, just like the armed activities of the counterrevolution, all necessitated that significant budgetary allotments had to be made towards the defense of the country. There was a massive mobilization of individuals that normally occupied positions in the productive apparatus. Moreover, the reorientation of foreign trade almost in its entirety towards the former Socialist Bloc had generated tremendous objective difficulties. The long distances by then involved with trade urgently required the enlargement of the storage infrastructure. The technological base of production was then significantly different, making it nearly impossible to substitute spare parts in the national industrial apparatus previously based upon U.S. designs.

On the other hand, the economic strategy upon which the plan for the Cuban economy rested on since 1961, considered that sugar production should not be maintained as the country's principal means of earning wealth. Anything short of this would have amounted to reproducing the problems of Cuba's neocolonial past. But while the industrial sector had become positioned in a more central role, it had not yet managed to compensate for the declining production within the sugar sector, thus provoking a serious deficit in the balance of trade. The inability of the industrial sector to reach their anticipated productive levels called into serious question the overall strategy of development that was being applied. Fidel Castro put it this way:

> There was a time when we didn't know well what we were going to do with agriculture, when we were being influenced from among other things by a series of ideas from the past related to sugar cane, the lack of markets, and the suppression of the sugar quotas. All of this kept us disoriented for some

time, until we discovered the possibilities that the Socialist Bloc could offer our products as a market. . . . But all of us are now absolutely convinced and we know very well that in agriculture rests the base of our development and that we have very fine conditions for the development of that agriculture.[15]

During 1963, important decisions were taken in the economic order, among others, to modify the direction in which it was best thought necessary for moving forward. A new economic strategy was being elaborated, based upon the development of the agricultural sector, and with sugar as the lynchpin of that development. That converted industrialization into a "support lever" for this effort. A second Agrarian Reform Law was promulgated in that same year, depriving the largest members of the rural bourgeoisie of their social and political influence, and setting the limit of 67 hectares of land as the maximum size that could now be privately owned. In this manner, 70% of the country's land was then placed in the hands of the state while the remainder belonged to small- and medium-sized producers.

To the extent that Cuba was changing profoundly and in an accelerating manner, it also became crucial to carry out a transformation of the population's mindset. This was particularly essential in view of the ideological lag that existed on account of what was inherited from the previous regime. To achieve this in short order, the society as a whole had to be transformed into a gigantic school. As Che put it:

In our case direct education acquires a much greater importance. The explanation is convincing because it is true; no subterfuge is needed. It is carried on by the state's educational apparatus as a function of general, technical and ideological education through such agencies as the Ministry of Education and the party's informational apparatus.[16]

During this first decade of the Revolution, significant educational advances were accomplished in terms of universalizing the principle of work and study. With this, the practice of one of the most notable ideas of Marx concerning the creation of integral individuals was established, consistent with the profoundly wise postulate developed by José Martí about the way in which future generations of Cubans should be educated.[17] Prior to this point, illiteracy had been eliminated by 1961 through a mass campaign, adult education programs had been initiated, and the formation of Worker and Campesino Schools had been accomplished, already making it possible for working people to gain access to the universities. Also accomplished in 1961 was the nationalization of teaching that made possible the declaration of the principle of universal free education for all Cubans. Gradually, the design of the national educational system was taking shape, continually refining its objectives and its curricula in accordance with the developing character of the new society.

During the very first minutes of power, the Revolution had also adopted measures to eradicate unemployment. It extended agricultural activities, undertook widespread construction projects, and intensified industrial production. This resulted in tens of thousands of people becoming incorporated into the activities of education, public health, and other social services.

During the first decade of the Revolution, nearly a million people were incorporated into the nation's workforce (a 58.5% growth). Breaking this down by gender, male employment grew by 23% while females grew by 40%. The annual mean rate of employment growth was 3.6%, while the population was growing at 2.1%.[18] Full employment was soon reached for males. Low salaries became the object of gradual reform beginning even earlier when, in 1959, the daily wage for sugar cane cutters was increased. At the same time, the state guaranteed year around employment for 73,000 workers who had previously suffered from chronic seasonal unemployment that revolved around the sugar harvest cycle. Up until 1970, the mean salary for such workers was 130 pesos.

The important results of this decade can be observed in the following:

Table 1

Growth of the Cuban Economy Annual Mean Rate of Growth (at constant prices) (%)	
Indicators	1960-70
Global Social Product*	2.8
Global Social Product per capita	0.8
Gross Material Product**	3.6
Gross Material Product per capita	1.6

*. Gross Social Product is the sum of material goods produced in a society during a specific period.

**. Gross Material Product is equivalent to the gross production of the agricultural and livestock sector, the fishing and mining industries, manufacturing, construction andelectric energy production.

SOURCE: José Luis Rodríguez and George Carriazo, *La erradicación de la pobreza en Cuba* [The Eradication of Poverty in Cuba], 49.

These advances that began during the breaking up of the backward, unjust, and dependent social order which existed previously, were achieved in the midst of systematic aggression and a total economic blockade imposed by imperialism. They were carried out in a significant context of creative effervescence, of theory and practice, and of ideology and political struggle.

Within the thought and practice on how to achieve Socialism and Communism, there existed two theoretical positions which when simplified could be defined as follows: one position considered that revolution and socialist transition were the results of a rupture within the correspondence between the existing productive forces and the social relations of production. The other considered that revolution is a historical movement that can advance in accordance with the conscious and organized revolutionary action of people, circumscribed within the limits of the objectively possible.

In reality, both positions are not so far apart from each other and their counterposition is something which can be mostly explained by the history of Marxist thought and practice. Putting it more precisely, social determinism does not fail to recognize the active and conscious role of people in the course of revolution nor does the position that privileges revolutionary action reject the existence of objective conditions as factors influencing social change. The issue amounts to a question regarding *which theoretical—and consequently, political and ideological position—best contributes to the making of revolution, the latter understood as the capture of political power with the aim of transforming reality into something which is in its essence contrary to capitalism.*[19] Marxist thought within the Cuban Revolution recognizes that in the era of the socialist transition, there exists a dialectic of both factors in which the dominant pole has to be the subjective one.[20] In other words, Cuban revolutionaries believed that Socialism and Communism did not arise spontaneously.

It is worthwhile to point out that during the decade of the 1960s, what came our way from the former Soviet Union was a Marxist literature made up of various manuals of Philosophy and Political Economy. Their ostensibly didactic contents contributed to the impoverishment of authentic Marxist thinking and ultimately promoted a dogmatic understanding of revolutionary practice.[21] In short, the Soviet manuals tended to encourage a justification of Socialism rather than teaching the techniques of objective analysis. They affirmed, to the point of elevating to the status of scientific truth, the notion that the experience of achieving Socialism in the former Soviet Union was coincident with the science of socialist transition per se. In that context, the model of economic and social management (economic cost accounting or financial self-management dynamics) that

28

was generalized from the former Soviet Union's particular experience posed as the only possible one.

Early on in the process, Fidel Castro and Che Guevara among others in the Cuban revolutionary leadership had questioned those ideas associated with the search for greater efficiency in Socialism by means of the utilization of individual material incentives. That is to say, they questioned the belief that socialist economic progress can only be achieved when economic relations achieve a certain grade of autonomy that guarantee its own smooth functioning by the use of regulations, controls and incentives.[22]

In the thought of Che Guevara, one essential idea continually resurfaced. Namely, that from the first day of the construction of Socialism, work has to proceed in the direction of the practical realization of the communist project. As Che stated:

> . . . we are, relatively speaking, very young in the communist revolution that is already our goal. . . . We are fully immersed in a period of transition, an era of construction prior to reaching Socialism and moving from there on to the construction of Communism. But we have already set our objective as the communist society. In this, the new society . . . is already in our view, absolutely new, without classes, and consequently without class dictatorship."[23]

For Che Guevara, as for Fidel Castro, the strategic objective of the model for leadership in the socialist transition should simultaneously anticipate the socialist-communist advance. As an essential part of this conception, Che affirmed that the economic structures of Socialism should propose to gradually eliminate self-interested, individualism within human conduct. In other words, the generalization of a new consciousness is the result of the gradual process of transforming social structures and the correct selection of motivational incentives behind human action. "To build Communism it is necessary, simultaneous with the new material foundations, to build the new man."[24] He also assures: "The pipe dream that Socialism can be achieved with the help of the dull instruments left to us by capitalism (the commodity as the economic cell, profitability, individual material interest as a lever, etc.) can lead into a blind alley."[25]

At the very onset of the revolutionary socialist process, Che Guevara had arrived to various theoretical conclusions about which system of management would be ideal in Cuba for accelerating the transition to Socialism and Communism. By 1962, at the Bimonthly Meeting of the Management Council of the

Ministry of Industries, he affirmed: "We continue in the polemic concerning the financial cost-accounting system verses the budgetary system . . . personally, I am each day more convinced that the budgetary system is an extraordinary step forward."[26] The basic principles that sustained this model can be appreciated in the following which Che offered as a response to a journalist's question:

> Economic socialism without communist morality doesn't interest me. We are struggling against misery, but at the same time, we are struggling against alienation. One of the fundamental objectives of Marxism is to make selfishness and individual self-interest disappear from the field of psychological motivations.

> Marx was as concerned with economic acts as he was with how they became transformed in their mind. He called this a "conscious act." If Communism fails to pay attention to conscious acts, it can become a method of distribution but will remain far from constituting a revolutionary morality.[27]

In 1963-64, a constant economic debate took place that was carried out by various foreign and Cuban economists (including Che Guevara). In the course of this debate, Che formulated his conception about the construction of Socialism that subsequently came to constitute an enduring contribution to the contemporary theory of socialist transition and the means of practicing it. The content of the debate revolved around the possible ways of building Socialism, the possible and necessary ways of structuring the system of social decision-making and the concrete forms of economic management, i.e., the feasibility of utilizing economic cost-accounting or the centralized, budgetary finance system.

During those years in Cuba, two systems coexisted in the national economy. In the agricultural and livestock sectors, the cost-accounting system was utilized while the industrial sector experimented with the budgetary system. Nevertheless, throughout the decade of the 1960s, neither one nor the other system was completely decided upon.

In the central report to the first congress of the Communist Party of Cuba, Fidel Castro referred to the debate, displaying an exceptional sense of self-critique in announcing the decision taken to create a new procedure. The new system would annul the monetary-market relations between the enterprises of the state sector, expand the policy of gratuities, encourage more voluntary work, do away with the payment of overtime, and suppress the monetary interest that had been placed upon campesinos as well as the taxes that had been levied upon the general population, along with various other measures.[28]

In 1968, the "Revolutionary Offensive" took place which included the nationalization of the small businesses owned by the urban petty bourgeoisie. In the last three years of the 1960s, there was a growing conviction that Socialism and Communism were only possible if the values and principles that rule bourgeois society could be negated and transcended at the ideological level. In other words, the socialist revolution had to be lived as a new form of life that is materially and spiritually different from the preceding one. Only in the new reality created on a day-to-day basis with all of its limitations, deficiencies, and risks, can the glimmer of the future society be glimpsed.

As part of the economic strategy elaborated after 1963, a program of large investments was conceived of with the aim of rapidly modernizing the Cuban sugar industry. It was foreseen that by 1970, the country would be in conditions to produce ten million tons of sugar, a goal that would be sufficient for generating the financial resources necessary for the implementation of the revolutionary economic project. But despite the enormous efforts carried out with the aim of reaching this achievement, the goal of a ten million ton sugar harvest was ultimately not realized. What instead followed was the beginning of a complex and very difficult period internally for the country. Intense criticisms surfaced concerning the methods and procedures utilized for managing the economy between 1967 and 1970, means that now became qualified as "idealistic."

Many analyses were carried out with the aim of initiating a social reordering that took as its point of departure, the criterion of the "proven non-viability" of the preceding model. It was of course impossible to deny that previous socialist projects had confronted numerous difficulties in the course of their enactment. The fact that the socialist revolutions constituted "revolutionary islands" immersed in an ocean of a world capitalist system became recognized as a major obstacle for all of them. This does not remain confined only to the persistence of market relations within the interior of each society nor to the enormous material and ideological power of money, even under circumstances of enclosure and liquidation provided by the driving force of revolution, but also and above all, to those market relations at the international level that firmly establish the commercial and financial patterns that favor the polarized reproduction of the global system.

Neocolonialism had historically imprinted development with its real, structural relations of subordination and its resulting creation of underdevelopment. The insufficient level of technical development and insufficient productive capacity at the social level that typify the underdeveloped countries constitute a constant limitation on the accelerated advance of the process of its social transformation.[29] This situation is made even more difficult by imperialist aggression that was consistently utilized in a clever variety of forms to torpedo, destabilize and overthrow unfolding revolutionary processes throughout the Third World.

By the end of the 1970s, it had become evident that another factor no less decisive than those just mentioned was becoming critical in determining the future of the Cuban socialist project, namely, that "the hoped-for liberation of other Latin American countries had not occurred, thwarting the possibility of a regional integration of revolutionary countries that was indispensable for the process."[30]

It was in this complex national and international context that a new era began in the Cuban Revolution, a period that for our purposes can be dated from 1971 and extending forward until 1986.

The Cuban Revolution in the 1971-86 Period

Between 1971 and 1974, a variety of actions for reordering Cuban society were decided upon, concretized and gradually implemented. Many of these actions were based upon a new model of socialist management composed of experiences obtained by their application by the former Soviet Union and Eastern European socialist countries. The nation was also marked by the adoption of a new political-administrative map. A new system of participatory government was organized and established across the entire national territory, known as People's Power. This was based upon experiences that had already been accumulated by the Revolution and by considerations regarding the need to institutionalize them. A unified system of tribunals was established that consolidated changes begun in 1963 with the Popular Tribunals. In 1975, the Family Code was promulgated that defined the equality of rights and duties between marital partners as well as the rights of children.

In 1976, after having been debated all across the nation and approved by an ample majority in a referendum, the new socialist Constitution of Cuba was promulgated. By October of that year, the regular holding of elections for the organs of People's Power was carried out with the participation of 95% of the eligible citizens of voting age (16 years and older). It was during that period that the respective functions of the state and the Communist Party were further delimited as were those of the mass organizations and the nationwide confederation of labor unions. In December 1975, the first Congress of the Communist Party of Cuba was convened.

At the first party congress, among other measures approved was the System of Management and Planning of the Economy and the Directives for Social and Economic Development for the 1976-1980 five-year period. This defined the accelerated industrialization of the country as the central task while sugar production and the diversification of agricultural and livestock production were identified as the sources of its financing. In 1972, Cuba entered into the CMEA (Council of Mutual Economic Assistance), the commercial trade pact of the former Socialist Bloc. This confirmed that two ideas had been placed into practice: first, that economic integration into the former Soviet Union and Eastern European countries was being pursued because it had not been possible to do something similar in the region of Latin America. Second, that Cuba was an underdeveloped country, a sugar producer and that its objective was to cease being so in the shortest time possible.

In effect, it was during all of these years that an intense investment effort was made to broaden the industrial base and develop the metal and heavy industrial branches of the economy (something that was practically non-existent prior to the Revolution), the industries of construction materials, textiles, and part of the chemical and pharmaceutical industries as well as workshops for reconstruction and repair of agricultural and other types of equipment. With the entry into operation of new cement factories, the construction sector became transformed into one of the most dynamic branches of the economy. Between 1971 and 1983, the average rates of growth of the previous period were substantially surpassed as can be seen in the following comparative chart:

Table 2

Dynamics of the Growth of the Cuban Economy Annual Mean Rate of Growth (at constant prices) (%)			
Indicators	1960-70	1971-80	1981-83
Global Social Product	2.8	5.7	7.3
Global Social Product per capita	0.8	4.5	6.3
Gross Material Product	3.6	5.2	6.7
Gross Material Product per capita	1.6	4.0	5.7

SOURCE: José Luis Rodríguez and George Carriazo, op. cit., 49.

Data concerning the dynamics of gross investment during the period considered shows investments of 17,870.4 millions of pesos during 1981-85, with a growth in work productivity at an annual average rate of 5.2%.[31] If the existing data from previous periods are analyzed, it can be observed that the figure for cumulative gross investment during 1959-85 rose to 47,524.3 millions of pesos and the average rate of work productivity stabilized at an annual 2.9% rate for that period.

During the 1980s, Cuba further advanced in its industrialization process. The capital goods industries grew as did the production of machinery in general, including that which was used in producing plant and equipment for biotechnology, pharmaceutical and chemical industries, foodstuffs industry and construction materials. High quality equipment used for construction was produced with a national integration of between 50% and 80%, including concrete mixers, levelers, vibrating cylinders, compacting cylinders, freight elevators, semi-tows, front end loaders and others. By the end of the decade, the production of bulldozers had leveled off in what was the most complex industrial project that had been undertaken to date.

The automobile industry managed to produce a modular-type diesel motor upon which the development of bus and truck production could be based. The production of gear boxes was initiated and a major goal was set to achieve a national integration of between 70% and 80% in the production of buses and other goods.

Likewise produced during those years were automatic furnaces that utilized the importation of non-automatic furnaces for the purpose of converting them to digital control. Also produced were drills, saws, presses, metal cutters, seeder ploughs, accessories and cutting utensils for using throughout the country.

The medical equipment industry has produced a wide range of items for hospitals and laboratories. In addition, this industry has assembled some medical and non-medical equipment in cooperation with various countries including Colombia and Argentina. Industrial and commercial refrigeration equipment has been produced as well as items for acclimatization, kitchen items, domestic refrigerators, and small boilers for hospitals and hotels. Another industrial complex has produced a wide variety of railway equipment minus the locomotives. Agricultural machinery factories have developed ploughs, harrows, diverse types of irrigation systems, tows, and fumigators. Especially important was the production of sugar cane cutters that served to elevate the productivity of the sugar harvest while improving the conditions of work in carrying out this extremely arduous agricultural labor. Also produced was cane processing equipment, lamination equipment, quarry equipment, reducers, centrifuges, compressors, turbines, and small depth pumps. As a collaborative effort of various national enterprises, the elements were put into place that will eventually lead to the first Cuban cement factory.

The electronics industry was born in 1960 with the assembly operation of radios and in 1970, the first Cuban mini-computer had been constructed known as the CID-201. By the end of the 1970s, however, its development had stagnated. Subsequently, the production of a broad line of domestic consumer goods, including television, radios, communication equipment, and calculators, was implemented.

By the beginning of the 1980s, the biotechnology industry took its first steps forward and since then has obtained international recognition for its state of the art production.[32]

Undoubtedly, "the technological capacity of Cuba has begun to achieve obvious benefits . . . the domestic production of innovations in medicine and biotechnology, world leader in sugar industry technology, the new methods of electronic production and the growth in various non-traditional exports are linked to the development of the capital goods sector. . . . The key to Cuba's success in the capital goods industry rested in the early emphasis the country placed on general and technical education, and in the creation of research and development institutes. Cuba was graduating in its universities 40% more students than Czechoslovakia and 31% more than the German Democratic Republic."[33]

There is no question that in the area of education, Cuba obtained significant achievements during the period under consideration. By around 1985, 97.3% of primary school age children were going to school while 84.4% of adolescents between 12 and 16 years of age were attending secondary school and 11.1% of young people were entering into higher education.[34]

At the onset of the 1980s, the educational pyramid had evolved as follows:

Table 3

Educational Pyramid (%)		
Grade level	1958	1980
Primary	88.7	54
Secondary	11.0	40
Higher Education	0.3	6

SOURCE: "Presentación del informe del Ministro de Educación a la Asamblea Nacional" [Presentation of the Report of the Ministry of Education to the National Assembly], *Granma* daily, June 26, 1981.

The rate of illiteracy over the decade of the 1980s was at 1.9% for the population between 15 and 49 years of age. The average grade level of schooling was 6.4 years as compared to 1953 when it was scarcely 2 years.[35]

With respect to health, the unquestionable progress made by 1989 could be seen in the average Cuban life expectancy that reached 74.2 years (61.8 years for 1955-60), the infant mortality rate at 11.1 per thousand live births (60.0 in 1958), the rate of maternal mortality at 29.2 per thousand live births (118.2 in 1960), and the availability of 302 physicians per inhabitant (1067 in 1958). Practically 100% of births were being performed in healthcare institutions. Only 7.3% of live births in 1989 displayed characteristics of low birth weight and child malnutrition had been practically eliminated.[36]

Errors and Negative Tendencies (1986-91)

. . . we had ideas, indications, that some things seemed a little strange; but we did not immediately become aware of the problems that were developing.

The figures were there, the data were there, and it seemed that there were a variety of difficulties pertaining to the introduction of new methods, of new mechanisms, but that in one way or another, these problems were definitely going to be overcome. What reality began to demonstrate was that these problems were not in fact on the path to solution, but rather heading towards further aggravation, and that it was not just a question of simple errors but instead problems of a conceptual kind, and that there were also problems of an ideological sort wrapped up in all of this, some reactionary beliefs.[37]

To begin to comprehend the errors and negative tendencies that took root in Cuban society as a consequence of the application in 1976 of the System of Economic Management and Planning (SDPE), we must take into account some prior considerations. In the first place, exactly what was the SDPE? This referred to the total collection of principles, subsystems, methods and procedures that were initiated in order to carry out the organization, planning, management and control over Cuban economic activities.[38]

The SDPE was designed to function by means of economic calculation and financial cost accounting. The style of economic calculation employed considered that the functioning of the socialist economy takes place by means of monetary-commodity relations that were based on the law of value. In both economic categories, it was recognized that their character had an objective existence in a society engaged in a socialist transition although it was insisted that they presented a "new content."[39]

The following general criteria characterize the principles, methods and procedures that were used by the SDPE in order to direct the economic processes of Cuban society:[40]

- Direct material incentives to workers according to the Marxist formula of socialist distribution: from each according to his/her ability, to each according to his/her work.
- The increase of material incentives to workers as collectively organized in the enterprise based on the efficiency that they achieve in their economic management.
- The measurement of enterprise efficiency based on the performance of a group of indicators that integrally reflect the enterprise's functioning.
- The formation of economic incentive funds based on the profits obtained by the enterprise, after its basic responsibilities to the national budget were met, and all payments of bank credits were satisfied, etc.

The explicit objectives to be satisfied as defined by the SDPE included the following in order of their importance: the conjugation of the general social interest with those of the particular interests of institutions, enterprises, provinces, municipalities and individual workers, performed in a manner such that the mechanisms applied could contribute to slowing and eliminating tendencies towards sectorialism, regionalism and individualism. Likewise essential was the conjugation of centralized decision making with the principle of the maximum level possible of workers' participation. The establishment of mechanisms for work discipline was seen as indispensable for increasing productivity and the quality of production of goods and services. Above all was the notion of achieving an adequate correlation between material and moral incentives so that both could contribute to improving the efficiency of the economy and serve as instruments for the development of socialist and communist morality.[41]

Among other aspects, the SDPE defined the socialist enterprise as the central link of the national economy, with its own juridical personality, capable of covering its costs with its income, doing so while leaving behind a margin of profit for the economic incentive funds.[42] Also contained in the Resolution concerning the SDPE was the principle that enterprises could form associations with other enterprises if they considered that a greater economic rationality could be achieved.[43] For its implementation and development, the SDPE required the creation of certain prerequisites which were seen as indispensable such as the reestablishment of the relations of costs and payments in the state sector, the elaboration of a methodology for planning at various levels, the formation of economic statistics and accounting, the creation of national and local budgetary systems, the creation of systems of wholesale and retail prices as well as the restructuring of the banking system in accordance to the important new functions that the SDPE assigned to finances.

A price reform was put into practice in 1981 that modified wholesale prices within the stock of agricultural products, construction goods and the technical services used in production.

The organization of work based upon technical training requisites constituted the point of departure for a new salary regime that became envisioned. In 1980, a general salary reform was put into effect that modified the salary scale and levels that had characterized Cuban industry since 1963. The 1980 reform introduced changes with respect to the prior system in that its intention was to increase the monetary income of workers within certain occupational groups.[44] In this way, not only were salary scales adjusted according to the specified labor norms[45] but the pay for individual workers was also adjusted for abnormal conditions of work as well as for the surpassing of established performance quotas. The payment of bonuses was authorized in accordance with individual increases in work productivity as well as for increases in the overall profitability of the enterprise. Those bonuses would together form supplementary sources for increases in salary. All of this meant that the relationship between work and salary would generally depend upon the satisfaction of established norms and the possibilities of salary increases would be associated with efforts made by workers to exceed those expectations.

So what happened in Cuba once the SDPE was implemented? Without intending to establish any order of priority, the following items address some of the errors and negative tendencies that eventually became seen as decidedly negative in their consequences.

First, there was a generalization of an "enterprise spirit." This can be defined as a strengthening of the particular interests of a workers collective of an enterprise and of the individual self-interest of the worker, making it nearly impossible to accord sufficient importance to the general social interest (despite the fact that the SDPE has proposed an adequate reconciliation of these interests).[46] This "enterprise spirit" as it was first called by Che Guevara refers to the development of a selfish spirit in work that tends to isolate the worker from his or her general social surroundings, i.e., a society undergoing a transformation towards Communism. It promotes the proliferation of a socially harmful sectorialism and individualism. Che insisted on warning about this negative tendency and sanctioning it. As Minister of Industries, he had created an educa-

38

tional sanction for administrators who violated socialist and communist norms of conduct, consisting of their transfer to Guanahacabibes, an inhospitable zone in the western portion of the country so as to carry out agricultural activities for a certain length of time.[47]

With the SDPE, the negative aspects of the "enterprise spirit" managed to become extended throughout all of the various branches of the economy. Sectorialism at that level contributed to obstructing an adequate distribution of the country's financial resources according to the lines of development prioritized by the state, something that constituted one of the negative tendencies that was most rapidly detected.[48]

In reality, there were innumerable examples of how the economic mechanisms applied via the SDPE entered into conflict with the general interests of society and most have been criticized by Fidel Castro in practically all of his speeches since 1986 to the present.

Another of the most serious errors was to have maintained at a very elementary level the country's existing labor norms, because it was upon those norms that all of the scaffolding associated with the salary reform and the SDPE's material incentives was constructed. The State Committee of Work and Social Security recognized in 1984 that "at the national level, 77% of all the existing norms are elemental in nature, with 23% semi-technical, and those norms that are technically argued are practically zero, which means that there are essentially no technically argued norms in the country."[49]

Salary levels in the productive sphere, in reality, mostly in the industrial sector, became associated with the completion of the norms of production. Despite the recognized proliferation of elemental norms, a conception of wages was applied in which compliance with productivity norms was remunerated but also when they were surpassed. In that situation, there were norms that became surpassed two, three and up to four times the original target. This also signified a kind of braking effect upon the introduction of technological innovations since that would have implied a modification of existing norms. A factory with easy targets was well-situated to elevate the amount of over-compliance on the part of worker collectives. Many workers began to earn very high salaries without the corresponding productivity.[50]

The principle of socialist distribution—of each according to their capacity and to each according to their work—became distorted to such an extent that work became associated with the easy acquisition of wages, and that in turn resulted in a regrettable process of corruption among workers.[51] Salary is the individualized form of material interest, whose genesis forms a constitutive part of the history of the capitalist regime. In the new social conditions created by the socialist revolution, should salary have the same connotation that it had during the previous regime?

In our judgment, the wage-labor relation in Socialism becomes the object of an urgent process of transformation, without which it is impossible to reproduce life itself. Work has to become transformed into a *social duty*, i.e., the comprehension of the essential importance of each person's work in making their contribution to the cause of production within a society that seeks to shorten the historical periods of development. In this, the economic order constitutes the enabling factor that propels the revolutionary socialist project forward.

In the first years of the Revolution, the fulfillment of production targets signified the completion of a social duty for every societal member. If the target was exceeded, there existed a greater benefit for society, with the worker deserving a material compensation. Yet, this was not understood as a payment in function of the percentage of the over-compliance with a given target. Why?

Because to the extent that the very transformation of society permits a progressive improvement in the historical standards of living of the population, workers progressively receive more of what they were contributing to society. The priority attention given by the socialist state to the educational system, to health care, to developing the spiritual conditions of people, to sports and recreation, and to the security and tranquility of everyday life, all constitutes a superior form of distribution according to work that came closer to the system of distribution (according to needs) of a communist society.[52]

Elsewhere, the conceptions established for evaluating efficiency and enterprise profitability also had negative consequences. Efficiency and profitability were "achieved" by the enterprises when they increased their bottom-line surplus. For the SDPE, this reflected an increase of the volume of production in excess of its costs. By prioritizing enterprise surplus as a fundamental indicator for efficiency and viability, the results led to non-compliance with the plans of production (in absolute terms and in variety), developing instead into a tendency to produce only those products whose prices were more lucrative. In this manner, the increased production of exchange value was being sought rather than that of use-values, thereby increasing enterprise profits at the expense of the overall society.

This extremely serious deformation had catastrophic consequences, especially in the sector of construction. It became known that more value was created during the movement of land and the construction of structures, and so, these works were initiated but often not finished. Many projects became paralyzed even while the plans of production were nonetheless being fulfilled in terms of calculated values.

The rush to achieve growth in surplus so as to increase viability and to obtain access to the economic incentive funds eventually led state enterprises to charge exorbitant prices for carrying out specific services.[53]

The self-contained justification for the extent to which monetary-market mechanisms were being utilized in economic management, in creating work incentives towards the end of socialist transition where workers' interest in increasing their productivity and economic efficiency would systematically increase over time, in time all resulted in a complete fraud. The consequence of privileging individual interest as well as collective material interest in the most narrow and sectorial sense was to effectively diminish the real advances in revolutionary ways of thinking and behaving that Cubans had achieved during the early years of the Revolution.

In essence, it amounted to a situation where economic calculation made monetary material interest predominant because it was considered as a motivation per se. Even though the Resolution that established the SDPE recognized the need for an adequate correlation to exist between material and moral incentives, in reality, it had unleashed an unbalanced shift towards reliance upon individual material self-interest. As a consequence, the conviction that monetary and market mechanisms were the optimal way of smoothly regulating social relations became rapidly generalized. This served to dangerously elevate the prestige of money on the ideological and organizational levels.[54]

From the beginning of the 1960s, Che Guevara had already anticipated this:

In our view, direct material incentives and consciousness are contradictory terms.

. . . For the advocates of financial self-management, direct material incentives extending into the future and accompanying society in all of the various stages of building Communism are not counterposed to the "development" of consciousness. For us they are. It is for this reason that we struggle against the predominance of material incentives, for it would signify delaying the development of socialist morality.

If material incentives are counterposed to the development of consciousness, but are a great lever for increasing production, does this mean that giving priority to the development of consciousness retards production?[55]

41

Nevertheless, Che knew that material interest still maintained a mobilizing capacity among workers as a habit inherited from the old society. For that reason, it was a problem that needed to be treated intelligently (or "correctly" as he would have said). For that reason, he proposed that we take best advantage of the possibilities that the new relations of production brought along with them, i.e., "the interrelationship between education and the development of production." As he put it:

> . . . although in a general historical sense, consciousness is a product of the relations of production, we must still take into account the characteristics of the current epoch, whose principal contradiction (on a world scale) is the contradiction between imperialism and socialism. Socialist ideas have touched the consciousness of all the world's peoples. That is why the development of consciousness can advance ahead of the particular state of the productive forces in any given country.[56]

The economic model of the socialist transition should propose *the gradual extinction* of the conditions that permit the existence and proliferation of bourgeois economic categories and its ideological and political reflections in peoples' consciousness. The socialist transition is not a mode of production that should somehow be consolidated before the construction of Communism begins. Rather, it is during the socialist transition that *society should be radically transformed in a communist sense*. The communist project does not emerge *by itself* as an extension of the dynamism and development of the economy.[57]

Che would say that the new society in formation has to strongly compete with the past given the manner in which the residual effects of an education that previously isolated the individual still weighs upon people just as does the persistence of market relations.[58]

The entire foundation of the subsystem of enterprise management and the subsystem of incentives of the SDPE was based upon beliefs of a neo-capitalist type, far from the most genuine and creative ideology that was forged out of the Cuban Revolution. The educational and mobilizing value of the conception of work as a social duty was gradually being lost in this context, being substituted by money as a fundamental mechanism for providing work incentives.

The conception of work as a social duty is consequently transformative of the larger social reality. The social context is revolutionized by people and people are revolutionized by the social context. The machine provides the trench where this duty is fulfilled (the most important duty after that of defending the Revolution itself). The consideration of work as only the means of satisfying "animal" needs tends to drift further and further way from human perception.[59]

42

Without doubt, the SDPE degraded the relationship between people and work by furthering the growing monetarization of motivations and the labor interests of workers. As if it meant little, it also placed the practice of voluntary work within the context of monetary-market relations. Thus, it established the notion that enterprises would pay a corresponding retribution for voluntary work to the mass organizations or state entities that had mobilized such efforts, so that such funds would be transferred to their budgeted activities. But the realization of voluntary work, although compensated, did not fit well into the criteria of the SDPE. The SDPE's logic considered the mechanisms of material interest as the determinant factor in the short term for increases in productive efficiency at the social level. It understood that voluntary labor would be rendered unnecessary in the course of its development. Such criteria are certainly distant from the Marxist appreciation of the correspondence between the modification of circumstances and human activity.[60]

Voluntary work has occupied a principal place in the ideology of the Cuban Revolution. It represents the germination of a new communist attitude towards work that implies that part of a worker's spare time can be dedicated to production without any additional economic remuneration. In a progressive manner, voluntary work contributes to the eradication of the alienation of work in the minds of people. People begin to little by little see themselves expressed in their work, seeing it as a projection of themselves and a contribution to the life that they share in common.[61]

Alienation did not have time to be fully uprooted from Cuban society and the frustrations associated with a retreat in this process are associated with the SDPE. Beyond all of those elements already discussed, this is also true because the SDPE exercised a notable influence upon the concept of planning and organization as a "top-down movement of directives, figures and papers."[62] This bureaucratic-technocratic approach to planning contributed to reducing workers' participation in the production process and increasingly led to a distancing between production and its results.

The production assemblies that were created in the era of Che remained in existence during the entire period that the SDPE was operative. Nevertheless, these meetings that were originally convened for analysis and discussion became instead converted into a formalistic exercise. Bureaucratism in economic management obstructed the recognition of errors, insufficiencies and deficiencies, and aggressiveness towards poorly done work gradually lost ground, silencing criticism in the process, and eradicating the basis for genuine self-criticism. A conformist attitude (something strange in the Cuban idiosyncratic discourse) became extended in all directions.

Little by little, the values that had become developed through the exercise of revolutionary power and assimilated by working people were in the process of being lost. These were values and ethical principles associated with socialist consciousness that in the thought of Fidel Castro and Che Guevara are indispensable in the process of modeling new patterns of human conduct. The gradual displacement of these values and principles in the ways that Cuban think and behave was giving way to motivations that were strictly market-based and individualistic in nature. Gaining force was an undesirable conception concerning the basic objective of revolutionary transformation, one relegating the human being to a second place status. Forgotten was the notion that the new society has its own transformation as its core just ninety miles from the shores of the United States.

To understand this problem, it should not only be analyzed at the theoretical level even though that is extraordinarily important in its own right, but above all on the political and ideological levels. One would have to wonder if Cuba could compete at the level of material wealth with U.S. imperialism, something that would seem "objectively" impossible. At the meeting of delegates of the Third Congress of the Association of Latin American and Caribbean Economists, Fidel Castro referred to this issue:

Are we going to compete with the United States either in material goods or material incentives? . . . Is it only upon material incentives that we could build Socialism in this country? . . . I think that we have to use both kinds of incentives in order to apply the socialist formula . . . but it has to be seen where the secret is in efficiency. It is a totality of technical and economic factors, but also moral factors, political factors and factors of consciousness. . . ."[63]

Another far reaching error of this period was the alteration of the traditional prioritization of investments in the social sphere, as it was considered that Cuba had achieved an adequate level of development in that regard. Unsatisfied social needs, especially in the city of Havana, were accumulating in the daycare centers, in housing, in special schools for physically and mentally handicapped, in hospitals and in the polyclinics.

In production, the country's hydraulic program fell to extremely low levels, something that plays a fundamental role in the search for higher yields in sugar and other agricultural harvests. The plans of agrarian development began to become paralyzed to the point that the production of foodstuffs for the internal market became relegated to a lesser priority.

From 1990 forward, the tremendous limitations of the Cuban insertion into the international division of labor (CMEA) promoted by the former-socialist countries had become dramatically evident. In reality, this had not only deepened the traditional productive scheme of specialization in just a few products: sugar, citric fruits, nickel, but also maintained the singular market focus of the country's exports, now towards CMEA and principally, the former Soviet Union. This type of insertion deprived Cuba of its productive diversification such as the creation of an iron and steel industry for which it possesses one of the principle reserves in the world of iron as well as nickel and cobalt reserves. These resources would have guaranteed the possibility of producing the country's own means of production. Instead, the assimilation of generally second class, Soviet technology left the Cuban industrial sector dependent upon imported raw materials and resulted in highly inefficient patterns of industrial energy consumption. In spite of having been a pioneering force in research concerning the derivatives of sugar cane and the wide range of byproducts out of the sugar industry, the production of these goods remained sparse and has only recently existed in the aftermath of the CMEA period. The economic model that had been implemented was based upon an extensive approach that promoted low yields and a marked tendency towards the shrinking productivity of labor.[64]

At the same time, it was during the period from between 1971 and 1986 that Cuban society was influenced, in greater or lesser part, by the post-revolutionary ideology that prevailed during that time in the former Soviet Union. This had repercussions in numerous and dangerous ways for our transition to Socialism, despite the fact that it coexisted alongside of many real material advances, an international policy of solidarity that was extremely important, and had occurred during a time in which impressive achievements were being made in the areas of public health and education.

A process of political critique and rectification, based on national ideological roots and native revolutionary conceptions managed to detain in a timely manner the over-assimilation of that previous model of Socialism. Under the direction of Fidel Castro, the process of *rectification of errors and negative tendencies* constituted a broad political movement that shook up the entirety of Cuban society, de-legitimating the main ideological bases of the so-called "real socialism" of the former Soviet type, and proposing a continuation of the project of national liberation that could place the Cuban revolutionary process solidly back on track.

45

The Economic Crisis (1991-)

A powerful mobilization of the political power of capital that unfolded beginning in the 1980s managed in relatively short order to bring about fundamental changes in the international order. The reactionary wave of Perestroika led to the end of Socialism in the former Soviet Union and the countries of Eastern Europe.

In that context, a profound economic crisis was unleashed upon Cuba, leading its GDP to contract around 35% in 1993, especially since the new political elites of Eastern Europe and Russia decided to break the prior existing trade accords based upon fixed prices and external credits over a pre-established plan for the medium and long term.

For the second time in a period of thirty years, Cuba abruptly lost its preferential markets. This time, the United States sought to exploit the situation to the maximum extent possible by tightening the economic blockade. In 1992, the Torricelli Act was put into effect followed in 1996 by the Helms-Burton Act. Together, they formed the juridical interventionist framework for a heightened blockade. Fidel Castro argued that this amounted to a double blockade, one on the part of the United States that represented a virtual economic war against Cuba, and the other on the part of the regimes now in power in the former socialist countries.

In that context, an economic adjustment became indispensable to the country's survival. Between 1994 and 1995, the Cuban population debated various survival measures in the Workers Parliaments that were formed to contemplate the alternatives. There, they decide upon the means by which a new strategy of development could be initiated under conditions of the country's reinsertion into the international market.[65] These new circumstances have given rise in Cuba to considerable reflections about the objective possibilities for an underdeveloped country to break its relations of subordination within the international capitalist system. In this process, as in everything, practice has shown that the accumulated advances in mass education and the advances made in cultural, technical and scientific capacity still offer Cuba this possibility. This remains so only as a direct consequence of its sovereignty and its existence as an independent nation and people.

Notes

1. Andrew Zimbalist and Claes Brundenius, *The Cuban Economy,* chapter X, tables 10.2 and 10.6 (The full facts of publication of all the sources are found in the Bibliography at the end of the essay. *Ed.)*

2. Carlos del Toro "Algunos aspectos económicos del movimiento obrero cubano (1933-1958)" [Some Economic Aspects of Cuban Workers Movement (1933-58)], in: *La república neocolonial* [The Neocolonial Republic], vol. 1, 224 and 233.

3. José Luis Rodríguez and George Carriazo, *La erradicación de la pobreza en Cuba* [The Eradication of Poverty in Cuba], 26.

4. Instituto de Desarrollo de la Salud, 1982.

5. José Luis Rodríguez and George Carriazo, op. cit., 25-26.

6. Ibid.

7. Ibid.

8. Fernando Martínez, *Desafíos del socialismo cubano* [Challenges of Cuban Socialism], 85.

9. *Plataforma Programática del Partido Comunista de Cuba* [Programmatic Platform of the Communist Party of Cuba], 40.

10. The self-defense argument by Fidel Castro on October 16, 1953, in the trial for the attacks of the Moncada and Carlos Manuel de Céspedes garrisons in Santiago de Cuba and Bayamo, respectively, that same year on July 26. *Ed.*

11. Fidel Castro, *History Will Absolve Me*, 67.

12. In declarations expressed in the daily *Revolución* in November of 1959, Che Guevara stated on the occasion of assuming the position of President of the National Bank of Cuba: ". . . the government will follow the same policy already taken in this sense, trying to orient private investment towards industrialization and looking for the jeans to gain their collaboration but without utilizing compulsory methods." In Ernesto Guevara, "Al tomar posesión en el Banco Nacional de Cuba. Noviembre 27, 1959" [On Taking up at the National Bank of Cuba. November 27, 1959] in *Discursos* [Speeches], vol. 2 of *El Che en la Revolución Cubana* [Che in the Cuban Revolution], 124.

13. Ernesto Guevara, "Ciclo de conferencias del Banco Nacional de Cuba. Enero 1960" [Lectures at the National Bank of Cuba], in *Discursos* [Speeches], vol. 2 of *El Che en la Revolución Cubana* [Che in the Cuban Revolution], 154.

14. "Naturally, the conditions for the definitive liberation of our country in the national and social terrain were established by the new correlation of forces in the world scenario, but in that period, more than cold calculation of all the possibilities prevailed a spirited mood among the people and a decision on the part of their

leaders to be free at any price. . . ." In *Informe Central al I Congreso del Partido Comunista de Cuba* [Central Report to the 1st Congress of the Communist Party of Cuba] (1975 ed.), 35.

15. Fidel Castro, "Dos discursos de Fidel Castro" [Two Speeches by Fidel Castro], in *Obra Revolucionaria* journal, no. 21, August 12, 1963): 21.

16. Ernesto Che Guevara, "Socialism and Man in Cuba," in *Che Guevara and the Cuban Revolution. Writings and Speeches of Ernesto Che Guevara*, p. 250. (This article was written in the form of a letter to Carlos Quijano, editor of *Marcha*, a weekly published in Montevideo, Uruguay. *Ed.)*

17. *Informe Central al I Congreso del Partido Comunista de Cuba* [Central Report to the 1st Congress of the Communist Party of Cuba] (1982 ed.), 123.

18. Ibid., 146-147.

19. ". . . we have found that the process of historical development of societies under certain conditions can be abbreviated and that the vanguard party is one of the fundamental arms for making this happen," written on March 24, 1963 by Ernesto Che Guevara, "Sobre la construcción del Partido" [About the Construction of the Party], in *Obras escogidas, 1957-1967* [Selected Works. 1957-67], vol. 2, 193. Also, "Socialist ideas have touched the consciousness of all the world's peoples. That is why the development of consciousness can advance ahead of the particular state of the productive forces in any given country," written in February, 1964 by Ernesto Che Guevara, "Planning and Consciousness in the Transition to Socialism ('On the Budgetary Finance System')," in *Che Guevara and the Cuban Revolution*, op. cit., 214.

20. The basic concepts concerning these aspects have been rigorously developed by Fernando Martínez in his essay—Extraordinary Casa de las Américas Award—, *Che, el socialismo y el comunismo* [Che, Socialism and Communism], 57-69.

21. In our judgment, the Cuban Revolution began as an armed insurrection against that theory and by taking its own paths "encountered" the theoretical presuppositions and the essential truths of Marxism. On July 26, Che who was in Bolivia among guerrilla forces, entered into his diary: "July 26, a rebellion against oligarchies and against revolutionary dogmas." *(The Bolivian Diary of Ernesto Che Guevara, 239. Ed.)*

22. "The new society in formation has to compete fiercely with the past. This past makes itself felt not only in the individual consciousness—in which the residue of an education systematically oriented toward isolating the individual still weighs heavily—but also through the very character of this transition period in which

commodity relations still persist." Ernesto Che Guevara, "Socialism and Man in Cuba," in *Che Guevara and the Cuban Revolution*, op. cit., 249-250.

23. Ernesto Che Guevara, "En la entrega de certificados de trabajo comunista" [Giving the Certificates for Communist Work], a speech at the Revolutionary Cuban Workers Union, on January 11, 1964, in *Obras escogidas, 1957-1967*, op. cit., vol. 2, 245.

24. Ernesto Che Guevara, "Socialism and Man in Cuba," in *Che Guevara and the Cuban Revolution*, op. cit., 250.

25. Ibid.

26. Ernesto Che Guevara, «Reuniones bimestrales» in Ministerio de Industrias [Ministry of Industries], 1962, vol. 6 of *El Che en la Revolución Cubana*, op. cit. At the beginning of the 1960s, Che had gradually consolidated his budgetary finance system which was applied in the industrial sector of the Cuban economy as supervised by the Ministry of Industries. The system incorporated centralized planning, the most advanced techniques left behind by the monopolies, techniques of computation, programming and control, using budgetary means to achieve this planning, alongside an excellent method of economic control and a salary system that was coherently articulated with a system of incentives and emulation, whose objectives were to stimulate work through the ways and means that would best strengthen the development of socialist morality and revolutionary consciousness.

27. Ernesto Che Guevara, "Entrevista concedida a Jean Daniel en Argelia. Julio 25, 1963" [Interview Given to Jean Daniel in Algeria. July 25, 1963], in *Discursos* [Speeches], vol. 4 of *El Che en la Revolución Cubana*, op. cit., 469-470. It was entitled "La profecía del Che" [Che's Prophesy] and published for the first time in *L'Express*, July 25, 1963.

28. *Informe Central al I Congreso del Partido Comunista de Cuba* (1982 ed.), 106-107.

29. As Che would put it: "A complete education for social labor has not yet taken place in these [underdeveloped] countries, and wealth is far from being within the reach of the masses through the simple process of appropriation," in Ernesto Che Guevara, "Socialism and Man in Cuba," in *Che Guevara and the Cuban Revolution*, op. cit., 250.

30. Fernando Martínez, *El socialismo en Cuba: desafíos y perspectivas* [Socialism in Cuba: Challenges and Perspectives], 4-8.

31. *Informe Central al I Congreso del Partido Comunista de Cuba* (1982 ed.), 3.

32. The summary of advances in industrial production has been taken from: Miguel Figueras, "Análisis de las políticas de industrialización en el período revolucionario y proyecciones futuras" [Analysis of Industrialization Policies in the Revolutionary Period and Future Projections].

33. Andrew Zimbalist, "Does the Economy Work?," in *NACLA Report on the Americas: Cuba Facing Change*, vol. 24, no. 2, 17.

34. José Luis Rodríguez, *Crítica a nuestros críticos* [Criticism to Our Critics].

35. Ibid.

36. Data taken from diverse sources: State Committee of Statistics of Cuba, *Anuario Estadístico de Cuba, 1988* [Statistical Yearly of Cuba: 1988], 99, 174 and 175; Ministry of Public Health, *Anuario estadístico, 1999* [Statistical Yearly: 1999], 21, 57, 96 and 110.

37. Fidel Castro, during the 53rd Meeting of the Nacional Council of the Cuban Workers Union, in *Por el camino correcto. Compilación de textos (1986-1989)* [Along the Right Way. Compilation of Texts (1986-89)], 96.

38. *Tesis y Resoluciones del Primer Congreso del PCC* [Thesis and Resolutions from the First Congress of the PCC], 189-205.

39. Ibid., 191. The resolution from the Party Congress likewise points out that economic cost-accounting is consistent with the wider experience accumulated by the socialist countries over the course of various decades. On this, I would like to interject the following personal opinion: the critical political economy set forth by Marx has as its specific objective the study of the capitalist mode of production. In the course of his explanation, he elaborated a specific conceptual framework based in a method. From there, the categories and the reality that these concepts explain are understood as relations of a different nature, i.e., the process of knowledge and the historical process. The theory of value explains the operation of the capitalist mode of production, i.e., a society in which the production of commodities rules, with the means of production in the form of private property, and where the class who does not own the means of production is forced to sell labor power and become exploited by virtue of that social relationship. With the elimination of private ownership over the means of production and the achievement of the principal revolutionary transformations that modify the social relations of production toward the aim of Socialism-Communism, the conceptual apparatus of Marx's *Capital* is unable to explain the new realities that are created. Unfortunately, the more than seventy years of Socialism that had transpired by the time of these policy debates in Cuba had not yielded a theory of socialist transition with its own categories and concepts for application to *a new social content*. Instead, the conceptual understanding was extrapolated from Marx's *Capital* in a pro forma "dialectic."

40. Ibid., 203.

41. Ibid., 190-191.

42. The funds of economic stimulation are aimed at individual and collective material incentives for the workers. In the former USSR, there existed three types of incentive funds: material incentives aimed at worker productivity and high-quality production, socio-cultural activities aimed at satisfying important needs for child care, housing, workers cafeterias, etc., and the economic production fund which was aimed at reestablishing fixed capital funds, such as for automation, etc., at the point of production. *Diccionario de Economía Política* [Dictionary of Political Economy], 170.

43. *Tesis y Resoluciones,* op. cit., 199.

44. Assuming that the principle of each according to their capacity, to each according to their work in quantity and quality, is respected in accordance with the letter of the Resolution of the First Congress of the Communist Party of Cuba concerning the SDPE.

45. The norm or target is a measured quantity of work that creates a given product in a specified period of time, with the average skill level, and under specific conditions of the utilization of equipment.

46. In a speech given for the 25th anniversary of the Victory at Playa Girón (Bay of Pigs) on April 16, 1986, Fidel Castro denounced that "From the moment in which we have so-called managers that are more concerned with the enterprise than with the interests of the country, we have a full-bodied capitalist. The system for managing and planning the economy [SDPE] was not formed for so as to begin to play with capitalism. . . . In Fidel Castro, *Por el camino correcto,* op. cit., 3-4.

47. ". . . not everyone who errs or makes mistakes goes there [to Guanahacabibes], because if everybody who made mistake went, there would be a city there with skyscrapers. Those who go are those who have committed a violation, something that goes against socialist morality, but which is not a crime. Guanahacabibes is not so grave, so bad, but it is a sanction of a moral type. Recently, the manager of an enterprise was sent there after "pirating" another official, something that results from the spirit of the enterprise. And what we have to have is a socialist spirit, not the spirit of the enterprise." Ernesto Guevara, "Con los trabajadores vanguardias del Ministerio de Industrias" [Remarks Honoring Vanguard Workers of the Ministry of Industries], in *Discursos* [Speeches], vol. 5 of *El Che en la Revolución Cubana,* op. cit., 51.

48. Fidel Castro, *Discurso en el IV Forum Nacional de Energía* [Speech at the 4th National Forum on Energy].

49. J. Benavides, address at the Ministry of Basic Industry, in A. Vilariño and S. Domenech, *El sistema de dirección y planificación de la economía, historia, actualidad y*

perspectivas [The System of Economic Management and Planning, History, Topicality and Perspectivas], 158.

50. "It is even more painful when some of the measures of rectification are going to affect the worker, someone who is not to blame for the negligence, indolence, tolerance and lack of responsibility that put into place a target that is regularly filled four times over . . . yes, there were weaknesses that led to the distorted salaries." Fidel Castro, speech at the 3rd CDR Congress, in *Por el camino correcto*, op. cit., 62.

51. "The first person to be cheated is the same worker who is given this money, almost by being bought with money and is bought with the help of money, paper, transforming the money into paper." Ibid., 63.

52. Concerning this, Fidel Castro expressed the following: "the socialist formula can lead to egoistic selfishness and individualism as well, if the individual has everyday not been spoken to other than to discuss what they are going to earn for doing what and how much," during the 53rd Meeting of the Nacional Council of the Cuban Workers Union, in *Por el camino correcto*, op. cit., 97. Some of the conceptual problems related to the norms of production and salaries in socialism were taken from Ernesto Che Guevara, "Planning and Consciousness in the Transition to Socialism ('On the Budgetary Finance System')," in *Che Guevara and the Cuban Revolution*, op. cit., 203-230.

53. Fidel Castro referred to this problem in a very critical manner: "Just a few days ago, I visited the Ameijeiras hospital and saw that they had elevators very well maintained, reinforced with sheets of stainless steel . . . and they told me: Do you know how much they charged us to put these sheets of stainless steel into place? 10,000 pesos . . . In the end, they installed them for 5000. . . . The sheets belonged to the hospital and the enterprise charged those prices, a state enterprise. . . . In this way, one can be profitable. This disgusting spirit we have seen in action." Speech for the 25th anniversary of the victory of Playa Girón (Bay of Pigs), in *Por el camino correcto*, op. cit., 4.

54. Fernando Martínez, *Desafíos del socialismo cubano*, op. cit., 23.

55. Ernesto Che Guevara, "Planning and Consciousness in the Transition to Socialism ('On the Budgetary Finance System')," in *Che Guevara and the Cuban Revolution*, op. cit., 213.

56. Ibid., 214.

57. "On one occasion, with the motive of constituting the Central Committee, we said that we didn't believe that Communism could be fully constructed independently from the building of Socialism; that Communism and Socialism must be build, in

a certain sense, in a parallel manner, and that to invent a process and to say: up to here we have built Socialism and up to here, we have built Communism can come to constitute an error, a big mistake. That, since then, among other things, in the rush to reach socialist goals, the development and formation of the communist person should never be left aside or mortgaged." Fidel Castro, speech on May 1, 1966.

58. I do not even remotely intend here to deny the importance of salary and the role of "correct utilized" material incentives as a form of human motivation in the productive process. Indeed, Che was explicit in his considerations with respect to this issue. I refer the interested reader to his numerous writings on the subject, especially in: Ernesto Che Guevara, "La planificación socialista, su significado" [Socialist Planning, Its Meaning] in *Escritos y Cartas* [Writings and Letters], vol. 1 of *El Che en la Revolución Cubana*, op. cit., 235-248 and "Socialism and Man in Cuba," in *Che Guevara and the Cuban Revolution*, op. cit., 246-261.

59. Ernesto Che Guevara, "Socialism and Man in Cuba," in *Che Guevara and the Cuban Revolution*, op. cit., 253-254.

60. In "Theses on Feuerbach," Marx expressed that: "The coincidence of the changing of circumstances and human activity can only be conceived of and rationally understood through revolutionary practice," in Karl Marx and Frederick Engels, *Obras escogidas* [Selected Works], 397.

61. ". . . a complete spiritual rebirth in his attitude toward his own work, freed from the direct pressure of his social environment, though linked to it by his new habits. That will be communism." In Ernesto Che Guevara, "Socialism and Man in Cuba," in *Che Guevara and the Cuban Revolution*, op. cit., 254.

62. J. Benavides—as president of the Commission of Improvement of the SDPE—, interview to the *El militante comunista* journal: 13-18.

63. Fidel Castro's dialog with the participants at the 3rd Congress of the Association of Economists of Latin America and the Caribbean, November 26, 1987. In *Por el camino correcto*, op. cit., 285.

64. Fernando Martínez, "Un laboratorio," in *Cuadernos del Tercer Mundo* journal, no. 152, year XVI (July 1993).

65. Given all of its specific characteristics and repercussions, it is impossible to briefly review them all in the present work. I have written in detail about then in the article "Período especial y democracia en Cuba" [Special Period and Democracy in Cuba], in *Cuadernos de África y América Latina* journal, no. 16 (1994), as well as in "Adjustment, Economic Crisis and Democracy in Cuba," in *Cuba in the 1990s*.

Bibliography

CASTRO, FIDEL. *Discurso en el IV Forum Nacional de Energía.* Havana: Ediciones DOR, 1984.

————. "Discurso pronunciado por el Comandante Fidel Castro, Primer Ministro del Gobierno Revolucionario y Primer Secretario del CC del PCC, en la conmemoración del Primero de Mayo, Día Internacional del Trabajo. Plaza de la Revolución, 1ro. de Mayo de 1966." *Granma* daily, 2 May 1966.

————. "Dos discursos de Fidel Castro." *Obra Revolucionaria* journal, no. 21 (August 12, 1963).

————. *History Will Absolve Me* (Annotated Edition). Havana: Editorial José Martí, 1998.

————. *Por el camino correcto. Compilación de textos (1986-1989).* 3rd ed. Havana: Editora Política, 1989.

Diccionario de Economía Política. Moscow: Editorial Progreso, 1985.

FIGUERAS, MIGUEL. "Análisis de las políticas de industrialización en el período revolucionario y proyecciones futuras," an advisory report done for the Latin American Economic System (SELA), 1991.

GUEVARA, ERNESTO CHE. *The Bolivian Diary of Ernesto Che Guevara.* New York: Pathfinder Press, 1994.

————. *El Che en la Revolución Cubana.* 7 vols. Havana: Editorial MINAZ, 1966.

————. *Obras escogidas, 1957-1967.* 2nd ed. 2 vols. Havana: Editorial Casa de las Américas, 1970.

————. *Che Guevara and the Cuban Revolution. Writings and Speeches of Ernesto Che Guevara.* Edited by David Deutschmann. Sydney: Pathfinder / Pacific and Asia, 1987.

————. *Che Guevara Reader.* Edited by David Deutschmann. 2nd expanded edition. Melbourne, New York: Ocean Press, 2003.

Informe Central al Primer Congreso del Partido Comunista de Cuba. Havana: Editorial DOR, 1975.

Informe Central al Primer Congreso del Partido Comunista de Cuba. Havana: Editora Política, 1982.

LÓPEZ, DELIA LUISA. "Adjustment, Economic Crisis and Democracy in Cuba." In José Bell Lara (Coordinator), *Cuba in the 1990s.* Havana: Editorial José Martí, 1999.

————. "Período especial y democracia en Cuba." *Cuadernos de África y América Latina* journal (Madrid), no. 16 (1994).

MARTÍNEZ, FERNANDO. *Desafíos del socialismo cubano.* Havana: Centro de Estudios sobre América, 1988.
———. *Che, el socialismo y el comunismo.* Havana: Casa de las Américas, 1989.
———. "Un laboratorio." *Cuadernos del Tercer Mundo* journal, no. 152, year XVI (July 1993).
———. *El socialismo cubano: desafíos y perspectivas.* Guadalajara, Mexico: Ed. IMDEC, 1990.
MARX, KARL and FREDERICK ENGELS. *Obras escogidas.* Moscow: Editorial Progreso, 1955.
MINISTRY OF PUBLIC HEALTH. *Anuario estadístico, 1999.* Havana: MINSAP, 2000.
OJEDA FERNÁNDEZ, SUSANA. "Entrevista al Ministro Presidente de la Comisión Nacional del SDE. Nuevas respuestas a viejas preguntas y viceversa." *El militante comunista* journal, no. 9 (September 1989).
Plataforma Programática del Partido Comunista de Cuba. Havana: Ediciones DOR, 1977.
"Presentación del informe del Ministro de Educación a la Asamblea Nacional." *Granma* daily, 26 June 1981.
RODRÍGUEZ, JOSÉ LUIS. *Crítica a nuestros críticos.* Havana: Editorial de Ciencias Sociales, 1988.
RODRÍGUEZ, JOSÉ LUIS and GEORGE CARRIAZO. *La erradicación de la pobreza en Cuba.* Havana: Editorial de Ciencias, Sociales, 1987.
STATE COMMITTEE OF STATISTICS OF CUBA. *Anuario Estadístico de Cuba, 1988.* Havana: Comité Estatal de Estadísticas, 1988.
Tesis y Resoluciones del Primer Congreso del PCC. Havana: Editorial de Ciencias Sociales, 1981.
TORO, CARLOS DEL. "Algunos aspectos económicos del movimiento obrero cubano (1933-1958)." In vol. 1, *La república neocolonial.* Havana: Editorial de Ciencias Sociales, 1973.
VILARIÑO, A. and S. DOMENECH. *El sistema de dirección y planificación de la economía, historia, actualidad y perspectivas.* Havana: Editorial de Ciencias Sociales, 1986.
ZIMBALIST, ANDREW. "Does the Economy Work?" In *NACLA Report on the Americas: Cuba Facing Change,* vol. 24, no. 2, August 1990.
ZIMBALIST, ANDREW and CLAES BRUNDENIUS. *The Cuban Economy.* Baltimore: The Johns Hopkins University Press, 1989.

Ethics, Economics and Social Policies: Cuban Values and Development Strategy, 1989-2004*

EUGENIO ESPINOSA MARTÍNEZ

*. This is an updated version of the paper published in the journal *Impulso*, no. 21 (September-December, 2002, Methodist University of Piracicaba, Brazil). An earlier version was presented at the 13th National Congress of Economics, National University of Ancash, Perú, October, 2003.

EUGENIO ESPINOSA MARTÍNEZ

Ph.D. in Social Sciences. An economist and expert on development strategies, he is currently researching the processes of globalization, regionalization and integration. He is professor at the University of Havana and senior researcher in the FLACSO-Cuba Program.

There are values that are priceless.
There are prices that are worthless.

EUGENIO ESPINOSA MARTÍNEZ
December 3, 2000, Havana.

Introduction to Another Possible Economy

Economics as a science situates us in the terrain of values and prices, of the social relations of production, distribution, exchange, and consumption[1] while ethics leads us into the world of values and principles. Apparently, a great distance separates one from the other and yet there is an essential proximity that consists in something more than a simple coincidence of the word "values."

There are prices that are without value. Karl Marx gave the example of land in that masterful section of *Capital* dedicated to the derivation of land-rent. He also gave examples of honor and virtue, among others, when he wrote of commodities and the capitalist market in the first section of that work. He could have referred to water and air, the so called "public" goods, to the life of a human individual, to an idea; indeed, the capitalist market could put a price on everything, or almost everything. This is the terrain of Economics.

Nevertheless, there are values to which no price can be fixed. Sovereignty, independence, dignity, liberty, honor and virtue are all values that are priceless. This now places us on the terrain of ethics, or within the confines of a new economy. It is the market that sets prices, but it is the human being that exhibits values. This is a product that doesn't want to be sold, regardless of what it may be, and it has value but no price. Karl Marx did not theorize about this,[2] but he lived his whole life consciously demonstrating it. It comes to mind that he once wrote in a letter that nobody had previously ever written so much about money while having so little of it!

The new economy does not disregard the market or money, it does not reject it nor does it fear it or fetishize it. It values goods and services, both tangible and intangible, not only on account of the human work embodied within it, as postulated by the labor theory of value, and not only on account of its scarcity or its utility as expounded by marginalist theory. Or to put better, it procures the *utility of virtue* as expressed by José Martí (or in the terminology of Marxist political economy, it would be the use-value of virtue) and considers that the human labor that is contained throughout history in the defense of ideas and values is so high that there is insufficient money in the world to set a price

59

on it. Here, we return to the labor theory of Marx and observe that in this case, it would have value without exchange value, without price.

For example, what can the value be of an idea? The publicity market has considerable experience in setting a price on ideas. The project market likewise has, or to say it more appropriately, in the process of economic project assessment, there is an accumulated experience in the valorization of knowledge.[3] Nevertheless, in the value of an idea, of a principle, of an ethical value, is the previous labor contained within them as the result of a historical evolution involving hundreds or perhaps thousands of years?

With permission from the economists, the politicians, or the academics, I would like to add the following: When Ho Chi Minh said that there is nothing more precious that liberty and independence, or when Fidel Castro says and reminds us that we lived a revolution that has more than a hundred years, these are ideas, values that take on material force in the life of many men and women over time. What value can these ideas, these values have?

An example somewhat closer at hand could be the following: When a person invents something new, when this invention becomes materialized in a product, in a tangible or intangible good or service, such as a new theory (Marxist political economy), or a method, or a new machinery, or a new way of doing things that incorporates, for example, the valorization of experts, game theory, rapid communications, and computer data processing, what value can this product have? We could add to the preceding the mobilization of social actors (in this case, university students) in collecting the primary information through interviews, interactions with the larger population and knowing close-up the existing social reality. Marx spoke of the symbols of value devoid of value,[4] but what we refer to here is the value of ideas, not only of an innovation. What is the socially necessary labor time of an idea? Scientific economics still has a lot of ground to cover in this area as does the field of ethics or we could say axiology.

This issue may seem to be quite far from the practical questions of life but I would argue that in fact, it is not. How can we measure, for example, the contribution in value offered by education and health within the Gross Domestic Product (GDP) of the Cuban economy? In a session of the Cuban Parliament, the sentiment was put forth at one point: "It is entirely correct that Comrade Fidel has asked that the Gross Domestic Product be reviewed so as to see in what way it expresses the services of education and health care."[5]

These varied reflections, that perhaps might have been better accompanied by an exploration into the etymology of the crucial words, and a methodological proposal for more adequate measurement—which would be more useful—, are addressed to introduce the topic of Cuban development strategy of the 1990s.[6]

60

The preference, here, has been the concept of development strategy as opposed to public policies or social and economic policies, because the notion of development strategy seems more appropriate for a society such as Cuba than the notions of public, environmental, social, economic policies, and so on.

The basic reason for this resides in the notion that concepts of public polices or development planning (or programming) presuppose that they are elaborated by states and governments.[7] As such, they do not always take into account the interests and needs of the populations to which they are directed, and still less frequently, permit diverse social actors to participate in the design and implementation of policies.

In a society such as Cuba's, where organized social actors not only express their interests freely but actually form part of the consensus-building process that leads to a strategy of national, sectorial or local development and from there to policies,[8] the concept of development strategy constitutes a more useful tool and better expresses the real processes taking place.[9]

Cuban Development Strategy in the 1990s: Principles and Values in Cuban Thought

Cuban development strategy in the 1990s was guided by a set of values and principles that have been present throughout a whole history of struggle and ideas since at least the 19th century and which have characterized state and government policies since 1959. Here we shall analyze only the period of the 1990s, one of the most difficult decades that the Cuban people have experienced in their entire history and certainly the most difficult period since 1959.

Nobody is saying that these values and principles are unique to Cuba. Indeed, these ideas have been present in the history and struggles of many peoples. Nevertheless, there are not many countries where they have actually materialized into policies. The values that favor human development are rarely rejected as ideas, but their concretization into state and government policies and their embodiment into the everyday life of a people is in fact a truly difficult process. There is a gap, and not a small one, that exists between ideas and reality that can be closed only through the design of a strategy, through the implementation of policies and a process of follow-up of the same.

The following is a list of values, principles and concepts that guided Cuban development strategy through the 1990s and which can likewise be found throughout different periods of Cuban thought:

- Economic independence as a foundation for political sovereignty, continuity in social policy and of the preservation of the human, historical, cultural and spiritual heritage of the nation.
- Economic growth and social development.
- The human being as a subject and object of development.
- Political sovereignty, economic independence and justice, and social equity.
- Dignity, ethics, participation and democracy, liberty, honor and honesty, solidarity and internationalism, preservation of material, spiritual and human heritage, and peace.
- Socialist society.

Independence, sovereignty, freedom, justice and social equality have been explicitly formulated in Cuban thought since the 19th century. It is in the pro-independence thought of José Martí that they reached their highest expression. Martí's thought has enriched and fertilized the spiritual and intellectual soul of Cubans, Latin Americans and Caribbean peoples, and Ibero-Americans and Americans alike.

More recently, Ernesto "Che" Guevara wrote his extraordinary essay "Soberanía política e independencia económica" [Political Sovereignty and Economic Independence] in which he ties "these two concepts that must always go together"[10] with the history of Cuba and the Americas. Here, the new strategic objective for Cuba to achieve began on January 1st, 1959 in the "conquest of economic independence,"[11] with the principles of freedom and democracy, because "We don't talk of economics purely for the sake of economics, but of economics as a foundation for meeting all the country's other needs: education, a clean and healthy life, the need for a life not only of work but of recreation,"[12] with the aim of drawing up "a whole plan to be able to predict the future,"[13] with the objectives of "diversification of foreign trade, and raising the people's living standards,"[14] with the "birth date of the true republic, politically free and sovereign, that takes as its supreme law the full dignity of man"[15] and woman.

From a very early date, Cuban thought distinguished between growth and development,[16] pointing out that

. . . the basic problem of development was the structural alignment of the economy and the fact that there is no economic development when the growth of the productive forces is brought about in a manner such that it leads to an economic structure which instead of moving the country forward out of its condition of underdevelopment towards one more developed, contributes to maintaining or aggravating its underdeveloped status . . . because there can be no economic development without simultaneous growth and within certain limits of diverse branches of production. This problem was anticipated brilliantly by Karl Marx and applised with great foresight by Vladimir Lenin in the first scientific work on these issues, *The Development of Capitalism in Russia*, written about a half century prior to the "discovery" of the topic of development made by the decadent bourgeois economists. Among the bourgeois theorists of economic development was Raúl Prebisch who left things in their right place when he postulated that development was not a mere augmentation of what presently exists. It is a process of intense structural change. . . .[17]

Subscribing "without reservations to the words of Prebisch," Rodríguez points out that

. . . we are going a bit further than Wallich, beyond Pazos and beyond Prebisch . . . in our second thesis. Given that in contrast to those countries that developed in the 19th century and the first part of the 20th century, the basic strategic factor of the fundamental economic development of Cuba and other countries that share its conditions is not the private entrepreneur, but rather the State with a popular democratic content. . . . With this, we are not declaring ourselves in favor of a premature socialization. . . . What we want to say is that the popular democratic state has to be the first actor in motion.[18]

Economic development has always been closely associated with social development in Cuban thought in the sense that men and women are both subjects and objects of development. This vision is present from the earliest actions and written thought of Fidel Castro, where abundant references can be found in the thematic selection made of his speeches over the thirty-year period 1959-1988 that were published in 1991.

Development is not only economic but social as well. There can be economic growth, deformed or dependent, that does not serve this social objective or at all lead to the hoped for ends. A correct economic and social policy should have a concern for people at its core. If a policy is followed that does not correspond to this content, there will be no development or even peace.[19]

63

Development brings with its solutions for poverty and contributing through education and culture to our countries achieving rates of growth that are rational and adequate.[20]

There are governments that come to power through popular or revolutionary struggle and which then find that the shocking conditions of poverty, indebtedness and underdevelopment impede them from responding to the most modest hopes of their peoples . . . if the system is socially just, the possibilities of survival and of economic and social development are incomparably greater.[21]

In this kind of vision, there is a strong presence of democracy and participation. As Che Guevara put it:

. . . the government cannot dictate norms, make plans, and set goals without the participation of the people, because that would be a cold, bureaucratic plan. For this same reason, the enterprise must rely upon its personnel and workers to discuss plans, to involve the people in production and in the problems of the workplace in such a way that the final result be a dynamic product of practical discussions about specific issues that can offer completed conclusions. It is important to add to this that in accordance with the present principles of enterprise management in socialist countries, the administrator and the managing council are those who have the sole and absolute responsibility for completing the tasks assigned to them. . . .

The establishment of the socialist system does not eliminate contradictions but rather modify the form for resolving them.

. . . Harmonizing all of these in the framework of discussion and persuasion is a basic method for acting correctly.

. . . This totality of revolutionary organs, the Advisory Technical Council, the trade unions and the management.

. . . There should exist a broad integration of these sectors, discussing among themselves continually, establishing a continual communication that permits the exchange of opinions at every moment and achieves the advisement of all the political and technical factors necessary so that the managers, in the final instance and under their full responsibility, make a decision.[22]

This is not about abstract categories or faceless collectivities but rather about the individual person. There is nothing further from Cuban socialist thought than the hypocritical accusation that the individual disappears in the masses of the people. In the essay that is considered by many as a synthesis of his thought, Che Guevara treats this issue:

I would now like to try to define the individual, the actor in this strange and moving drama of the building of socialism, in his dual existence as a unique being and a member of the society.

. . . It is the twenty-first century man whom we must create, although this is still a subjective and unsystematic aspiration.

. . . The reaction against 19th century man has brought a recurrence of the 20th century decadence. It is not a very serious error, but we must overcome it so as not to leave the doors open to revisionism.[23]

Given the depth of Cuban thought, the illuminating sparks have were briefly presented above runs the risk of overlooking the importance of other essential themes that have figured prominently, such as the environment, the determinant role of science and technology, history and the nation's material and spiritual heritage, and the particular significance that international relations have had for Cuba in development.

With respect to the environmental issue, it is surprising that José Martí had already made this notion present in his writing where he taught that development in the present should not compromise future generations, a theme that re-emerges today in the concept of sustainable development. Likewise found in the thought of Martí was the perception that environmental themes had and would have a significant connotation in international political relations. This was something which he analyzed at the end of the 19th century with respect to the United States' utilization of the issue of North Pacific whales against Canada and England.[24]

With respect to the particular significance that international relations has for Cuba, and vice versa, much has been written. As Professor D'Estéfano states:

Every nation has an international presence, but some—as is the case for Cuba—have an especially large relevance. Very few of the smaller countries have had the kind of impact that Cuba has.

. . . Cuba could be the way of tying together three continents, America, Europe and Africa, and it would constitute a fair reflection of the wars that have occurred over the centuries between imperial powers, all of which explains why we have been at the center of the policies of diverse European and American countries. . . . The disputes of the powers over Cuba have extended over a period of centuries, beginning in the 16th century. . . .

Only in one case had there been an accord between the United States, England, France and the other European powers with respect to Cuba, and it was that the Island[25] could not pass into the hands of any of these, so for that reason, it was important that it remain in the hands of Spain, the weaker power. . . .

The attitude of the powers in the face of the country's independence, if indeed it made for a long and hard struggle, led to a contrary effect that could be followed by other countries: the development of a firmer and more resolute Cuban nationality, more convinced of the just nature of its cause and more conscious that it had powerful enemies.[26]

But Cuba, just like the Caribbean overall, not only had been a place of confluence and confrontation of the interests of the world powers, but also had been and continues to be a space for the fusion of races and cultures, constituting a unity from diversity, and a primordial issue in any development strategy. Nobody has catalogued this better than Fernando Ortiz, named as the third discoverer of Cuba with that new concept of *transculturation*, incorporated by him into the social sciences.

The true history of Cuba is the history of its very intricate transculturations. First the transculturation of the Paleolithic Indian to the Neolithic and the disappearance of them on account of refusing to accommodate to the impact of the new Castilian culture. Later, the transculturation of an unceasing current of white immigrants, Spaniards but from distinct cultures, themselves torn away from their Iberian peninsula and transplanted to a New World which was all new to them—nature and human beings—, and where they had to adjust themselves to a new syncretism of cultures. At the same time, there was the transculturation of a continuous human current of Black Africans, from diverse races and cultures, arriving from the African coastal regions of Senegal, Guinea, the Congo and Angola on the Atlantic side, to the coasts of Mozambique on the eastern side of the African continent. All of these peoples uprooted from their social origins and with the native cultures destroyed, oppressed under the ruling cultures of their new destination, found themselves as if they were the sugar cane ground in the thatched sugar mills. And still more migrant cultures would be assimilated from the sporadic and continuous waves of the Orient: from the subcontinent of India, Jews, Portuguese, Anglo Saxons, French, North Americans, and even Oriental peoples from Macao, Canton, and other regions of the Celestial Empire. . . .[27] This immense racial mixture of cultures overshadows in importance every other historical phenomenon.[28]

That cultural democracy that underlies the acceptance of the other in the process of racial mixing, that cultural tolerance towards the different and the diverse, something with deep roots in Cuba and our mixed America as "our America" was referred to by Martí, that does not segregate or discriminate, but melds in a pot of mixed identities into the creation of a new identity; this is the base line of that political democracy that through the construction of consensus has been and remains an essential component of the Cuban development strategy in the 1990s.

Solidarity, to both offer and to receive it, and internationalism are values that not only correspond to the external projection of Cuba since the time of the 19th century Republic in Arms but is likewise associated with the sphere of internal policies and interpersonal relations. This solidarity that goes to the deepest levels of the human condition is rooted in radical humanism.

Appreciation of the importance of history, the nation's material and spiritual heritage, projection towards the future and continuity in the process of development are the elements of highest importance. As Raúl Castro Ruz concurs:

The history of this country . . . has not been accomplished for free. It has cost dearly. The war for independence.

. . . This last year, it can be more than demonstrated that the indestructible force of the unity of this country which began with Martí and which Fidel has brought to bear.

. . . you know that at our age, of course, one thinks in the future. . . . I think that the best homage that they could ever pay us, in the first place, would be to those who fell in this heroic struggle and than were unable to see, as we can do, the end of the century and at the 42nd anniversary of the triumph of the Revolution, which remains in force. This is what one most thinks, that the process not become diverted, that the people remain alert, and very especially that the experience of what happened in the former

67

Soviet Union not come to pass here, that self-destruction of the largest country in the world.

We need to have the institutions of the Revolution, in the first place, the Party, functioning with an efficacy such that the very first negative steps can be detected in time. . . . And that not even a well intentioned act of stupidity come to surprise us nor any heinous act of a betrayal. . . . we have to be thinking about the future, about a future that has to be better. . . . The enemy will continue to exist. Now they are talking about the post-Castro era and that the transition has to be a pacific one, and clearly there will always be a transition, but to a Socialism ever more superior. . . . And when I spoke of perfecting our institutions as not being sufficient, the fundamental role has to be paid by the vigilant attitude of the people when they see some deviation because they are always noticeable and this is an informed people, a studied people, a people ever more politicized.

. . . Now we have the battle of ideas. What is this? New methods of struggle. The emphasis is in the trench of ideas. . . .[29]

Here I leave this brief exposition of values, principles and concepts that serve as a preamble to the list of objectives that have permitted the materialization of Cuban policies during the 1990s.

Objectives for 1989-93

- Attenuate the social impacts on the population of the economic crisis.
- Preserve the work of the Revolution and the achievements made by Cuban Socialism.
- Diversify Cuba's foreign relations.
- Maintain growth and development in selected branches of the economy: tourism, biotechnology and basic industry.
- Conserve the strength of the political system.
- Reinforce primary attention to health.
- Prioritize environmental policy as a basic component of development strategy.
- Diversify the forms of property and management while at the same time allotting a space for foreign capital and the operation of a market in the domestic economy.

Objectives for 1994-2000

- Initiate and maintain the economic recovery.
- Conduct monetary, budgetary and fiscal policies in such a manner as to contain inflation and the public deficit without affecting the quality of life and work of the population.
- Reinforce the sociopolitical consensus through participation, representativeness and democracy.
- Continue reducing vulnerability to foreign economic factors.
- Restructuring, reorganizing and re-dimensioning the economy while at the same time undertaking improvements in its forms of management and administration.
- Improve economic efficiency without renouncing efficiency and social equity.
- Situate culture at the center of the country's development.

The Present Situation

- Cuba's society and economy are more complex now than it was ten years earlier, both in its structure and in the means of its regulation.
- The forms of property and management are more diverse and are not completely harmonized.
- The ranges of social inequity are greater now than they were ten years ago, but much less than those of other countries.
- New social phenomena have arisen that are more proper to capitalism than to socialism, bringing with them a certain erosion of values.
- The policy of blockade and aggression on the part of the United States against Cuba has been maintained and intensified in spite of the growing opposition that can be found in numerous countries and political sectors throughout the world and in the United States itself.
- Cuba maintains economic, political and cultural relations with a large number of countries, companies, and political and social sectors from around the world.
- A foreign trade deficit has persisted, compensated for by the dynamism in the export of services.
- The Cuban population retains high levels of health and education, favorable levels of technical and cultural training, and a strong scientific potential.
- The dependence upon foreign energy sources has been substantially reduced, while the efficiency in the production and consumption of energy has been substantially increased.

69

- The levels and overall amount of vulnerability upon foreign factors has been reduced in the Cuban economy, increasing the levels and overall amount of its autonomy, although the optimal levels have not yet been achieved.[30]

Cuba's Economic and Social Strategy in Times of Globalization: 1989-2001

The Secretary General of the 71 ACP countries (African, Caribbean and Pacific) recently took note of the interest of this group in Cuba on account of its development in education, health, and production achieved over the last ten years without the benefit of foreign assistance.

The significance of the Cuban case is that despite being a small, Third World country with a Gross Domestic Product of around U.S.$14.5 billion, a product per capita of scarcely U.S.$1300 and a 45% dependence upon its sugar exports, it has had to sort out the challenges of competitiveness in globalization, of the global neoliberal trend, of the policy of blockade and aggression of the United States amounting to an average annual cost of approximately U.S.$2 billion over the last 42 years, of the loss of 85% of its foreign trade relations with the disappearance of the Socialist Bloc and the disintegration of the USSR, and of the damaging effects of global climatic changes.

It is known that one of the impacts of neoliberal globalization has been to abandon the debate over development strategies within the social and economic sciences. Nevertheless, the notion of strategy continues to be elaborated in the macroeconomic and corporate management literatures.[31]

In the case of Cuba, the consensus of the citizens around the values, objectives and strategies of economic and social development—the two first tasks in the formulation of any development strategy—has been present since early times and has maintained its continuity beyond the changes introduced in policies and even in economic and social structures.[32]

This set of values and objectives is one found across the long Cuban tradition of political, economic and social thought and that differentiates between economic growth and development; that points out the very necessary interaction and balance between economic development and social development; and that places human beings as subjects and objects of development. It recognizes political sovereignty, social justice and equality, autonomy and economic independence, and the full dignity of people as the basis of the Republic. It implements a consultative democracy, representative and participatory in the exercise of political, economic and social rights of citizens and promotes solidarity. In sum, it puts forth the preservation of the spiritual, cultural, environmental, historical, material and human patrimony of the nation as indispensable values and objectives of Cuban socialist society.

These values and objectives that are clearly not exclusive to Cuba and its history have been present in the policies and strategies employed since January 1st, 1959 up through the years 1984-2004. It is their presence in the design and implementation of social and economic policies that gives continuity and coherence to the forty-five years of Socialism in Cuba and it is what permits us to speak of a socialist strategy or of a Cuban model of Socialism, with all of its variations over time that go beyond one way or another of the virtues and limitations inherent in the concept of a model.[33] The changes in policies, that have not been few, have not impeded the continuity that underlies the strategies.

Although it is not the objective of this essay to go into detail on the issue of socialist reform processes, it should suffice to point out that based on the collapse of Eastern European Socialism and the contrasting capacity of Cuban Socialism to survive and reinitiate development, the debate once again has arisen with respect to the recent reforms in Cuba. For some authors who assume a pre-established logic in that the reforms (or the transition) should follow a linear itinerary that goes from centrally-planned socialism to a market-based, mixed economy, the Cuban case displays neither a strategy nor a model.[34]

In this essay, however, exactly the contrary is argued: the Cuban economic strategy is clear, well-defined, and coherent with respect to its socialist objectives and values as established over more than forty-four years in Cuba. The changes and transformations that have occurred and become implemented over this period, and specifically, those over the last decade, reveal that the application of social and economic policies constitute the placing in action of those values and objectives, adjusting them to the new external and domestic conditions of the economy and the larger Cuban society. During the decade of the 1990s, two great moments of transformation, continuity and change within social and macroeconomic policies could be observed: the period of 1989-1993 and that of 1994-2000.

The entire five-year period that extended from 1989 through 1993 could be characterized as a severe economic crisis that was expressed in the abrupt fall of the island's principal macroeconomic indicators. The economic recovery that was initiated in 1994 and which maintains its dynamism up to the present, has still to overtake the value of production realized back in 1989.

71

Table 1

Cuba: GCP, 1981 (millions of pesos)				
Year	GDP per capita	GDP	Cumulative growth	1998/1989
1989	1851	19,585	n/a	n/a
1993	1168	12,776	-34.8	n/a
1998	1568	17,481	36.8	89

Figure 1

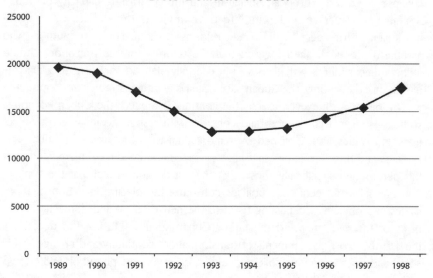

Gross Domestic Product

SOURCE: Oficina Nacional de Estadísticas (National Office of Statistics), *Cuba: estadísticas seleccionadas* [Cuba: Selected Statistics], various years.

Figure 2

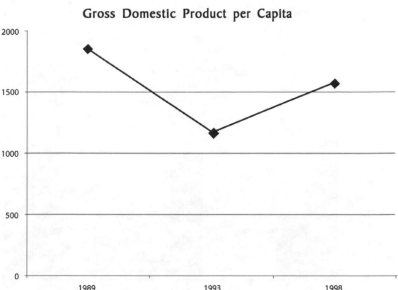

Gross Domestic Product per Capita

SOURCE: Oficina Nacional de Estadísticas (National Office of Statistics), *Cuba: estadísticas seleccionadas* [Cuba: Selected Statistics], various years.

The macroeconomic policy designed and implemented so as to confront the crisis and initiate the recovery led to a lesser contraction of consumption than that of accumulation. Many projects and investment programs were postponed while others were accelerated towards a more rapid completion than initially envisioned. Yet, the basic social policies were maintained, even to the point of increasing the rate of consumption and decreasing the rate of accumulation, in the larger context of an absolute decline in both categories.

Table 2

Cuba: Consumption and Investment (millions of pesos)				
Year	Consumption	GDP	Consumption /GDP	Investment /GDP
1989	12,244	5063	58.8%	24.3%
1993	10,685	965	64.3%	5.8%
1996	18,800	1900	74.6%	7.5%

Figure 3

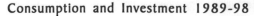

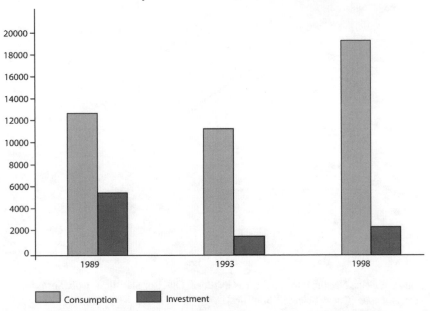

SOURCE: ECLAC, *La economía cubana. Reformas estructurales y desempeño en los noventa* [The Cuban Economy. Structural Reforms and Operation in the 1990s].

These figures not only reflect the priority that was given to the Cuban people (who constitute the principal wealth of the country by their high levels of education, training, and culture), but also show that the economic strategy was different than the social strategy in terms of the distribution and allocation of resources. In an economy in crisis, with limited resources, the policies opted for included:

- A strategy of concentration of the critical mass of investment resources, that is, the concentration of available resources into selected branches, sectors and investment projects.
- Distribution of the resources destined towards social and personal consumption, following the criteria of universality and of the greatest possible social equity and justice, maintaining subsidized the basic food basket, increasing coverage of welfare services and social assistance, keeping health and educational services free, pursuing a full employment policy up until 1993, and a low unemployment policy since 1994, and maintaining subsidies for basic services of water, sewage, electricity as well as cultural programs.

74

In summary, the approach involved a relatively equitable distribution of resources destined to personal and social consumption with the selectively concentrated allocation of resources destined to investment. This is one of the elements of continuity present in the economic and social strategies applied during the 1989-1993 and 1994-2000 periods. Although the continuity rests in the underlying values and the objectives, the change was to be found in the means and the instruments of macroeconomic and microeconomic policymaking and in the social dynamics that they implied.

The results of that strategy for the Cuban population has been recognized by respected international agencies, such as in the ECLAC study that showed that "contrary to what has been occurring throughout Latin America, the liberalization of markets in a setting of social solidarity has served to mitigate some of the regressive twists in the distribution of costs of the so-called 'special period' that is being experienced"[35] in Cuba. "In the face of the magnitude of external shock, the costs of the stabilization policy were in the end relatively low and the distribution of them was more equitable as compared with other Latin American economies, thanks to the policies that guaranteed employment and income to the population."[36]

The UNDP also favorably evaluated Cuba in this period "due to the policy of the government to engage in well-structured social spending."[37] While these studies recognized the efficiency of social policies, they tended to forget the economy and the macroeconomic policies that constituted the base for sustaining such policies.

In a similar manner, the World Bank through the declaration of its president, recognized that Cuba has done great work in education and health, and he was not ashamed to admit it. These April 30, 2001 declarations of James Wolfensohn were made during the presentation of the annual World Bank publication *2001 World Development Indicators,* in which Cuba appeared in the same category as the leading countries of the Third World on account of its social indicators, this in spite of the loss of its trade relations with the CMEA and the ongoing U.S. blockade. Such results have only been possible on account of the macroeconomic policies that were, in some very basic respects, the antithesis of the orthodox, neoliberal policies promoted by the Washington Consensus.[38]

The counterposing of economic efficiency and social equity is not a new item in economic theory much less in studies on the Cuban economy. In the debates back in the 1980s, analyses of the Cuban case for the 1959-85 period served to demonstrate that it was possible to reconcile economic growth with the satisfaction of basic human needs.[39]

Conditions changed in the 1990s both for the Cuban economy as well as for the world economy. But the Cuban case during that decade served to demonstrate that it is possible to maintain the satisfaction of basic needs during the economic crisis—as effectively occurred during the 1989-93 period. Even more so, the economic recovery and the productive reconversion of the economy included a redirection of investment towards advanced technologies and in more efficient areas without (or with very little) foreign financing, showing that it was possible to restructure without significantly sacrificing social objectives. This was the case during the 1994-2001 period. The debate rebounds back to the present situation of Latin America to the extent that it previsions a possible post-neoliberal scenario[40] in a context of ebbing flows of speculative capital.[41]

What occurred during the 1990s also demonstrates another thesis, namely, that it is possible, convenient, and desirable to pursue political sovereignty and economic independence, and that a small, Third World country can sustain itself, develop itself and assure its broader reproduction. The thesis of the non-viability of the small economies has been debated on numerous occasions in economic theory and the political sciences. In the case of Cuba, it has assumed various formats over the course of its history. In the 19th century, it consisted of the myth that Cubans could not govern themselves, that the Cuban colonial society could not survive without Spain, and that the Cuban economy could not reproduce itself without the European economy. The unfolding of the independence struggles demonstrated the opposite. During the first half of the 20th century, the myth consisted of the argument that the Cuban economy could not function without the U.S. economy, and that the Cuban government was not possible without the support of the U.S. government. The triumph of the 1959 Revolution demonstrated the contrary. In the second half of the 20th century, the myth consisted of the argument that the Cuban economy could not reproduce itself without the "Soviet subsidy" and that the Cuban government was not possible without the protection of the Soviet nuclear umbrella. The 1990s demonstrated that it was possible to restructure the Cuban economy in a way that enabled it to survive the crisis and develop itself based on its own resources.

The key to the Cuban experience in the 1990s rests in the principle that it is possible to achieve social and economic results with few resources. This consists not only of maintaining the level of social spending but also in elevating the social efficacy of spending. In health, the prioritizing of primary care and prevention and the improvement of the health indicators achieved by the Family Physician Program permitted the maintaining and improvement of basic health indicators. That was expressed, for example, in the rate of infant mortality which was at 6.5 per thousand live births in 1999,[42] this in spite of the deterioration of the hospital system and the scarcity of medicines. In education, similar achievements were made through reinforcing school-community relations at the local level and by developing pedagogical methods that elevated the quality of educational programs without requiring greater resources. The results of the international research project carried out by the Latin American Laboratory for Evaluation and Quality in Education (LLECE) sponsored by the Regional Office of Education for the Latin America and the Caribbean Countries/UNESCO attested to this fact by placing Cuban education very high in the regional rankings.[43]

Other factors that influenced the depth of the crisis, and at the same time, figured in the recovery and reinsertion of the island in the world economy was the policy of the U.S. blockade, redoubled in 1992 and again in 1995 through the implementation of the Torricelli and Helms Burton acts, as well as the vulnerability of the Cuban economy derived to a large extent from its external openness and other structural characteristics[44] and in larger economic and global climatic changes.

U.S. policy toward Cuba in its over forty-four years of harassment, something without precedent in world economic history, has nonetheless failed in its political, diplomatic and economic aims to destroy the Cuban Government, isolate it internationally, and prevent its reinsertion into the global economy.[45] It is certainly the case that such policies managed to inflict great economic, social and human costs, the former of which has been estimated in its totality at over 181 billion dollars over the period of 1959-2004.

The international opposition against the U.S. policies of blockade and aggression has been expressed in various declarations and actions on the part of a large majority of countries, by regional entities such as the European Union, the Rio Group, CARICOM, the Ibero-American Summits, as well as by national laws that have sought to protect and stimulate private sector investors which are negotiating and planning to negotiate with Cuba, and by a variety of social, religious and diverse political sectors, including within the United States itself as revealed in various Congressional votes in the 2000 and subsequent sessions.

A significant moment in this international rejection of aggressive U.S. policies has been the Resolution on the "Necessity of ending the economic, commercial and financial blockade imposed by the United States of America against Cuba" that has been approved by the UN General Assembly on numerous occasions since 1992.

With the collapse of East European Socialism and the redoubling of U.S. policies of blockade and aggression, the Cuban strategy has been to diversify its political and economic foreign relations, both geographically and sectorially, and to decentralize them to the level of the enterprise, with around 500 enterprises now carrying out relations directly with foreign entities, along with diverse associations with foreign capital both within and outside of Cuba. The reform of the foreign sector included a new style and implementation of foreign policy in bilateral, multilateral, intergovernmental, inter-enterprise, and between NGOs. The entry of Cuba as a member of the Caribbean Forum and the Latin American Integration Association (ALADI), as an observer in the negotiations of the Lome Accords and as a country seat for the 9th Ibero-American Summit are examples that reflect upon the successes achieved in this sphere. According to experts, "the Havana government has more amply practiced an open regionalism that is the official strategy of its subregional partners."[46] We could qualify this affirmation by making the observation that there are aspects which do coincide and others that do not coincide with the notion of open regionalism as seen from the vantage point of Havana.

A special mention should be made of the favorable assistance package developed by the Ibero-American Program of Integral Health for the Central American countries and the Dominican Republic as proposed by Cuba after the disasters caused by hurricanes Mitch and Georges towards the end of 1998, as recognized by the program heads of the Ibero-American Cooperation meeting in Guatemala that ended with the Declaration of Antigua in November of that year. Up through October of 2000, over 3400 Cuban health workers had been practicing their profession as volunteers in 57 countries throughout Latin America, the Caribbean, Africa, Asia, European Union and the United States.

The creation of the Latin American School of Medicine on the outskirts of Havana became a reality with the convocation of the First Scientific-Methodological Workshop held in February 1999 and the arrival in March of that year of the first 600 Central America students. Up through November of 2000, there were well over 3000 students matriculating from 23 countries. This huge effort of solidarity on the part of a poor country such as Cuba reflects the potential that exists with South-South cooperation even when resources are scarce. That kind of cooperation is also reflected in the presence of over 2300 Cuban technicians in 18 countries and the over 11,000 foreign students that presently study in Cuban universities.

In sum, the changes put into effect since 1990 have been profound ones, but with varying levels of importance:

• With respect to the structure of property and in the forms of their use; cooperative property as well as private property have when taken together moved from 24.8% of lands in 1992 to 67.2% in 1998.

78

- In economic policy and in the criteria for resource allocation, greater emphasis has been placed on efficiency, self-financing, competition and the reduction of monopolies.
- Asymmetrical sectorial policies, favoring investment in selected enterprises, branches and designated sectors, have been implemented.
- Introduction of new techniques of planning and management, characterized by indirect methods of regulation and by a gradual and segmented decentralization.
- A steady opening in the space of operation of the market (agricultural and livestock, industrial, services, foreign currency and directly regulated).
- Greater reliance upon foreign investment under diverse modalities, protected by the constitution, Laws 77 and 165, and by thirty-four intergovernmental agreements with thirty-five countries.
- Financial monetary policies that actively tend towards a budgetary equilibrium with a lower level of deficit, reduction of subsidies to enterprises, greater control over monetary emission, the reduction of excess liquidity and inflation, greater stability in currency exchange through the use of multiple rates, the appreciation of the value of national currency, and the dual circulation of currencies.
- Reduction of the central administration role of the state and the strengthening of its regulatory capacity of enterprises along with a territorial decentralization.
- Reinforcing the role of the organized civil society and of legislative parliamentary activities.
- Greater emphasis on environmental sustainability and historical and cultural heritage.
- Reforms of the banking system.
- Developing strategies of community and territorial development.
- Placing culture into the role of a key element in the overall development strategy.
- Maintaining the importance of the high tech sectors, especially that of biotechnology.
- Promoting tourism as a sector of key importance to the economy.
- Prioritizing the efficiency and diversification of the sugar sector.
- Improving the indices of energy self-sufficiency.
- Enlarging the role of enterprise beginning in 1999, with a greater amount of economic and financial autonomy.

Figure 4

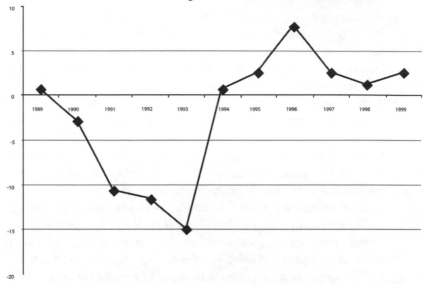

Cuba: GDP, Average Annual Rate of Growh (%)

The 2000-2004 Period

Beginning in 2001, a group of programs was initiated in Cuba aimed at increasing the quality and quantity of educational, health, social assistance, professional and cultural training programs, as well as in increasing the levels of employment. These social programs continued to expand during the 2001-2004 period in spite of the relative drop in the growth of tourism that occurred during 2001-2002. As it is well known, world tourism was gravely affected by the terrorist attacks[47] of September 11, 2001 and subsequently by the international war policies implemented by the U.S. administration beginning in 2002.

The declines in GDP growth experienced in Cuba for 2001-2003 were principally the result of low levels of world economic growth as well as the negative impact of two hurricanes.

Table 3

Cuba: GDP, Average Annual Rate of Growth (%)					
	2000	2001	2002	2003	1998-2002
GDP	5.3	2.5	1.4	1.6	3.4
GDP per capita	4.9	2.1	1.1	1.2	3.0

SOURCE: Economic Development Division - ECLAC, *Current Conditions and Outlook. Economic Survey of Latin America and the Caribbean, 2000-2003; ECLAC. Preliminary Overview of the Economies of Latin America and the Caribbean.* See http://www.cepal.cl. (The author consulted the Spanish version books. *Ed.*)

However, those rates of growth are higher than the average rates for Latin America and the Caribbean during the same period. Nevertheless, of equal importance to the amount of growth is the quality of the growth, that is, in which activities is growth being fostered. An important characteristic shown during these years has been that of a strong investment in social policies without neglecting the fundamental productive sectors.

Presently, there are more than a hundred social programs being developed in Cuba in the sectors of education, culture, health, employment and foodstuffs, some of which are new and others are continuing from previous periods:

- Over 81,000 color TV sets and more than 22,000 VCRs have been installed in schools and daycare centers, which represents one VCR for every 100 pupils and one TV set per classroom in all teaching centers of the country.
- In the most remote areas, over 2300 schools were installed with electricity, with 1944 of them using solar panels, and it was projected to install solar panels in over 12,500 communities that currently utilize conventional electric plants and in 43 settlements that previously relied upon mini-hydroelectric generators.
- During the 2002-2003 school year, 84% of the 48,433 groups of students at the primary level of instruction received their classes with 20 pupils or less. This is an indicator reached by very few countries in the world. Prior to 2000, 80% of pupils in primary education studied in classes of 30-50 children. In order to achieve this figure of 20 students per classroom, repairs had to be carried out in 848 schools while 33 new schools had to be constructed, resulting in a net gain of 4453 classrooms.

81

- Over 21,000 new teachers, principally youths, were prepared for primary school teaching, while they were continuing their university studies in 8 specialty areas of the humanities.
- During the 2001-2002 school year, just under 45,000 computers were installed in primary schools, costing U.S.$25.7 million.
- By the end of 2002, there existed a little less than 20,000 computer instructors in schools, 14,593 of which were teaching at the primary school level, resulting in over 12,600 new jobs, principally for youths who would continue their university studies in computer sciences.
- In total, 1,077,879 children in primary schools were the beneficiaries of the improvements.
- An educational television channel was created that by the end of 2002 had reached 4 million Cubans or around 40% of the total population. In 2004 another education channel was created.
- Four schools have been created for the training of Social Workers in which 8500 youths presently study. Upon graduation, they will be able to continue their university studies in 8 different specialty fields in the humanities.

For a poor, Third World country with few resources like Cuba, these figures are extremely favorable ones.

In the sphere of health, Cuba has made a significant effort in the area of international cooperation, principally directed towards the countries of Latin America, the Caribbean and Africa. International collaboration through the Integral Health Program mentioned earlier has continued as an expression of international solidarity:

- By the end of 2002, 2642 Cuban health workers were practicing in 18 Central American, Caribbean, South American and African countries, located in those communities where primary health care did not exist.
- At the Latin American School of Medicine, 5853 pupils from 24 countries in Latin America, the Caribbean and even the United States had studied by the end of 2002. Of them, 1440 were now completing their third year of studies.[48]

The complete and detailed listing of these kinds of programs would be a lengthy process. The above simply serves to illustrate the continuity in the values and objectives discussed at the onset and seeing them in action with respect to programs aimed at increasing the people's quality of life.

The policy of blockade and aggression employed against Cuba on the part of the United States has been intensified during this 2000-2004 period. Just in 2002 alone, the estimated losses attributed to these policies have been:

- U.S.$685 million in the area of foreign trade, a value that is higher than the total exports of Cuba in a year.
- U.S.$403.5 million on account of contracting at higher prices.
- U.S.$62.3 million on account of unfavorable terms of financing.
- U.S.$65.8 million due to higher freight and transportation costs.
- U.S.$119.2 million due to non-sugar exports that were unable to be realized.
- U.S.$182.9 million in actual sugar exports affected.
- U.S.$4.5 million in increased costs of carrying out citric exports.
- U.S.$25 million in thwarted exports of other tropical fruits.
- U.S.$157 million due to greater costs in exploration, perforation and extraction of petroleum.
- U.S.$16.32 million in increased costs for nickel exports.
- U.S.$28 million due to forced cancellation of two cinema projects.
- U.S.$13 million in lost compensation for rights to authors.
- U.S.$576 million in unrealized tourist revenues and U.S.$70 million of losses in unrealized cruise ship stopovers.
- U.S.$142.6 million in civil aviation losses.[49]

The preliminary estimates of costs to Cuba since 1959 just on account of the economic blockade amounts to around U.S.$72 billion, a figure various times greater than the Cuban GDP or the total gross foreign debt. This figure does not include frozen funds and a whole host of other aggressive actions, some of which were referred to earlier.

Not only has Cuba been affected, but these policies have also cost certain sectors of U.S. business. Cuban purchases of foodstuffs made from the United States under very onerous conditions have in the last three years ascended to U.S.$512 million,[50] this in spite of the intensification of the blockade and other new policies of aggression, and this has signified the possibility of a potential new market that could also help generate employment for the U.S. economy. At present, agricultural products such as those being purchased by Cuba are difficult to place in the tight international markets and in the internal U.S. market.

The continuity of strategic objectives during the 1989-2004 period was by no means an obstacle for the changes that were initiated back in 1992-93 when new forms and new instruments of social and economic management were introduced. The civic consensus concerning the new measures, different from the sterile and false unanimity often found elsewhere, were produced through a sustained national and public debate (assemblies held from October, 1993 to May, 1994, the most difficult moment of the crisis, in which 3 million workers, 158 thousand campesinos and 300 thousand students participated), in two sessions of Parliament (May and August, 1994) and in the substantial incorporation of social and economic research in designing these policies, although it remains necessary to build more systematic and coherent forms of participation. The opposition, although a minority, constitutes a new social phenomenon with peculiar aspects in the Cuban case given the U.S. policy of aggression against the island that has included attempts to finance an opposition from abroad.

The changes that have taken place in all of the economic, social and institutional spheres have had successful results. Economic growth has been maintained, with low inflation, low budgetary deficit, and the external vulnerabilities of the economy have been reduced while the coefficient of national production in energy consumption has increased as it has in the product inputs demanded by national tourism, this while social and cultural services have expanded.

In summary, the experience of social and economic policies during the 1989-2004 period in Cuba demonstrates a profound continuity in the values that have characterized Cuban Socialism since 1959, and which have become expressed in the Cuban conception of development. The changes in social and economic policies have signified an adaptation to the new national and international conditions that exist while at the same time preserving the underlying values and principles inculcated by the Revolution.

The combination of continuity in values and changes in policies has permitted effective results in the economic and political spheres, and in the social conditions of life and work of the population. While the difficulties that remain to be resolved are not few, and many projects remain to be completed, it can be said that the 1989-2004 period represented a very tough test for the Cuban model of socialist development which it has successfully passed.

Appendix

These tables, prepared by the author, synthesize the statistical information that supports the thesis developed in the essay.

Table I

Cuba: Exports for Selected Products (%)					
	1990	1993	1996	1998	2001
Fish and seafood	1.8	7.5	6.7	6.7	4.7
Citric fruits	2.7	1.2	0.6	1.2	0.7
Fruit preserves	0.3	1.1	1.5	1.0	3.1
Raw sugar (96 quality level)	79.7	56.2	51.3	38.6	33.2
Tobacco and manufactured	2.1	5.4	5.8	14.2	15.8
Minerals	7.5	15.5	23.2	22.9	28.9
Medicines and pharmaceuticals	1.6	5.7	2.9	2.5	2.5
Non-metallic manufactures	0.1	1.3	1.0	1.8	2.1

SOURCE: National Office of Statistics, *Anuario estadístico de Cuba, 2002* [Statistical Yearly of Cuba, 2002].

Table 2

Cuba: Geographical Distribution of Foreign Trade (percentage breakdown; totals in millions of pesos)						
Regions	Exports			Imports		
	1990	1998	2001	1990	1998	2001
West Europe	7.9	32.9	24.1	7.9	35.6	32.5
East Europe	73.2	27.3	39.7	79.6	6.3	2.7
North America (Canada and U.S.A.)	7.3	25.1	23.1	5.2	48.5	44.7
Latin America & Caribbean	5.4	10.2	9.4	5.2	42.6	37.1
Asia	8.1	12.8	12.2	5.8	16.4	19.7
Africa	3.5	1.8	0.9	0.4	0.8	0.4
Total	5414.9	1512.2	1660.6	7416.5	4181.2	4787.7

SOURCE: National Office of Statistics, *Anuario estadístico de Cuba, 2002* [Statistical Yearly of Cuba, 2002].

Table 3

Cuba: GDP 1990-2001 (constant prices 1981 and 1997)		
Years	Millions of pesos	Annual growth rate
1990	19,008.3	-2.9
1991	16,975.8	-10.7
1992	15,009.9	-11.6
1993	12,776.7	-14.9
1994	12,868.3	0.7
1995	13,184.5	2.5
1996	14,218.0	7.8
1997	14,572.4	2.5
1998	14,754.1	1.2
1999	15,674.4	6.2
2000	16,556.4	5.6
2001	27,273.7	3.0

SOURCE: National Office of Statistics, *Cuba en cifras, 1998* [Cuba in Figures, 1998] and *Anuario estadístico de Cuba, 2001* [Statistical Yearly of Cuba, 2001].

Table 4

Cuba: GDP per capita	
Years	Pesos
1990	1787
1993	1175
1998	1327
1999	1405
2000	1478
2001	2469

SOURCE: National Office of Statistics, *Cuba en cifras, 1998* [Cuba in Figures, 1998] and *Anuario estadístico de Cuba, 2001* [Statistical Yearly of Cuba, 2001].

Table 5

Cuba: Population. Macro-indicators (constant 1981 prices)			
	1990	1996	1998	2001
Resident population (thousands)	10,694.465	11,038.602	11,139.875	11,243.358
Working-age population (thousands)	6,398.984	6,650.619	6,621.522	6,642.718
Employed population (thousands of individuals)	3941.0	3626.7	3753.6	3968.9
Average monthly salary (pesos)	187	202	206	245
Income of population*	11,928.2	13,341	15,516.3	21,696.5
Spending*	11,104.4	13,057.7	15,248.4	20,347.8
Cash circulation*	239.4	433.4	267.9	1348.7
Savings*	584.4	−150.1	0.1	499.2
Household consumption*	10,588.5	16,101.1	18,087.0	19,180.1
State markets (non-agricultural goods and services)	10,155.8	12,188.6	12,853.5	13,479.0
Agricultural, meat and poultry markets	n/a	1229.3	1382.1	2048.0
Self-employed workers market	n/a	1574.2	1444.2	1597.7
Other sources	432.7	1109.0	1278.3	2005.4
Consumer Price Index (%)	2.4	−4.9	2.9	−2.3

*. Millions of pesos at current prices.
SOURCE: National Office of Statistics, *Cuba en cifras, 1998* [Cuba in Figures, 1998] and *Anuario estadístico de Cuba, 2001* [Statistical Yearly of Cuba, 2001].

Table 6

Forms of Management and Property							
	1981	1990	1992	1996	1997	1998	2001
Agricultural land (%)							
State	n/a	n/a	75.2	n/a	n/a	n/a	n/a
Non-state	n/a	n/a	24.8	n/a	n/a	n/a	n/a
Thousands of workers							
employed	2897.6	n/a	n/a	3626.7	3705.2	3753.6	3968.9
(%)	100			100	100	100	n/a
State entities	2632.8	n/a	n/a	2817.5	2837.0	2815.7	n/a
(%)	91.8			77.7	76.6	75.0	76.5
Cooperatives	30.7	n/a	n/a	348.8	338.6	328.8	n/a
(%)	1.1			9.6	9.1	8.8	8.1
Joint ventures and							
trade societies	n/a	n/a	n/a	110.3	134.7	151.9	n/a
(%)				3.0	3.6	4.1	4.9
Political, social and							
mass organizations	n/a	n/a	n/a	38.4	37.8	39.1	n/a
(%)				1.1	1.0	1.0	
Nacional private	157.6	n/a	n/a	191.7	227.9	305.2	n/a
(%)	5.5			5.3	6.2	8.1	14.7
Self-employed	46.5	n/a	n/a	120.0	129.2	112.9	n/a
(%)	1.6			3.3	3.5	3.0	3.8
Monetary income							
of population							
(millions of pesos)	n/a	11,982.2	n/a	13,341.0	13,895.4	15,516.3	21,696.5
Wages and other							
compensations	n/a	9369.8	n/a	8159.4	8248.1	8457.5	10,579.7
Income from							
cooperatives	n/a	157.2	n/a	198.9	195.4	203.9	227.9
Private campesino							
income	n/a	319.5	n/a	483.5	586.5	798.8	1253.3
Non-agricultural							
sector income	n/a	88.4	n/a	243.3	218.7	197.4	574.7
Income from UBPC	n/a	n/a	n/a	765.1	739.2	676.5	694.9
Other income*	n/a	1993.3	n/a	3490.8	3907.5	5182.2	8366.0

(Cont.)

Monetary spending of population (millions of pesos)							
	n/a	11,104.4	n/a	13,057.7	13,988.6	15,248.4	20,347.8
Goods purchases	n/a	9047.1	n/a	9976.5	10,240.7	10,571.1	12,199.9
Services payments	n/a	1402.6	n/a	1346.1	1404.8	1414.0	1776.6
Other spending**	n/a	654.7	n/a	1735.1	2343.1	3262.3	6371.3
Liquidity among population	n/a	823.8	n/a	283.3	−93.2	268.0	1847.9
Cash in circulation	n/a	239.4	n/a	433.4	32.9	267.9	1348.7
Savings	n/a	584.4	n/a	−150.1	−126.1	0.1	499.2

*. Other income: social security & assistance payments; student stipends, from financial system and elsewhere.

**. Other spending: in financial system, obligations and voluntary contributions, contributions to the public budget, insurance, debt payment and payment of quotas to social institutions.

SOURCE: National Office of Statistics, *Cuba en cifras, 1998* [Cuba in Figures, 1998] and *Anuario estadístico de Cuba, 2002* [Statistical Yearly of Cuba, 2002].

Table 7

Cuba: Monetary Circulation. Entries and Exits (millions of pesos at current prices)				
	1992	1996	1997	1998
ENTRIES	11,871.2	13,133.2	14,154.4	15,467.3
Market circulation	9135.3	9945.7	10,237.5	10,571.8
Transportation services	513.6	329.0	301.6	280.6
Housing payments, electricity, gas, water	480.4	523.7	534.7	547.8
Saving accounts variation	544.4	n/a	n/a	n/a
Others	1197.5	2334.8	3080.6	4067.1
EXITS	12,110.7	13,567.3	14,187.3	15,735.7
Wages, salaries, UBPC payments	9238.5	8839.7	8888.6	9011.1
Social security	1396.5	1749.6	1707.4	1705.0
Saving accounts variation	n/a	320.0	226.1	85.4
Others	n/a	1475.7	3658.0	4934.2
BALANCE	239.5	434.1	32.9	268.4

SOURCE: National Office of Statistics, *Cuba en cifras, 1998* [Cuba in Figures, 1998].

Table 8

Cuba: State Budget Earnings and Expenditures (millions of pesos at current prices)				
	1996	1997	1998	2001
Total Earnings	12,242.8	12,203.6	12,502,2	15,033.5
Transaction taxes and sales	5079.0	4876.2	5076.4	5721.6
Utility taxes	468.5	849.6	1131.8	1717.5
Contributions to social security	959.2	1070.5	1025.0	1247.8
State enterprise apportions	2685.0	2014.7	1907.5	1661.2
Other non-tax earnings	1589.0	1614.7	1342.7	1974.9
Total expenditures	12,813.5	12,662.6	13,061.7	15,771.0
Education	1421.3	1453.9	1509.7	2368.6
Health	1190.3	1265.2	1344.9	1796.6
Defense	496.7	637.5	537.1	1273.8
Social security	1630.2	1635.9	1705.1	1870.3
Social assistance	128.4	135.2	145.4	215.2
Administration	397.5	431.2	437.8	565.2
Housing and construction	462.4	487.6	565.5	827.2
Science and technology	113.6	109.2	104.1	163.6
Sports	117.5	121.5	125.9	163.4
Arts and culture	165.2	164.7	168.8	310.7
Inventory. Bills for payment	187.6	−264.8	−206.3	n/a
Enterprise losses subsidy	1 624.4	1350.0	1139.4	393.4
Differential price subsidy	867.3	757.9	1352.0	1900.2
Assistance to agricultural coops	600.6	718.1	384.8	63.8
Investment expenses	2043.4	1839.0	1580.8	1989.7
Extraordinary expenses	239.1	680.6	1000.0	n/a
Balance	−570.7	−459	−559.7	−737.5

SOURCE: National Office of Statistics, *Cuba en cifras, 1998* [Cuba in Figures, 1998] and *Anuario estadístico de Cuba, 2002* [Statistical Yearly of Cuba, 2002].

Table 9

Cuba: Foreign Earnings (millions of U.S. dollars)					
Years	Totals	Goods	Services	Tourism	Other Services
1990	5940.0	5414.9	525.1	243.4	281.7
1998	4182.0	1539.5	2642.5	1416.0	1226.5
2001	3874.3	1661.5	2212.8	1840.4	372.4
Annual growth rate 1990-98 (%)	-3.7	-8.9	50.4	60.2	41.9

SOURCE: National Office of Statistics, *Anuario estadístico de Cuba, 2002* [Statistical Yearly of Cuba, 2002] and I. Mañalich, N. Quiñones, N. Nieves, *El sector externo cubano en los '90s* [The Cuban External Sector in the 1900s].

Notes

1. Karl Marx, *El Capital: crítica de la economía política* [Capital: Critics on Political Economy] (The full facts of publication of all the sources are found in the Bibliography at the end of the essay. *Ed.)*

2. Or if he did theorize about this, it would be worthwhile to re-read the work done in this regard.

3. Eugenio Espinosa, "Evaluación económica de proyectos: proyectos Biotec" [Economic Assessment of Projects: Bistec Projects].

4. Karl Marx, op. cit., 87.

5. "Informe sobre los resultados económicos del 2000 y el Plan Económico y Social para el año 2001, presentado por el diputado José Luis Rodríguez, Ministro de Economía y Planificación, en el VI período ordinario de la Asamblea Nacional del Poder Popular" [Report on the Economic Outcome of the Year 2000 and the Economic and Social Plan for the Year 2001, Presented by the Deputy José Luis Rodríguez, Minister of Economy and Planning, during the 6th Ordinary Period of the National Assembly of People's Power].

6. There are various background studies concerning the analysis of the Cuban economy based upon the notion of strategy. In this regard, the reader can see: Fidel Castro, *Desarrollo, subdesarrollo y Tercer Mundo* [Development, Underdevelopment and

91

the Third World]; Carlos Rafael Rodríguez, "Estrategia de desarrollo de la economía cubana" [Development Strategy of the Cuban Economy], in *Letra con filo* [Sharpened Word], vol. 2, 444-460; Alfredo González, *Modelos económicos socialistas: escenarios para Cuba en los años noventa* [Socialist Economic Models: Scenarios for Cuba in the 1990s]; Alfredo González and Estela Espinosa, *La economía sumergida en Cuba* [The Submerged Economy in Cuba]; Eugenio Espinosa, "Estrategia de desarrollo entre la rectificación y el período especial" [Development Strategy between Rectification and the Special Period]; Eugenio Espinosa, "La economía cubana en 1989-1995: crisis, reformas y relanzamiento, vulnerabilidades y perspectivas estratégicas" [The Cuban Economy during 1989-95: Crisis, Reforms and Recovery, Vulnerabilities and Strategic Perspectives].

7. J. Benard, N. Kaldor, et al., *Programación del desarrollo* [Programming of Development]; Raúl Prebisch, *Transformación y desarrollo: la gran tarea de la América* [Transformation and Development: The Great Task of the Americas]; N. Fedorenko, *Desarrollo económico y planificación perspectiva* [Economic Development and Prospect Planning]; UNESCO and SELA, *Empleo: un reto para el crecimiento* [Employment: A Challenge for Growth]; UNESCO, "Environment and Society: Education and Public Awareness for Sustainability."

8. Eugenio Espinosa, "La economía cubana en 1989-1995," op. cit.

9. Eugenio Espinosa, "Comunidad, medio ambiente y desarrollo, estrategias de desarrollo local y nacional: el caso del municipio Habana Vieja en la Ciudad de La Habana" [Community, Environment and Development, Local and National Development Strategy: The Case of the Habana Vieja Municipality in Ciudad de La Habana Province].

10. Ernesto Che Guevara, "Political Sovereignty and Economic Independence. March 20, 1960," in *Che Guevara and the Cuban Revolution. Writings and Speeches of Ernesto Che Guevara*, 86.

11. Ibid., 92.

12. Ibid., 100.

13. Ibid., 86.

14. Ibid., 93.

15. Ibid., 91.

16. See Carlos Rafael Rodríguez, "América Latina y el Plan Clayton" [Latin America and the Clayton Plan], vol. 2, 15-30; "A propósito del empleo en Cuba" [With Regard to Employment in Cuba], vol. 2, 31-53; and "Las bases del desarrollo económico de

92

Cuba" [The Foundation of the Economic Development in Cuba], vol. 2, 55-70, all of them in *Letra con filo*, vol. 2, op. cit.

17. Carlos Rafael Rodríguez, "Las bases del desarrollo económico," in vol. 2, op. cit., 41-42.

18. Ibid., 56-59.

19. Fidel Castro, op. cit., 78.

20. Ibid., 82.

21. Ibid., 93.

22. Ernesto Che Guevara, "Discusión colectiva; decisión y responsabilidades únicas" [Collective Discussion; Sole Decision and Responsibilities], in *Obras escogidas. 1957-1967* [Selected Works. 1957-67], 122-131.

23. Ernesto Che Guevara, "Socialism and Man in Cuba." In *Che Guevara and the Cuban Revolution*, op. cit., 249-257.

24. Eugenio Espinosa, "La iniciativa para las Américas y la Conferencia Internacional Americana: 1989-1990" [The Initiative for the Americas and the American International Conference: 1889-90].

25. The Cuban archipelago.

26. Miguel A. D'Estéfano, *Cuba en lo internacional (1510-1898)* [Cuba in the International Setting (1510-1898)], 1-6.

27. Also, Japanese, Germans and Italians as well as Caribbean and Latin American peoples can be included here, although Ortiz does not mention them.

28. Fernando Ortiz, "Del fenómeno social de la transculturación y de su importancia en Cuba" [On the Social Phenomenon of Transculturation and Its Importance in Cuba] in *Contrapunteo cubano del tabaco y el azúcar* [Cuban Counterposition of Tobacco and Sugar].

29. "Transcripción de conversación sostenida con el Ministro de las FAR General de Ejército Raúl Castro Ruz, por la periodista Marta Moreno, de los Servicios Informativos de la Televisión Cubana, a propósito del aniversario 42 de la Revolución Cubana" [Transcription of the Conversation Held with the Minister of the Revolutionary Armed Forces, General Raúl Castro Ruz, by the Journalist Marta Moreno, of the Informative Services of the Cuban Television, with Regard to the 42nd Anniversary of the Cuban Revolution].

30. This conclusion is based upon my unpublished article "Indicadores de vulnerabilidades externas y grados de autonomía de la economía cubana en los '90"

[Indicators of External Vulnerabilities and Degrees of Autonomy of Cuban Economy in the 1990s].

31. Arthur Thompson and A. J. Strickland, *Strategy Formulation and Implementation;* Roberto Pérez Llanes, "Dirección estratégica: la experiencia en la empresa cubana" [Strategic Management: The Experience in Cuban Enterprise], in *Economía y Desarrollo* journal.

32. José Luis Rodríguez, *Estrategia del desarrollo económico de Cuba* [Strategy for the Economic Development in Cuba].

33. With respect to the virtues and limitations of the concept of "model," see: Michael Barrat Brown, *Models in Political Economy.*

34. M. A. Font, "Crisis and Reform in Cuba."

35. ECLAC, *La economía cubana: reformas estructurales y desempeño en los noventa* [The Cuban Economy: Structural Reforms and Operation in the 1900s], op. cit., 16.

36. Ibid., 66.

37. UNDP, *Informe sobre el desarrollo humano* [Report on Human Development], 1997 and 1998; UNDP, *Investigación sobre el desarrollo humano en Cuba* [Research on Human Development in Cuba].

38. Jim Lobe, "'Learn from Cuba,' Says World Bank."

39. Claes Brundenius, *Cuba: Redistribution and Growth with Equity.*

40. W. C. Smith, "Democracia, equidad y globalización: del Consenso de Washington al Consenso del Sur ¿y más allá?" [Democracy, Equity and Globalization: From the Washington Consensus to the Southern Consensus, and Beyond?], in *Globalización, América Latina y la diplomacia de las cumbres* [Globalization, Latin America and Diplomacy of the Summits].

41. ECLAC, op. cit.

42. Ministry of Health, *Anuario estadístico de salud, 2000* [Statistical Health Yearly, 2000], 39.

43. The comparative study was based on a simple of 100 schools and 4000 pupils in 11 countries including Argentina, Bolivia, Brazil, Chile, Colombia, Cuba, Honduras, Mexico, Paraguay, Dominican Republic and Venezuela. LLECE, *Estudios comparativos en educación. Primer estudio latinoamericano comparativo de matemática y lenguaje* [Comparative Studies in Education: First Latin American Comparative Study of Mathematics and Language].

44. Eugenio Espinosa, *La economía cubana en 1989-1995,* op. cit.

45. W. C. Smith, op. cit.; F. León, "ALCA-Cuba: participación o marginación" [FTAA-Cuba: Participation or Marginalization], in *Globalización, América Latina y la diplomacia en las cumbres*, op. cit.; Latin American Economy System (SELA), *Informe de seguimiento de la aplicación de la Ley Helms-Burton y análisis de expropiación e indemnizaciones en Cuba* [Follow-up Report of the Application of the Helms-Burton Act and Analysis of Expropriation and Indemnities].

46. F. León, "ALCA-Cuba: participación o marginación," op. cit.

47. Héctor Ayala and Roberto Llanes, "Impactos en el turismo del Caribe insular" [Impacts on Tourism in the Insular Caribbean].

48. Figures from the Department of Social Development of the Ministry of Economy and Planning and the Instituto de Investigaciones Económicas (Institute of Economic Research).

49. For more details, see Cuba's report to the UN Secretary General on General Assembly Resolution 57/11: "Necessity of Ending the Economic, Commercial and Financial Blockade Imposed by the United States of America against Cuba," currently available at: http://www.granma.cu/documento/ingles03/022.html.

50. The General Manager of ALIMPORT, Pedro Álvarez, stated on October 8, 2004 in Havana that 96% of these imports are dedicated to the subsidized food consumption of the Cuban population.

Bibliography

AYALA, HÉCTOR and ROBERTO LLANES. "Impactos en el turismo del Caribe insular." Tourist Study Center, University of Havana, 2002. Typescript.

BENARD, J., N. KALDOR, M. KALECKI, W. LEONTIEF and J. TINBERGEN. *Programación del desarrollo*. Havana: Instituto del Libro, 1969.

BROWN, MICHAEL BARRAT. *Models in Political Economy*. Middlesex, England: Penguin Books, 1987.

BRUNDENIUS, CLAES. *Cuba: Redistribution and Growth with Equity*. London: Blackwell, 1985.

CASTRO, FIDEL. *Desarrollo, subdesarrollo y Tercer Mundo*. Havana: Editora Política, 1991.

———. "Message Issued by Cuban President Fidel Castro to the UNCED, on June 12, 1992 in Rio de Janeiro, Brazil." *Latin American Network Information Center*. http://lanic.utexac.edu/project/castro/1992/19920614. Accessed September 11, 2004.

———. "Speech Given by President Fidel Castro Ruz, First Secretary of the Central Committee of the Communist Party of Cuba, at the Main Ceremony for the 45th Anniversary of the Attacks on the Moncada and Carlos Manuel de Céspedes Garrisons." Cuba.cu. http://www.cuba.cu/gobierno/discursos/ 1009/ing/f260798i.html. Accessed September 11, 2004.

D'ESTÉFANO PISANI, MIGUEL A. *Cuba en lo internacional (1510-1898).* Havana: Editorial de Ciencias Sociales, 1988.

ECLAC. *La economía cubana. Reformas estructurales y desempeño en los noventa.* Mexico City: ECLAC and FCE, 1999.

————. *Preliminary Overview of the Economies of Latin America and the Caribbean, 2003.* ECLAC, August, 2003.

ECONOMIC DEVELOPMENT DIVISON – ECLAC. *Current Conditions and Outlook. Economic Survey of Latin America and the Caribbean, 2002-2003.* ECLAC, August, 2003.

ESPINOSA, EUGENIO. "Comunidad, medio ambiente y desarrollo: estrategias de desarrollo local y nacional: el caso del municipio Habana Vieja en la Ciudad de La Habana." Paper presented at the CALACS Congress, Guatemala, February 2001.

————. "La economía cubana en 1989-1995: crisis, reformas y relanzamiento, vulnerabilidades y perspectivas estratégicas." Working Document no. 7 at FLACSO, University of Havana, 1996. Typescript.

————. "Estrategia de desarrollo entre la rectificación y el período especial." FLACSO, University of Havana, Cuba, 1988. Typescript.

————. "Evaluación económica de proyectos: proyectos Biotec." Paper presented in the Seminar on Management of Projects, CNIC, Havana, October 2000.

————. "From Crisis to Recovery." In José Bell Lara (Coordinator), *Cuba in the 1990s.* Havana: Editorial José Martí, 1999.

————. "Indicadores de vulnerabilidades externas y grados de autonomía de la economía cubana en los '90." FLACSO, University of Havana, Cuba, 2000. Typescript.

————. "La iniciativa para las Américas y la Conferencia Internacional Americana: 1989-1990." *Revista de Relaciones Internacionales* journal (National University of Costa Rica, San José), no. 39 (April-June 1992).

ESPINOSA, EUGENIO, ELENA DÍAZ, BEATRIZ DÍAZ, R. GONZÁLEZ, E. SALINAS and J. MATEO. *Investigaciones sobre medio ambiente.* Madrid: SODEPAZ, 1993.

FEDORENKO, N. *Desarrollo económico y planificación perspectiva.* Moskow: Editorial Progreso, 1976.

FONT, M. A. "Crisis and Reform in Cuba." Draft paper at American Sociological Association, Washington, 1995.

96

GONZÁLEZ, ALFREDO. *Modelos económicos socialistas: escenarios para Cuba en los años noventa.* Havana: Instituto Nacional de Investigaciones Económicas, 1993.

GONZÁLEZ, ALFREDO and ESTELA ESPINOSA. *La economía sumergida en Cuba.* Havana: Instituto Nacional de Investigaciones Económicas, 1993.

GUEVARA, ERNESTO CHE. *Che Guevara and the Cuban Revolution. Writings and Speeches of Ernesto Che Guevara.* Edited by David Deutschmann. Sydney: Pathfinder / Pacific and Asia, 1987.

————. *Obras escogidas. 1957-1967.* 2 vols. Havana: Editorial Casa de las Américas, 1970.

LEAL SPENGLER, EUSEBIO. Presentation to *Viaje a la memoria: apuntes para un acercamiento a la Habana Vieja,* by Patricia Rodríguez Alomá, Rafael Rojas Hurtado, Madeline Menéndez and Azalia Arias. Havana: Editora Oficina del Historiador de la Ciudad de La Habana, Pamplona: Colegio Oficial de Arquitectos Vasco Navarro, 1996.

LEÓN, F. "ALCA-Cuba: participación o marginación." In *Globalización, América Latina y la diplomacia de las cumbres.* Edited by Rojas Aravena. Santiago de Chile: FLACSO Chile and FIU, 1998.

LOBE, JIM. "'Learn from Cuba,' Says World Bank." *Hartford Web Publishing.* 1 May 1st, 2001. http://www.hartford-hwp.com/archives/43b/185.html. Accessed July 22, 2004.

MAÑALICH, I., N. QUIÑONES and N. NIEVES. "El sector externo cubano en los '90s." National Institute of Economic Research (INIE), Cuba.

MARX, KARL and FREDERICK ENGELS. *El capital: crítica de la economía política.* Mexico City: FCE, 1972.

MINISTRY OF HEALTH. *Anuario estadístico de salud, 2000.* Havana: MINSAP, 2001.

MONETA, CARLOS J. "Espacios económicos y globalización." In SELA, *Dinámica de las relaciones externas de América Latina y el Caribe.* Buenos Aires: SELA and ACECI, 1999.

NATIONAL OFFICE OF STATISTICS. *Anuario estadístico de Cuba, 2001.* Havana: Oficina Nacional de Estadísticas, 2002.

————. *Anuario estadístico de Cuba, 2002.* Havana: Oficina Nacional de Estadísticas, 2003.

————. *Cuba en cifras, 1998.* Havana: Oficina Nacional de Estadísticas, 1999.

"Necessity of Ending the Economic, Commercial and Financial Blockade Imposed by the United States of America against Cuba." *Granma Internacional.* http://www.granma.cu/documento/ingles03/022.html. Accessed July 22, 2004.

ORTIZ, FERNANDO. *Contrapunteo cubano del tabaco y el azúcar.* Barcelona: Editorial Ariel, 1973.

PÉREZ LLANES, ROBERTO. "Dirección estratégica: la experiencia en la empresa cubana." *Economía y Desarrollo* journal, no. 1 (1996).

PORRO MENDOZA, SOFÍA. "Un estudio social de la infancia: estudio de un grupo de niñas con nivel socio-económico bajo en Cuba." Ph.D. diss., University of Havana, 1999.

PREBISCH, RAÚL. *Transformación y desarrollo: la gran tarea de la América Latina.* Mexico City: FCE and ILPES, 1970.

QUIROGA MARTÍNEZ, RAYÉN and SAAR VAN HAUWERMEIREN. *Globalización e insustentabilidad: una mirada desde la economía ecológica.* Santiago de Chile: Instituto de Ecología Política, 1996.

RODRÍGUEZ, CARLOS RAFAEL. *Letra con filo.* 2 vols. Havana: Editorial de Ciencias Sociales, 1983.

RODRÍGUEZ, JOSÉ LUIS. *Estrategia del desarrollo económico de Cuba.* Havana: Editorial de Ciencias Sociales, 1990.

————. "Informe sobre los resultados económicos del 2000 y el Plan Económico y Social para el año 2001, presentado por el diputado José Luis Rodríguez, Ministro de Economía y Planificación, en el VI período ordinario de la Asamblea Nacional del Poder Popular." *Granma* daily, 23 December 2000.

SELA. Informe de seguimiento de la aplicación de la Ley Helms-Burton y análisis de expropiación e indemnizaciones en Cuba." Report presented at the 24th Ordinary Meeting of the Latin American Council, SELA, Caracas, December 1998.

SEN, AMARTYA. "Los bienes y la gente." *Comercio Exterior de México* journal, no. 2 (September 2000).

SMITH, W. C. "Democracia, equidad y globalización: del Consenso de Washington al Consenso del Sur ¿y más allá?" In *Globalización, América Latina y la diplomacia de las cumbres.* Edited by Rojas Aravena. Santiago de Chile: FLACSO Chile and FIU, 1998.

THOMPSON, ARTHUR and A. J. STRICKLAND. *Strategy Formulation and Implementation.* Boston: BPI / IRWIN, 1989.

"Transcripción de conversación sostenida con el Ministro de las FAR, General de Ejército Raúl Castro Ruz, por la periodista Marta Moreno, de los Servicios Informativos de la Televisión Cubana, a propósito del aniversario 42 de la Revolución Cubana." *Granma* daily, 8 January 2001.

UNDP. *Investigación sobre el desarrollo humano en Cuba.* Havana: Editora Caguayo, 1997.

————. *Investigación sobre el desarrollo humano y equidad en Cuba.* Havana: Editora Caguayo, 1998.

UNESCO. "Environment and Society: Education and Public Awareness for Sustainability." In *Proceedings of the Thessaloniki International Conference organised by UNESCO and the Government of Greece.* Edited by Michael Scoullos. Athens, 1998.

UNESCO and SELA. *Empleo: un reto para el crecimiento.* Caracas: SELA, 1997.

ZABALA, MARÍA DEL CARMEN. "Aproximación al estudio de la relación entre familia y pobreza en Cuba." Ph.D. diss., University of Havana, 1999.

A Guide for Understanding the Cuban Political System

DELIA LUISA LÓPEZ GARCÍA

Delia Luisa López García

Ph.D. in Economic Sciences. A specialist in the study of social class dynamics and economic strategies throughout the Latin American continent. She is a senior researcher in the FLACSO-Cuba Program and coordinator of the Cathedra Ernesto Che Guevara.

The origins of the present Cuban political system reside in the autochthonous popular revolution that triumphed out of armed insurrection on January 1st, 1959. This was the historical point when the rupture of the bourgeois neocolonial state was brought about. Along with it came the dissolution of the repressive apparatus long utilized by the ruling classes to ensure a tight dictatorial control over the vast majority of the population. For the first time ever in a Latin American country, a professional army was totally replaced by an insurgent army (the Rebel Army), thereby guaranteeing the nation's newly won sovereignty and providing for the subsequent defense of revolutionary transformations.

As these historic changes took place, the Revolutionary Government simultaneously promulgated various laws designed to benefit the popular sectors with the objective of redistributing national income. On May 17, 1959, the first Agrarian Reform Law was approved, resulting in the elimination of large landed estates, both national and foreign, and the transfer of those lands to those who had always worked them.

Starting with the radical political and redistribution measures taken during the first decade of transformation, the material and spiritual well-being of the most dispossessed sectors of the country began to sustain continual improvements as the process of socializing political power began to advance. From the very onset, the Revolution was under attack by U.S. imperialism. Millions of men and women who had now begun to feel as (and become) true human beings became immersed in the recently created mass organizations and popular militias for the defense of the Revolution. It was in that way that the political struggle of an entire people was born. Beginning with massive political acts that formed the base of the socialization of power, this constituted the formation of people's power in Cuba.

The revolutionary transformations that by the end of 1960 were already of a socialist nature began to change ever more radically the conditions of the population's existence. This was largely accomplished by means of ensuring equitable access to forms of social development never before contemplated. The doors became opened to knowledge, health, employment, culture and recreation, and along with these emerged levels of solidarity and a collective dignity that were previously unknown.

The Cuban political system of today forms part of a social totality that has been in continual transformation since 1959. In this sense, it is a sub-system whose basic objective is to achieve the social changes inherent to the larger society. The system does not exist as an end-in-itself, but rather for bringing about a larger social transformation. It envisions the creation of a way of life opposed to the neocolonial bourgeois system that existed in Cuba prior to the revolutionary triumph.

From that point of departure, it can be seen that the political system has since passed through diverse periods, with the institutional organization of the state experiencing periodic changes. Nonetheless, a central element has always been present with greater or lesser force from the first minutes of its existence, namely, that of popular participation. This participation was not only a new type of political and social practice but has in fact constituted a continual demonstration of consent by means of specific activities.

During the first revolutionary decade, new central organs of government were created. The Council of Ministers, an entity that existed prior to the revolutionary triumph, assumed legislative and executive functions. Meanwhile, a key element of decentralization at the base was found in municipal governance which passed through two experiences, first with the creation of the Boards of Coordination, Execution and Inspection (JUCEI) and later with the founding of Local Power. Both tried to concretize adequate forms of representation between the mass organizations (which had by then been already created) and the administrations at the municipal, provincial and national levels. Of the two experiences, Local Power was more significant despite its very brief existence as it created a series of precedents that would later become reevaluated for reincorporation in the system that is presently in place.

The early years of the 1970s were decisive for putting People's Power into full scale practice. As the general conception for Cuban state management was thought out, a decision was made to conduct a pilot project in the western portion of the country. On July 21, 1974, the Provincial Assembly of People's Power was constituted in the province of Matanzas. The follow-up to that experience provided for fine tuning and corrections of certain aspects that would soon afterwards permit the creation of the complete structure of the Organs of People's Power.

On April 10, 1975, the discussions for the proposed Constitution of the Republic of Cuba were initiated. More than 6 million people participated in them, giving rise to hundreds of suggestions. After the mass consultation process culminated in modifications, the draft was submitted to a referendum on February 15, 1976, in which 99.3% of eligible voters over the age of 16 participated, with 98.6% of the population voting to approve the Constitution.[1] This paved the way for it to enter into force on February 24, 1976. With that in place, a new political-administrative structure was established for the country and a calendar of elections was set for the establishment of the Organs of People's Power throughout the entire nation.

If a summary characterization were to be made about the Cuban political system, we would say that it is *popular participation* that typifies Cuba's socialist democracy. The nature, characteristics and functioning of the current Cuban political system clearly constitutes one of the least well known aspects of the new social reality created by the Revolution. We shall now offer a brief, synthetic description that emphasizes key elements for comprehending the overall system.

Key Elements of the Cuban Political System

The Cuban political system is presently composed of:

- *Political organization*, made up of the totality of state institutions and professional and mass political organizations that direct the complex process of creating the socialist society and whose praxis tends to privilege popular participation in the overall process.
- *Relations*, in that the system establishes a specific kind of relations at the interior of political organization as well as between it and the larger society.
- *Juridical norms and regulations*, in which the Constitution of the Republic of Cuba, its diverse laws, regulations and statutes emitted from the State, and the entities, institutions and political organization, including professional and mass organizations, are included.[2]
- *Cultural and political ideology*, oriented towards the transformation of the individual, projected in terms of the formation of a new human being whose values, conceptions and attitudes progressively approximate the socialist ideal.

In 1975, the political system was institutionalized, creating that which (with certain specific modifications made subsequently) exists at present. It is made up of the following constituent elements:

- Political organizations.
- Mass organizations and professional organizations.
- State institutions.

Cuba's *political organizations* constitute the political vanguard of the revolution. They include the *Communist Party of Cuba (PCC)* and the *Youth Communist League (UJC)*. The PCC has more than a million adult citizens that voluntarily belong, selected for membership by virtue of their moral and political character and their willingness to endure personal sacrifice. Among its objectives is the creation and socialization of a development program based on socialist transition, the mobilization of the population through mass organizations, and the reproduction of a political consensus.[3]

The UJC is made up of close to 800,000 young people between the ages of 14 and 30 who volunteer participate in this organization once selected. The UJC carries out tasks of political socialization, the reproduction of political consensus, and the cultural and ideological formation of Cuban youth.

The *mass organizations* actively group together diverse social sectors in order to carry out numerous actions in residential zones and neighborhoods, in cities and rural areas, across the plains and in the most remote parts of the mountains, and in the unions at the base of society and in classrooms of all kinds and levels of instruction. The principle mass organizations are:

- The *Committees for the Defense of the Revolution (CDRs)*, created in 1960 for the purpose of defending the revolutionary process of social transformation, being harassed and subjected to aggression during that period by U.S. imperialism and the internal counterrevolution. More than six million people of age fourteen and over voluntarily belong to the CDRs. They have carried out and continue to carry out various social tasks for the country. This is the largest and most diverse of the mass organizations that exist in the country.
- The *Cuban Women's Federation (FMC)*, created in 1960 in order to organize women around their gender interests and to educate them for their own defense as well as to carry out many other revolutionary tasks. Around three million women belong to this mass organization.
- The *Cuban Workers Union (CTC)* is a powerful trade union organization that was first created in 1939 for the struggle and defense of workers' interests during the period of the bourgeois republic. It is now made up of more than three million members and carries out tasks within the productive sector and in ensuring the revolutionary participation of workers.
- The *University Students Federation (FEU)* is another organization with a long history, founded in 1922. It initially assumed a patriotic attitude in confronting corrupt and anti-democratic governments during the era of the neocolonial Republic. Since that time, it has helped to defend the Revolution and has carried out important social tasks and actions related to the interests of university youth.
- The *Student Federation of Secondary School (FEEM)* was created in 1970 with the aim of incorporating adolescents who wish to belong to the organization, mobilizing them for carrying out tasks from within their student centers that are specific to their age group. They likewise perform work in the cultural and ideological formation of youth.

- The *José Martí Pioneers Organization (OPJM)* was created in 1960 with the aim of mobilizing children at the primary school level, preparing them for election and selection of leaders in the schools and classrooms. The OPJM promotes the analysis and discussion of problems faced by young students and possible solutions as well as participating in the tasks of the Revolution in a manner appropriate to their ages. Like the others, this too is a voluntary organization.
- The *Territorial Troop Militias (MTT)* were formed in 1980 during the especially hostile period of the Reagan administration in the United States. It is made up of around two million men and women who have voluntarily served to prepare for the military defense of the Revolution. Their training is based in the concept of an "All Peoples War" as learned from the Vietnamese experience in their struggle against U.S. aggression. As such, it constitutes an important support organization for the Revolutionary Armed Forces (FAR). As a mass organization dedicated to the country's military defense, its precursors were in the National Revolutionary Militias (MNR) that were created in 1959.

In addition to these mass organizations are the *professional associations,* some of which existed prior to the triumph of the Revolution while others have just been recently founded. These associations assume the tasks of professional development, organizing national and international congresses, workshops and seminars that encourage the debate of ideas and help to project the work of professionals. Among other activities, they all carry out at specified times the work of qualified advisement to state institutions and party organizations with which they are related to in the administration, distribution and quality control of economic, social, cultural and educational development plans and programs.

It is necessary to emphasize that all of the above-mentioned organizations (political organizations, mass organizations and professional associations) carry out tasks that are aimed at advancing social transformation and the progressive consolidation of socialist values and attitudes.

State Institutions

The institutions that make up the Cuban State include the:

- Organs of People's Power.
- Council of Ministers.
- Revolutionary Armed Forces.
- Judicial Organs of Justice.

The Organs of People's Power constitute an integrated system, including:

- The *National Assembly* (Parliament) is the supreme organ of State power in Cuba that represents and expresses the sovereign will of the people. It is the only organ of State with constitutional and legislative power in the Republic. Its faculties include partial reforms of the Constitution of the Republic; the approval, modification or derogation of laws; the approval of national plans for social and economic development as well as the State budget; the declaration of war in the case of a military aggression as well as the approval of peace treaties; the designation of the Council of Ministers; and the election of the president, vice-presidents and the judges of the People's Supreme Court, the Attorney General and Assistant Attorney General of the Republic. The members of the Assembly or *deputies* are elected by direct and secret ballot by the larger population. The deputies are not full time professionals dedicated to this legislative activity but rather each deputy continues working in their own occupation and as such receives no salary, food subsidy, per diem or any other payment or benefit associated with carrying out their elected duty. The National Assembly has a president, vice-president and a secretary who are each elected by the remaining deputies of the Assembly and carry out their duties on a paid, full-time basis.[4]
- The *Council of State* represents the National Assembly in between one or another session period, implements its accords and performs various constitutional duties. It has a collegial character and in the area of international affairs carries out the highest representation of the Cuban State. Its members and leaders are elected by direct and secret ballot by the deputies of the National Assembly. Members do not dedicate themselves full time to this activity and therefore do not receive salaries or other benefits for this duty. Only Council president and secretary work on a full-time basis and are exclusively dedicated to their posts.[5]
- The *Working Commissions* of the National Assembly are created by the Assembly and function continuously throughout the year, made up of deputies that have the responsibility of carrying out specified tasks, including: juridical and constitutional affairs; economic affairs; work concerning production, service, educational, cultural, scientific and technological activities; work relating to youth, children and gender equity issues so as to ensure the rights of women, among others.[6]
- The *Provincial Assemblies* (14 throughout the country) are made up of members or *delegates* who are elected by direct and secret ballot by the

population and who represent the highest level of State authority in the provinces. Its members, similar to the deputies, are not salaried professionals in their post. Each Provincial Assembly has a president, vice-president and secretary, who are the only full-time professionals and are elected by the Assembly delegates. Acting on behalf of their territorial jurisdiction, they implement and enforce laws while establishing the organization, operation and tasks of the administrative localities that are subordinated to them.

- The *Municipal Assemblies* (169 throughout the country) are made up of delegates from the local districts that define each, making up the base of the entire State apparatus. Like at the provincial and national levels, these delegates are not professionals, except for the president, vice-president and secretary elected by each Assembly. They implement and enforce laws throughout their territorial jurisdiction. The municipal administrative leadership is led and controlled by the Assemblies, the latter of which is empowered to designate and/or remove their leadership.[7]

As a consequence of the socioeconomic changes in Cuban society brought about by the Revolution, it became essential to elaborate a new constitution as mentioned earlier. The new Cuban Constitution that went into effect on February 24, 1976 exhibited a socialist character. In 1992, important modifications were introduced following a broad and open debate that came out of the Call to the 4th Congress of the Communist Party of Cuba in 1990. The Call was an important political document that critically focused on accumulated deficiencies and insufficiencies in the Cuban system and it included proposed courses of action designed to address them.

At that moment, the process of transition back to capitalism had already taken place in the Eastern European countries and the collapse of the Soviet Union itself was becoming foreseeable. For Cuba, this signified the lost of its markets and economic, financial and trade relations with those countries. That particular historical conjuncture was seized upon by ultraconservative elements in the United States so as to approve the Torricelli Act in 1992 and later the Helms-Burton Act in 1996. These measures attempted to extraterritorially expand the measures of economic war being waged against Cuba. The country had therefore entered into the 1990s immersed in a deep economic crisis. It was in that historical context that the 4th Congress of the Communist Party of Cuba convened in 1992 to put forward its suggestions to the Cuban State which included modifications to the system of People's Power.

The most important changes included the creation of the Popular Councils, a new level of power that resides between the neighborhood communities and the municipal assemblies, along with a new procedure for electing delegates to the Provincial Assemblies and deputies to the National Assembly. These and other changes were eventually incorporated into the Constitution as well as in the statutes of the Communist Party of Cuba and the Electoral Law.

From the point of view of democratic dynamics, what are the elements that essentially characterize the Cuban political system? In the first place, we could point out two important aspects that are very particular to this system as outlined above:

All elected representatives must periodically provide a full accounting of its work and their mandate can be revoked at any time by the very same deputies, delegates or people that have elected them.

The revocation of mandates is included in the Electoral Law and in 2000, a specific Law on the Revocation of Mandates was approved.

No representative (deputy or delegate at any level) receives salary, subsidies or any other type of payment or benefit for carrying out the work for which they were elected. As a rule, these representatives are not political professionals. Those who are elected to temporarily lead the Assemblies, working commissions or Popular Councils are salaried, at the very same rate that they earned at their place of work just prior to their selection and to where they are permitted to return at the conclusion of their mandate.[8]

Beginning with these two distinctive attributes, we can now offer the following characteristics:

- All Cuban citizens can vote upon turning sixteen years of age and can be elected upon turning eighteen if they are in full exercise of their mental faculties and civil rights.
- The right to vote is universal and is conducted in a direct and secret manner within the representative organs and posts of the People's Power.
- Neither the Communist Party of Cuba nor the Youth Communist League are electoral organizations. Neither organization puts forth or promotes candidates.
- The nomination of the candidates for delegates to the Municipal Assemblies is carried out in mass assemblies in the neighborhoods.
- Nominations of the candidates for delegates to the Provincial Assemblies and to the deputies of the National Assembly are carried out by Commissions of Candidacy made up of representatives of the mass organizations and are presided over by a representative of the Cuban Workers Union.

- A high percentage of delegates from local districts at the base are nominated as delegates to the Provincial Assemblies and as deputies to the National Assembly, the latter of which is made up of 50% of local delegates. The remainder includes scientific experts, cultural personalities, distinguished workers, athletes or students, and administrators from key sectors of the national economy and social services, among others.
- In order to be elected at any of the levels of the system of People's Power, it is necessary to obtain 50% plus 1 of the valid votes.

The electoral processes involve two basic types:

- *General elections* that are held every five years to elect the deputies of the National Assembly and the delegates of the Provincial Assemblies.
- *Partial elections* that are carried out every two and a half years so as to elect the delegates of the Municipal Assemblies.

With the idea of organizing, directing and validating the electoral processes, *electoral commissions* are created. The *National Electoral Commission* is created by the Council of State. Its faculties extend all across Cuba's territory and it selects the members of the *Provincial Electoral Commissions.* The provincial commissions in turn select the members of the *Municipal Electoral Commissions* who in turn are those that designate the *District Electoral Commissions.* The district commissions have multiple responsibilities that include organizing and conducting the neighborhood assemblies that nominate candidates to be delegates of the Municipal Assemblies; defining the schools and the electoral tables at each site and to make public the result of the voting that takes place at the selected schools.

Other institutions of the Cuban State include:

- The *Council of Ministers* is the government of the Republic of Cuba, its maximum executive and administrative organ that is articulated with the Council of State and is selected by it. The ministers direct, orient and control the development of the branches of production and services, of the national economy in general, of the armed forces, of foreign and domestic policy, of foreign and domestic commerce, in short, all of the essential activities of the country. The Council of Ministers has a president, a secretary and various vice-presidents and all of these are professionals.
- The *Revolutionary Armed Forces* are made up of the Western Army, Central Army, Eastern Army, and the Revolutionary War Navy. They are collectively administered by the Ministry of the Revolutionary Armed Forces.

- The *National Revolutionary Police* and the *Organs of State Security* are responsible for the country's domestic order and are under the administration of the Ministry of the Interior.

Cuba's Organs of Justice include:

- The *Popular Supreme Court* which is the highest level of justice in the Republic. Its judges are selected by the National Assembly.
- The *Provincial Tribunals* (14 throughout the country) which are presided over by magistrates selected by the Provincial Assemblies.
- The *Municipal Tribunals* (169 throughout the country), seated by judges selected by their respective Municipal Assemblies. All of these tribunals utilize non-professional or lay judges.

Other Considerations

We have argued that popular participation is the distinctive characteristic of the current Cuban political system. It forms part of the Cuban revolutionary conception of social transformation and the formation of a socialist consciousness. This participation takes on substance through the discussion and debate of proposed laws, regulations, economic adjustment programs, projections of national development, and in the systematic processes of accountability before the larger population that is required of the delegates to the Municipal Assemblies. In all of these processes, the population tends to progressively exercise decision-making power that essentially forms the raison d'être of their participation.

Other participatory mechanisms could also be mentioned, for instance, the social participation in projects of neighborhood and community development that takes place throughout the entire country. Even under the restrictions imposed by the economic crisis beginning in the 1990s, popular participation typified and characterized Cuban socialist democracy. It is precisely the socialist system that creates the conditions that makes such participation possible:

- *Participation arises, becomes developed and is maintained because it rests upon the continual redistribution of social wealth.* The socialist transition dramatically transformed the living conditions of the population through increased access to social development. During its most difficult moments, the Revolution has never renounced its policies of continual redistribution of wealth.

- *Participation arises, becomes developed and is maintained because it forms part of the new forms of comprehending and conducting politics.* The Revolution produced the socialization of political power; the effective distribution of social wealth that enhances welfare also creates power. It is this socialization of power on a mass scale that constitutes the exercise of popular power in Cuba. During the crisis and above all recently, popular participation has become deepened through the "Battle of Ideas" and the mass-mobilized culture, all of which contributes to making social participation an ever more conscious process.
- *Participation arises, becomes developed and is maintained because it has formed part of a new way of life; it is a systematic process of self-education.* The deeply dialectical interrelation between the modification of circumstances and human activity has effectively influenced the formation of attitudes, behavior and socialist values across the generations directly involved in the creation of the new way of life.
- *Participation is carried out as an active consensus towards revolution.* This participation can be identified not only as political and social behavior of a new kind but in fact also constitutes a demonstration of consent. Among other characteristics regarding participation that have not been treated here include the way in which it is organically functional for the development of Cuban society. This integral role of participation, rather than being a mere formality in institutional governance, is what affirms the democratic character of the Cuban political system. The practical forms in which that power is exercised as a socialist democracy has had to be created while being developed in action and of course are perfectively amenable to be perfected still further.

The extraordinary advances that the new socialist political power introduced in the democratization of society compared with that which existed prior to the revolutionary triumph does not exonerate us from recognizing the tensions that exist between power and the project; between the necessity to guarantee the consolidation of the current order and the inevitable necessity for the project to strive for that which is possible under the existing conditions of every period; and for the promotion of a radical reshaping of political behavior while helping to ameliorate the contradictory and negative consequences arising from the changes taking place.

It is essential to generalize the kind of popular political and ideological mobilization that can permit the neutralization of all negative consequences that arise from revolutionary change. In this sense, the "Battle of Ideas," a popular upsurge that began in late 1999 out of the popular struggle that demanded the return of the young boy Elián González to Cuba, kidnapped in the United States by counterrevolutionary groups, constituted a crucial moment in recent Cuban history.

Notes

1. E. Duharte Díaz, "El sistema político cubano: particularidades de su formación y desarrollo" [The Cuban Political System: Specificities of its Formation and Development], in *Teoría sociopolítica* [Socio-political Theory], 142. (The full facts of publication of all the sources are found in the Bibliography, at the end of the essay. *Ed.)*

2. Ibid., 130.

3. J. Valdés Paz, "El sistema político cubano de los años noventa: continuidad y cambio" [The Cuban Political System of the 1990s: Continuity and Change], in *Utopías* journal.

4. *Poder Popular. República de Cuba.*

5. Ibid.

6. Ibid.

7. E. Duharte Díaz, op. cit., 141-142.

8. *Poder Popular,* op. cit.

Bibliography

Duharte Díaz, E. "El sistema político cubano: particularidades de su formación y desarrollo." In *Teoría sociopolítica.* Havana: Editorial Pueblo y Educación, 2000.

López García, Delia Luisa. "Período especial y democracia en Cuba." *Cuadernos de África y América Latina* journal (Madrid), no. 16 (1994).

Martínez, Fernando. "La existencia de un poder muy fuerte es imprescindible." Interview done by Priscilla Pacheco, published in Mexico, 1993. Typewritten copy in author's possession.

———. "Transición socialista y democracia: el caso cubano." *Nuestra América* journal (Havana), no. 16 (1987).

Poder Popular. República de Cuba. Havana: Editora Política, 2001.

Valdés Paz, J. "El sistema político cubano de los años noventa: continuidad y cambio." *Utopías* journal (Madrid), no. 172, vol. 2 (1997).

Cuba's Struggle to Maintain the Social Safety Net in the Age of Globalization

José Bell Lara

José Bell Lara

Ph.D. in Philosophy. A sociologist, he is senior researcher in the FLACSO-Cuba Program and professor at the University of Havana. He has conducted various studies concerning development, social change and social policies in Cuba and Latin America. His numerous publications include *Globalization and the Cuban Revolution* and he was coordinator of *Cuba in the 1990s*.

In analyzing the recent experiences in social development in our continent, it is important to refer to the Cuban experience for two reasons:[1] one is the overall results reached between 1959 and 1989, which introduced radical changes in the quality of life of the Cuban people; the second is the severe economic crisis suffered by Cuba in the 1990s, and from which it is only now beginning to emerge. The State has assumed most of the negative impact of the situation by applying a compensatory social policy in order to protect the social gains of the Revolution; it is a veritable antishock adjustment policy that included daring measures that now, in 2004, we can qualify as unique.[2]

The purpose of this essay is to consider the results of Cuban social policies since 1990, with reference to three areas that constitute the central core of said policies: education, health, and social security. I would like to begin by making some observations that are necessary when dealing with social policies, since they refer to the larger circumstances of their application in Latin America. These factors and the present debates surrounding around them help to contextualize the application of social policies within the framework of the on-going transformation of the world system, something that has unfortunately placed our continent into a new situation of dependence.

Social Policy and Neoliberalism

My first observation refers to the processes of capitalist restructuring that promote globalization. These processes have led our countries into a situation in which the outstanding debt becomes the articulating axis of a mechanism promoting a reorganization of Latin American underdevelopment, designated by us as "the newest form of dependency."[3]

Judging from the characteristics involved in the negotiation processes surrounding the debt, they can be viewed as political and economic interventions through which the economic policies of the continent are dictated. The key is to be found in the conditions that are imposed. For negotiations to be successful and permit the granting of new loans, it is imperative to abide by certain guidelines and apply the entirety of measures advocated by the World Bank and the International Monetary Fund (IMF). Such measures are uniformly applied to the countries regardless of the specific problems of their diverse economies, and together they constitute the implementation of neoliberal adjustment policies.

The area of economic policy is thus defined by transnational forces, especially the international financial entities just mentioned above. Even when local officers are put in charge in a specific territory, the policies that are drawn up and implemented are contained in letters of intention and commitments established by the central offices of the World Bank and the IMF. The core economic policies that are implemented respond to a blind belief in the free market as the key to development and social wellbeing.

And this is my second observation: the market can have many useful purposes, *except that of social justice*. Its mechanism generates inequality instead of equality. Therefore, social policies cannot be left at the mercy of the market, but must be guided by the State for the benefit of all citizens. Only in this manner can a set of universal and individual policies (or "focused" policies, to use today's language) be aimed at sectors with certain degrees of vulnerability.

We believe that the state-market confrontation is not justified in the social area where efficiency should be measured by the capacity for systematic creation and implementation of policies that act in the interest of the majority. A state whose aim is the general wellbeing of the population must be in charge of social policies, and not leave them in the hands of the market. Beyond "state centrism" and "market centrism," we must keep insisting on "human centrism" where everybody, men, women and children, are the subjects and the objects of development.

Incidentally, it is important to note that all recently historical experience, even that of the Asian tigers, confirms that the State has played a critical role in development. Historical experience makes evident that State intervention is not irrelevant to development,[4] and even to non-development. This leads us to my third observation concerning social policies. Both academics and government officials agree that the objective of such policies is social development, understood as the concerted progress of wellbeing, equality, and personal fulfillment for all citizens.[5]

To achieve the above purpose, policies must be efficient and integral. This has not been the case in Latin America on account of the faulty design of policies, the actions of pressure groups, and chronic problems of dishonesty, technical deficiencies, and corruption on the part of those in charge of implementing them. Varies studies on this situation conducted by ECLAC and other institutions have confirmed these tendencies.

It is clear to us that privatization of an asset or a service is not necessarily any guarantee of efficiency. In the processes of privatization throughout Latin America, the norm has been increased corruption rather than greater efficiency. There is ample information on this, so it will not be repeated here. I simply wish to emphasize that efficiency in social as opposed to economic areas is not one and the same. Cost improvement has another dimension. It is necessary to measure costs, but if certain benefits are desired one must pay the cost. Education and preservation of the so-called human capital is costly, and without human capital it is not possible to talk about international competitiveness in the new global economy. If a State lacks the policies or institutional tools to invest in this area, the country will not be competitive in the long run. Rather, we could be condemned to remain as exporters of raw and semi-elaborated products which in fact is the aim of the neoliberal scheme.

We can pronounce endless dissertations and make all sorts of noise about the search of international competitiveness or a reentry into the world economy. But when the main exports of a country are sugar, coffee, bananas, crafts, or minerals, that country is wearing the "dirty face" of modern underdevelopment. Here, I would add that the reduction in expenditures for education, health, and research, decreases our opportunities to develop scientific and technological systems in keeping with the needs and possibilities of our countries.

It may be that my fourth observation is redundant. But it needs to be remembered that any privatization of social services implies "the abandonment of public criteria for services, leaving it to be replaced by the criteria of a private enterprise, i.e., maximum profits and profitability."[6] Numerous studies have been done on this worrisome process.

In my opinion, many disturbing deficiencies and destructive tendencies arise from the process of making a business out of social services such as education, health care, and social security. In most of our countries, the limitations of social policies derive from the very same model of accumulation which they reproduce.[7] This model, neoliberalism, imposes a growing dynamic of exclusion and inequality. While it, a matter of time before a regional consensus, determines that this is not the road to travel, we shall in the meantime have to unfortunately withstand the costs imposed by the present conjuncture of global forces.

Social Achievements: 1959-89

Underdevelopment is associated with hunger, abysmal living conditions, illiteracy, lack of education, high mortality rates, unemployment and underemployment, non-organized labor forces, and extreme social inequality. Cuba in 1959 was no exception to that situation. One third of the labor force was either unemployed or the victim of underemployment; illiteracy affected 23.6% of the population; less than one half of school-aged children attended elementary school; there was 1 physician for each 1076 inhabitants; life expectancy was 60 years; and infant mortality was over 40 for each thousand live births.

Social policies introduced by the Revolution gave priority to the most underprivileged, while proposing to improve living conditions for the whole population. Economic policies were characterized by an effort to combine the economic

119

and social aspects of development, resulting in drastic economic changes together with a notable improvement in the living standard of the population.

The State set in motion an integral and sustained social policy, supported by a wide margin of popular participation aimed at developing basic social services such as education, health care, and social security, with priority given to children, women, and the rural population.[8] Each of the areas had specific problems and situations that required special strategies. For example, the starting point in education was the training of volunteer teachers, the Literacy Campaign, education for adults, and university reform, establishing the preconditions for the country to arrive at its present educational system.

The program for health care started with the system of rural medical attention and with massive vaccination campaigns. Social security began with the merging of various institutions in charge of the so-called retirement or insurance funds (fifty-two institutions of this type were active in 1958) into a self-governing organization, the Social Security Bank of Cuba, along a program of reforms that kept growing until coverage was finally made available to the entire working population.

The financial system for social security was the object of drastic changes. Its funds are collected exclusively from the employers through the tax known as "contributions to social security." Insurance expenses became an item in the national budget and payment operations were entrusted to the National Bank of Cuba and its network of agencies all over the country.[9]

Law 1100 of 1963 required that all workers and their families be assured of social protection in cases of illness, maternity, work accidents, professional illnesses, disability, old age, and death. With the passage of Law 24 of 1979, the comprehensive system was given final form.

Given the large number of changes introduced by the Revolution and of all the social policies in force over three decades, Cuba reached remarkable results in social development as summarized in Table 1. In contrast to the situation of 1958, these figures for 1989 show that Cuba had achieved by the late eighties levels in the main indicators of quality of life that surpassed the averages for Latin America and the whole of developing countries for the same dates.

In order to measure the social development in Cuba by 1989, it would be necessary to compare the country with the industrialized capitalist nations, because the values measuring the results in this area were similar in both cases despite the fact that Cuba was a developing country. The comparison can be summarized briefly: same life expectancy as that in developed countries; the number of childbirth cases under health care personnel; infant mortality only slightly higher; the country had more physicians for the number of inhabitants; elementary and secondary schooling were similar.[10] The situation in the nineties affected the foregoing conditions and the social development.

Table I

Comparison of Social Indicators, 1989			
	Developed countries	Cuba	Latin America
GNP per capita	10,760	3245	1790
Daily calories per person	3390	2948	2700
As percentage of minimal needs	132	128	115
Life expectancy at birth (years)	74	75	67
Access to health care (% of population)	n/a	100	61
Infant mortality rate (per 1000 live births)	15	11.1	55
Mortality rate in those younger than 5 (per 1000 live births)	18	13.6	79
Childbirths under health care personnel (institutional)	99	99.8	77
Direct maternal mortality (per 10,000 live births)	24	29.2	100
Inhabitants per physician	500	300	1200
Adult literacy (%)	n/a	98	83
Net schooling – elementary education:			
Boys (%)	97	100	75
Girls (%)	97	100	75
% of children who start elementary school and quit, or not finish it in due time	11	7	55
Students per teacher in elementary schools	19	12.3	28

SOURCE: Beatriz Díaz, "Cuba: modelo de desarrollo equitativo" [Cuba: Model of Equitative Development], in ALAS-CEA, *Sistemas políticos, poder y sociedad (Estudios de casos en América Latina)* [Political Systems, Power and Society (Cases Studies in Latin America)].

The "Special Period"

At the onset of the 1990s, a conjuncture of several factors created an extremely difficult situation for Cuba, perhaps the worst crisis in the history of the Cuban Revolution, which came to be known as the "Special Period." These factors included the fall of "real Socialism" in Europe and the disintegration of CMEA along with the system of international relations in which Cuba participated, the worsening of the U.S. economic blockade, and a number of errors and deficiencies in the country's economy. The previous relations between Cuba and CMEA consisted of a mechanism of integration that included a system of prices, credits, production supplements, and a series of commitments that came with a high degree of security, allowing for a stable projection of economic development. The post-CMEA period can be defined as a time when, with all the features and tensions brought about by a huge crisis, Cuba managed to restructure its foreign relations as well as its system of production and services, with the aim of preserving as much as possible the achievements of the Revolution under changing world conditions. It was a time of crisis and also a time for searching.

Cuba is an open economy as evidenced by an aperture index estimated at 50%. Imports represented slightly more than one third of the product. The share represented by the CMEA countries accounted for more than 85% of total foreign trade, with the principal items and rates being as follows: food imports, 63%; raw materials, 86%; fuels, 98%, machinery, 80%. With regard to exports, sugar accounted for 63%; nickel, 73%; citric fruits, 95%; electronic units and parts, 100%. This helps to explain the severe magnitude of impact occasioned by the abrupt termination of these trade relations.

Between 1989 and 1993, the Cuban economy's capacity for imports was reduced by more than 75%; Gross Domestic Product fell slightly more than one third; and industrial production suffered a sharp decline by around 80%. The overall operation of the Cuban economy depends on the import of fuels and in 1989, Cuba imported 13 million metric tons of oil. In the years that immediately following, that amount became reduced by more than one-half. The official exchange rate had the Cuban peso on par with the dollar during the 1980s, but with the crisis, it became sharply devalued and by the first half of 1994, the dollar had reached a price of more than 100 pesos in the black market.

It is of course not possible to fully capture the magnitude of the crisis by just citing figures, rather; it can only be described as a catastrophe that affected the whole country as if it had been through an all-out war. Social conditions, however, did not suffer to the same extent despite all of these enormous difficulties.

The State bore the brunt of the crisis and took various measures in order to neutralize the most negative consequences. It is possible to identify two stages during the difficult and complex decade of the nineties when economic policies attempted to preserve as much as possible the social achievements of the Revolution.

The first stage that I would delimit between 1990 and 1993 could be characterized as a policy of shared shortages. Rationing of all consumer products went into effect with the purpose of assuring the utmost degree of equality in their distribution. It is precisely because of such measures that in 1993, the worst year of the crisis, the nation was able to maintain an average supply of 1983 calories and 46 grams of proteins, or 78% and 64% of the average per capita needs, respectively.[11]

Salaries and employment levels were maintained, despite the economic problems that resulted in a large scale paralysis of production centers. In 1993, for example, 80% of industrial capacity was at a standstill and the sugarcane harvest of 1993-94 reached only 4.3 million metric tons. There were also substantial losses in agriculture, particularly in those areas which had been developed through high technology and mechanized methods.

The policies designed to protect the population from the most negative effects of the crisis reached their limit in 1993, when the complex financial situation exhibited a large excess of currency in circulation at more than 11 billion pesos and a high fiscal deficit of 5050 million or practically a third of the Gross National Product. In that same year, a nationwide process of discussion was initiated along with a new stage of economic measures aimed at bringing the crisis under control. Some measures had already been taken in 1990 such as a selective opening to foreign capital investment, the promotion of tourism, and a concentration of investments in sectors of rapid economic recovery. But the new measures represented a broader shift in the national economy. Not necessarily in order of priority, these measures included:

- A wider opening to foreign capital, and a sharper definition of the legal framework for its operation through legislation regulating foreign investments.
- Decriminalization of the use and possession of foreign currency.
- Elimination of the state monopoly on foreign trade.
- Widening the sphere of activities eligible for self-employment.
- Setting up cooperatives on a large scale for state agriculture.

- Creation of a national tax system.
- Reorganization, simplification and rationalization of the institutions of central state administration.
- Creation of agricultural and industrial markets that would be governed by the law of supply and demand.
- Policies for financial reorganization that eliminated some goods and services which were formally free while raising the price of various other non-essential products.

While it is impossible within the scope of this essay to explain the logic of each of the above measures, or the extent to which each contributed to opening the way to a slow economic recovery, it can be said that in 1994, the decline of the economy was halted. In 1995, a 2.5% growth of the economy was registered, followed by a sharp fluctuation of 7.2% growth in 1996 and 2.5% in 1997. From that time on a slow and steady process of economic recovery is happening and, remarkably, in all the branches and sectors of the economy. In 2003 the GNP growth was 2.3%. Excess liquidity, which as mentioned above surpassed 11 billion in 1993, became reduced to one-fourth that level in those years that immediately followed. The large budget deficit went from 4.2 billion in 1993 or almost a third of GNP to a highly manageable level of 3.5% of the GNP.

The exchange rate for Cuban currency also strengthened, from over 120 pesos per dollar when it spiked on the black market in 1993 to 26 pesos per dollar, now under state control. While the basket of basic food products remained subsidized by the state throughout this period, it is also estimated that prices for other products on the free market have decreased by more than 40% since 1994.

All of the measures that were adopted during this period were not just the result of technical operations. Rather, each one had been introduced by taking into account its political character and the logical impact that it would have upon the majority of the population. For example, the creation of a dual monetary system that introduced inequality between those who have, and those without access to dollars, was accompanied by compensatory measures such as the introduction of a tax on foreign exchange, for social use, placed on products sold in a chain of state run stores operating entirely in dollars.

By granting authorization to enterprises to operate in dollars both in the tourist sector and by export companies, it was possible to connect the internal economy to the world economy without resorting to devaluation of the currency, thereby avoiding the social costs that such measures would have otherwise implied. Implementation of the financial program was preceded by a substantial process of discussion by the Cuban Workers Union (CTC), during which there was a call to hold Workers Parliaments (assemblies), making it possible to adopt the program by a majority vote.

It must be emphasized that this process did not take place within the framework of an ideal scenario, but rather against a worsening of the aggressive policies of the United States. In 1992, when the economy seemed to be in a freefall, the Torricelli Act was passed in order to intensify the blockade. In 1996, just as the process of recovery seemed to be gaining a foothold, the Helms-Burton Act was passed. Its purpose was to enact a total blockade against Cuba through the punishment of third countries doing business on the island. This law was firmly repudiated by the international community.

Social Policy during the Special Period

Given these conditions described above, let us examine Cuban social policies more closely. In general terms, it can be said that the crisis did not force the closing of schools or hospitals. Sick people were not neglected and no child had to quit school so to work selling trinkets in order to contribute to the survival of their family. The following is a brief account of the situation that resulted:

Achievements in education prior to 1989 included free educational services to the whole country and to all social segments, something which produced (a) a very high rate of literacy, more than 95% of adults; (b) a high percentage of young people who complete the mandatory level of 9th grade; and (c) a high skill level in the overall workforce where for every 100 workers, 13 are middle level technicians and 7 have a university education.

The impact of the crisis imposed extraordinary challenges to this educational system, but they were confronted not only with priority attention on the part of the government but also with a spirit of creativity and society's broad participation. Faced with the difficulties in continuing with construction of children's centers for preschool education, the Educate Your Child Program was developed "which is not academic but is supported by families and local communities, and covers 55% of preschool aged children."[12]

At other levels of learning, systematic efforts were made to sustain the quality of education, despite widespread problems with educational materials and support resources due to the shortage of convertible foreign currency. An academic course in Cuba requires more than 50 million notebooks and an even larger number of pencils. The State made huge efforts to guarantee such supplies. Problems are also encountered with textbooks, and efforts were also made to overcome them.

There were serious restrictions in food supplies for full boarding and semi-boarding schools. In the case of the latter, a solution was developed to connect school dining-rooms to workers' dining-rooms. As for full boarding schools, wherever possible the government helped to develop mechanisms of self-supply and other initiatives. Additional strains appeared when teachers were transferred to higher salaried positions. The resulting shortage was solved by the creation of Pedagogical Brigades, consisting of students from the Pedagogical Institutes that have begun teaching at the elementary level while finishing their professional training. By the year 2000, "emergency teachers" were being prepared to help guarantee adequate staffing for elementary schools.

In the face of all the above-mentioned difficulties, the educational achievements of the Revolution were maintained. In Cuba, there is presently 1 teacher for every 42 inhabitants. Schooling for the population aged 6 to 16 years was at 94% by the end of 1997. For pre-school and elementary school levels, 88.8% are included in the double shift program. In addition, 3 other indicators that had suffered during the Special Period had already recovered by 1997-98: 99% overall school retention; 99% retention of students graduating from the sixth grade, and 98.99% retention of basic secondary school. Cuba has a network of 57 centers for higher education, with a total enrollment of 126,000. There is no thought of canceling the right to free education at any level, including university studies, while the struggle continues to provide full coverage and to maintain and further increase its quality.

In the area of care, Cuba's achievements are symbolized by its constitutional right to comprehensive care. This is made possible through a network that provides coverage at the national, urban, and rural levels. Services are free and assistance, prevention, and treatment are provided to all citizens regardless of race, sex, or age.

As can be seen from Table 3, in 1989 Cuba had 1 physician for every 303 inhabitants and an oral health physician for every 1623. The number of physicians had increased 5 times the total that had been available prior to the Revolution, oral health specialists by 25 times, and the number of beds increased threefold. A growing medical-pharmaceutical industry was able to produce close to 90% of the medication needed by the country.

Cuba had eradicated polio (1962), tuberculous meningitis (1971), neonatal tetanus (1972), diphtheria (1979), congenital rubella syndrome (1989), and meningo-encephalitis due to parotiditis (1989). A transcendental step in the field of health care was the introduction of a plan back in 1984 for a family physician and a nurse; its main purpose was to decrease the morbidity/mortality rates induced by non-transmittable diseases and their risk factors, and improve the state of health of the population through well-integrated actions aimed at individuals, families, the community, and the environment. The office of every family physician covered an average of about 700 inhabitants. When preventive medicine is operative, the result is a decrease in medical treatments.

In the early years of the Special Period, the crisis predictably had a negative impact on the general state of health. Some of the consequences observed were an increase in underweight births and material mortality, a slight increase in cases of tuberculosis, and small increases in infectious and parasitic illnesses. However, mortality due to these illnesses did not exceed 2% of total deaths in the country.

There was also a certain degree of decline in some programs such as vector control and environmental sanitation. The latter was due to lack of equipment and fuels for proper control of solid waste. Also, there was a slight increase of morbidity rates in cases of some transmittable diseases, this being caused by the declines in sanitation and living conditions.[13] One serious problem was the onset of polyneuritis from various causes, requiring a mobilized effort to eradicate it. Considering the country's overall economic situation and the resources that were available, the problems could have been much more serious. The fact that this turned out not to be the case was due to concerted government actions, the priority that was given to public health, and the mobilization of citizen cooperation.

Despite all of the above problems, the general state of health of the Cuban population was for the most part maintained, and since 2000 has even improved in some indicators. Given the continuing lack of convertible foreign exchange, it presently remains difficult to acquire some medications necessary for testing and diagnostic care. Thus we find that the main causes of death continue to be chronic and degenerative illnesses. Life expectancy remains unchanged and infant mortality, which in 1989 was 11 per thousand live births, decreased in 1999 to 6.5 per thousand live births, with 99.9% of births taking place in hospital facilities. Since 1994 no diphteria or measles cases have been reported. Illnesses preventable by immunization, such as tetanus, diphteria, rubella, and parotiditis, show morbidity rates lower than 0.1 per 100,000 inhabitants. Data concerning the main indicators of health for 1999 and 2002 appear in Table 2.

Table 2

Main Indicators of Health, 1999 and 2002		
	1999	2002
Birth rate per 1000 inhabitants	13.5	12.6
General mortality rate per 1000 inhabitants	7.1	6.6
Infant mortality rate per 1000 live births	7.2	6.5
Maternal mortality per 100,000 live births	52.4	41.7
Children under 2 years of age protected against 11 illnesses (%)	98.5	95.5
Percentage of population in the care of family physicians	97.6	99.2
Beds for medical assistance per 1000 inhabitants	6.1	5.0
Beds for social assistance per 1000 inhabitants	1.3	1.3

Sources: Ministry of Health, *Situación de la salud en Cuba. Indicadores básicos, 1999* [Situation of Public Health in Cuba. Basic Indicators, 1999]; Ministry of Health, *Anuario estadístico de salud, 2002* [Statistical Yearbook of Health, 2002]; National Office of Statistics, *Estadísticas seleccionadas, 1999* [Selected Statistics, 1999].

Since the crisis of the early nineties, Cuba has reached the goal set by the World Health Organization for the year 2000 under the Extended Program of Immunizations: 98% of children under 2 years of age are protected against 10 preventable illnesses. Efforts remain ongoing to guarantee national self-sufficiency in the production of vaccines. Among others, the country already produces anti-meningococcical, tetanus toxoid, anti-typhoid, and anti-hepatitis "B" vaccines.

One remarkable accomplishment during the last few years has been the improvements made in the system of family physicians (who reside next to their consultation offices in the neighborhood they serve). In each coverage area, the physician cares for an average of 125 family units (about 700 people). While the total number of physicians has almost doubled in these critical years, the number of family physicians has more than tripled (see Table 3). This guarantees that 98.3% of the population will be cared for by a family physician and nurse.[14]

Table 3

Some General Health Indicators					
	1958	1989	1996	1999	2002
Inhabitants per physician	1076	303	183	172	168
Inhabitants per oral health physician	27,052	1623	1148	1125	1130
Total physicians	6286	34,752	60,129	64,863	67,079
Family physicians	—	8965	28,530	29,648	31,059
Total oral health physicians	250	6482	9600	9918	9955

SOURCE: "Informe de Cuba a la Cumbre Mundial de Desarrollo Social" [Cuba's Report to the World Summit for Social Development]; ECLAC, *La economía cubana: reformas estructurales y desempeño en los noventa* [Cuban Economy: Structural Reforms and Performance during the Nineties]; Ministry of Health, *Anuario estadístico de salud, 2002* [Statistical Yearbook of Health, 2002]; National Office of Statistics, *Cuba en cifras, 1999* [Cuba in Figures, 1999].

How was this accomplished? Despite the critical economic situation, Cuba regarded health as a primary right of all citizens. Ensuring the continuation of this service was therefore a prioritized responsibility of the State. This protection is supported by programs that have been developed as part of the social policies designed to promote the integral improvement of living standards. The State has not given up its commitment to health care for the Cuban people. On the contrary, a whole series of policies, programs, and a network of health institutions have been developed to guarantee that all levels of medical attention, either by prevention or by treatment, reaches the entire population and remain free of charge. Table 4 contains additional information regarding medical assistance as it evolved through the years.

In spite of the severe crisis of the nineties, social security has also been sustained as a system that is universal and equitable. With the increase in life expectancy, the number of elderly people is constantly growing larger, and so is the number of retirees. At the present time, one in every ten Cubans is living on a pension. The main stress on the system is the growing deficit between the portion of the budget allocated to social security and the amount of income being derived for that purpose, which consists solely of contributions from employers. In today's pesos, this deficit is hovering around 700 to 800 million pesos.

In 1994, one of the subjects widely discussed among the emergency measures to be taken in confronting the crisis included that of workers' contributions to social security. While it was approved in principle, its eventual implementation will depend on the economic conditions of the country and to what extent it will impact on the income of working people.

Table 4

Medical Assistance Units				
	1958	1993	1990	1999
Hospitals	337*	265	268	276
Polyclinics	52**	421	419	442
Stomatology clinics	n/a	148	163	165
Maternal homes	n/a	153	152	241
Elderly's homes	n/a	n/a	155	225
Hospital beds	28,500	77,739	78,164	77,367

*. Includes 242 mutual clinics.
**. It refers to emergency posts known as Houses for Assistance.
SOURCE: National Office of Statistics, *Estadísticas seleccionadas, 1999* [Selected Statistics, 1999]; "Informe de Cuba a la Cumbre Mundial sobre Desarrollo Social" [Cuba's Report to the World Summit for Social Development]; Ministry of Health, *Anuario estadístico de salud, 2002* [Statistical Yearbook of Health, 2002].

The overall priority given by the government to social expenditures can be verified by the resources that the State earmarks in its budget (see Table 5). In 1989, 41% of the budget was assigned to social expenses while in 1996 it had grown to 58% of the budget. Despite these increased expenses for social security, however, the budget deficit had decreased by 80% compared to 1989, including unemployment subsidies for those who were working in companies affected by the crisis.

Social Priorities for the 21st Century

During the first 4 years of this new century, the priority list of social expenditures in the State budget has continued to be maintained. In 2004, 59% of the budget or 12,155 million pesos were allocated to social spending. That figure was equivalent to 37% of the GDP. There has been a profound renovation in social policies, with the implementation of various programs that clearly demonstrate that it is possible to have a society that fights for social justice and solidarity despite living in economically underdeveloped conditions. New, concrete initiatives in Cuban social policy in the areas of education, health care,

Table 5

Budget for Social Expenses (selected items)*			
	1989	1996	1997**
Total income	12,600	7654	7891
Total expenses	14,014	8013	8197
Surplus / deficit	−1415	−359	−305
Total social expenses	5178	4447	4702
Education	1664	903	962
Health	912	764	829
Transfer for social purposes	1883	2279	2372
Social security	1103	1044	1109
Subsidies for price differences	679	467	533
Subsidies to companies for underemployment	n/a	676	626

*. The series of current prices were deflated with the indexes of prices implicit in the Gross National Product.

**. Losses of state enterprises due to underemployment (ECLAC). Does not include food subsidies.

SOURCE: ECLAC, *La economía cubana: reformas estructurales y desempeño en los noventa* [Cuban Economy: Structural Reforms and Performance during the Nineties]; and data given by the Ministry of Finances and Prices.

employment and social security are integrated into and indeed form part of the larger ideological struggle for socialism known as the "Battle of Ideas." The policies have been carried out through social programs, including some that have a strong participatory role on the part of Cuban youth.

In the area of education, numerous programs have been implemented, including those directed at training new teachers, elevating the existing level of teachers, repairing and expanding schools, implementing the use of mass audio visual equipment as well as extending the reach of university and higher education. The progress made in these programs during the 2003-2004 period can be summarized as follows:

- At the primary level of schooling there is a student teacher ratio of 20 students or less per teacher, a television per classroom and a video recorder per 100 students.
- At the junior high school level, a double study session was introduced, there is 1 teacher per 15 students and there is extensive support of audio visual material.

- To the educational system at all levels 24,000 computers have been added, guaranteeing computer learning and access throughout the country.
- At the university level, 732 municipal venues throughout the country have been created at which 146,913 young students now study, thus contributing to the universalization of higher education.

These programs have increased the demand for professors and teachers at all levels. In order to satisfy this demand, 4000 integrated professors have graduated and work at the junior high school level in addition to the 30,000 new professors working in distinct parts of the country. At the university level, hundreds of associate professors have been integrated into the university body, stemming from the most diverse backgrounds. There is a general process of elevating the educational level in university education and the evidence of this can be seen in the fact that more than half of the faculty at the University of Havana now possess their doctoral degrees. Taken together, the social programs mentioned above suggest a profound revolution in the conception and functioning of the educational system.

In the area of health, multiple programs are being developed of which the following are deserving of mention:

- Senior citizens program.
- Program of prevention and control for vaccine-preventable diseases.
- Program of prevention and control of chronic, non-vaccine preventable diseases.
- Medicines program.
- Program of renovation and transformation of pharmacies.
- Maternal-Infant program.
- Optical care program.
- Program for the formation of "emergency" nurses.

As a result of these programs and others during the year 2003, a better system of coordinated functions was created between polyclinics and hospitals. In addition, 1927 pharmacies were repaired so as to improve service, a mass program dedicated to improved training of medical personnel was sustained, and research and development in the production of medications continued.[15]

In the current era, employment and social security constitute two major problems worldwide. Looking through the daily newspapers in almost every country, one can easily perceive the deterioration of the labor market and the rise in levels of unemployment. In Latin America, the 2003 unemployment rate was registered at 10.7%, higher than the levels which prevailed back in 1990 and 1980. While the challenge of employment and social security is also present in Cuba, a socialist perspective has prompted new methods to be utilized in confronting this challenge.

Beginning in the initial years of economic recuperation towards the latter half of the 1990s, employment policy has been oriented towards diminishing unemployment, redistributing displaced workers, protecting the income level of workers and vulnerable groups, and generating new jobs.[16] In addition, the development of urban agriculture has served to augment food production while creating 326,000 new jobs since 1996. With regard to youth, there is a new approach that utilizes studying as a form of work, giving more marginalized young people the opportunity to prepare themselves for a better future. This program benefited 107,923 people in the year 2004, 30,000 of whom have enrolled in university courses.

In accordance with revolutionary ideals, the restructuring process of the sugar industry has not led to high unemployment levels, thanks to simultaneous policies implemented to retrain displaced workers, with many being incorporated into the educational system or other activities. All of these social programs have themselves constituted an important source of employment. By the end of 2003, those employed in the social sector included 15,000 social workers, 13,000 computer instructors, 8000 primary school teachers, 1053 physical education teachers, 2713 nurses, 1055 health technicians and 3142 operators of audiovisual equipment.

As a whole, the result of policies that unfolded in the recent years of economic recovery led to over 1,180,000 new jobs, with the unemployment rate in 2004 at just 2.3%. This level allows us to state that full employment has once again been attained, something that constitutes the best possible guarantee of social security. In 2004, nearly 2 million persons were actively receiving social security benefits in Cuba, of which 1,464,049 were on pensions while 395,821 were receiving social assistance. In the previous year, the State had allocated 2561 million pesos for social security and social assistance or 11% of the GDP.[17]

Alongside of these quantitative indicators, there have been qualitative improvements in social service delivery. With new kinds of specific policies geared towards offering better solutions to vulnerable groups, including the orientation and social prevention work by a new generation of social workers, citizens in need of assistance and solidarity are being attended to. In the best of times as well as in the toughest, the policies and ideals of the Revolution has consistently followed the logic of the majority.

Our Own *Guayabera*

We do not intent to draw an ideal picture of the Cuban situation. Ongoing economic difficulties are very serious and they affect daily life. The State has taken measures to distribute these effects as equitably as possible and then to try to overcome them. It is at this juncture that we now find ourselves. There are numerous challenges, each one requiring a special strategy, imagination, and policy decision-making, since their complexity must be mirrored in their solutions.

The closing of some companies and the search for entrepreneurial skills represent a serious challenge to the situation of full employment that was enjoyed until 1989. Cuba cannot afford the luxury of applying shock therapy, and leaving thousands of workers in the street. The policy of plant closings has been introduced gradually and combined with a series of measures. On the one hand, workers' subsidies are preserved while they are offered other options of employment. The priority for newly available jobs is given to workers already available, while segments of the work force are retrained, and special attention is given to certain social groups, for example, the young. The shortage of supply has increased prices in the private market, which results in a deterioration of real salaries. In addition, the policy of financial reorganization has a general effect, so that some social groups are more affected than others.

Some segments of the population suffer from the great disparity between their income and their expenses, showing a deficit in the relation of expenses/income. That is why some of the newest policies are directed at such groups. One example is the system of family assistance through which food services are assured at modest prices to more than 100,000 low income people, with a perspective that it will eventually help all who need it. In addition, this system intends to have an effect on food prices so they can be lowered by 20%. The free circulation of the dollar introduced some new elements of social discrimination, but chains of state stores have been opened for the sale of products and services in dollars, at prices carrying a special tax that is applicable to social assistance.

In these complex and difficult years, it has been necessary to take some measures that may be viewed objectively as not being in line with the social project of the Cuban Revolution, either due to the type of inequalities that result, or the advantages they create for certain social segments. However, the logic still presiding over these changes consists of maintaining the basic socialist character of Cuban society. In other words, even though there are changes in social policies, there is no change of the overall social policy per se; only different ways to sustain its effectiveness under new and changing conditions.

It is not possible to end this report without referring to the blockade, which exacerbates most difficulties and is the main source of suffering for the population. The Helms-Burton Act has tried to perpetuate this situation.

In the midst of these difficulties, Cuban society has not lost its quality of solidarity and its citizens know that they will never be neglected. The State maintains a system of basic social services, which in the present circumstances is a minimum expression of our expectations of life in a society based on solidarity.

The aim of the Revolution was to solve the social problems involved in underdevelopment, and the fact that they have been solved is one of the strengths of the Revolution; to lose them is tantamount to losing the sense of the Revolution. It is true socialism for the masses, and its loss would affect the security of the Revolution. This is why, under current circumstances, that the non-introduction of neoliberal policies in the economy is a victory for the Revolution. In this sense, social policies are a weapon of the Revolution, and social development constitutes a vital area for its national security.

For those who promote neoliberalism, there are no alternatives to its policies. Steeped in their own fundamentalist and messianic vision, they are devoted to dismantling public health systems, education policies, and social security, rather than just making changes, and surrendering them to vagaries of the market. For these new fundamentalists, privatizing is a sacred commandment and the market is the altar on which social justice is to be sacrificed. For neoliberals, there is no other way for economic and social policies. However, Cuba shows that there are alternatives in the form of adjustment programs that will be successful in preserving social justice.

In ending, let me refer to the parable of the happy man. The legend tells us that there was a man suffering from numerous evils, for which the sages of the times had prescribed a remedy: to be happy, the king had to wear the shirt of a happy man. And the legend goes on to say that when the king found a happy man, it turned out that he had no shirt.

Cuba reminds us of the happy man's story. The wise and powerful of our times have prescribed for the people a remedy for their problems; it is a holy remedy, a kind of universal shirt, with the same formula recommended by the IMF and the World Bank, regardless of the characteristics of the economy of each country. By donning this shirt, all problems can supposedly be solved: hunger, misery, lack of culture, illiteracy, extreme poor health, dire poverty, unemployment, in short, all the evils of underdevelopment. What they refrain from saying is that Latin America has adopted different models of the same shirt over centuries, because the real name of that shirt is capitalism.

Now they have come up with a new model, with a more attractive look, clean, scented, fully wash-and-wear, with brighter colors than Benetton, and to top it all off, with excellent marketing strategies. This new model is neoliberalism. Its formula for salvation: an all-inclusive market. Deification of the market means that it is the only means of salvation, and the way to climb the stairs toward post-modernity, or so claim the advocates of neoliberalism.

A decade after donning the new shirt, Latin American societies are poorer and more unequal than before. Neoliberal policies have proven to be incapable of solving the continent's social problems; all they can do is develop formulas to manage them, which explains why there are countries where the economy is in fine shape while most of their people live poorly.

To those who emphasize the failures of Socialism, we wish to remind them of the failures of capitalism in the process of development. On this point we are fully knowledgeable. We experienced it in Cuba up through the decade of the fifties and we recognize it in today's Latin America. For us, this represents the past. It is the reason why we do not wear that shirt. We prefer to put on our own *guayabera*, a homegrown shirt that best fits our nation. And our *guayabera* is called Socialism.

Notes

1. Since 1978 ECLAC attracted attention to the importance of studying the Cuban experience on social development. See ECLAC, *Estilos de desarrollo y política sociales* [Social Development Styles and Policies]. (The full facts of publication of all the sources are found in the Bibliography, at the end of the essay. *Ed.)*

2. Delia Luisa López, "Crisis económica, ajuste y democracia" [Economic Crisis, Adjustment and Democracy].

3. José Bell and Delia Luisa López, "La novísima dependencia" [The Newest Form of Dependence], in *La nueva América Latina* [The New Latin America].

4. Carlos Vilas (coordinator), *Estado y políticas sociales después del ajuste* [State and Social Policies after Adjustment].

5. Irma Arriaga, "El debate actual de las políticas sociales en América Latina" [The Current Debate on Social Policies in Latin America], in *Nueva Sociedad* journal.

6. Consuelo Ahumada, "Política social y salud" [Social Policy and Health], 136.

7. Carlos Vilas, op. cit.

8. José Luis Rodríguez, "El desarrollo económico y social en Cuba: resultado de treinta años de revolución" [The Economic and Social Development in Cuba: Outcome of Thirty Years of Revolution], in *Cuba Socialista* journal.

9. Áurea Rodríguez, *La seguridad y asistencia social en Cuba* [Social Security and Welfare in Cuba].

10. Elena Díaz and Beatriz Díaz, "Cuba y los siete países capitalistas más desarrollados" [Cuba and the Seven Most Developed Capitalist Countries].

11. Centro de Investigaciones de la Economía Mundial (CIEM – Research Center on Worldwide Economy) and UNDP, *Investigación sobre el desarrollo humano en Cuba*.

12. Ibid.

13. Ibid.

14. Ministry of Health, *Situación de la salud pública en Cuba. Indicadores básicos, 2002*, op. cit.

15. Silvia Martínez, *Cuba Beyond Our Dreams;* José Luis Rodríguez, "Informe sobre los resultados económicos del 2003 y el Plan Económico Social para el 2004" [Report on the Economic Outcomes in 2003 and the Economic Social Plan for 2004], in *Granma* daily.

16. Alfredo Morales, "Batalla de ideas, empleo y seguridad social" [Battle of Ideas, Employment and Social Security], in *Granma* daily.

17. Ibid.

Bibliography

AHUMADA, CONSUELO. "Política social y salud." Paper presented at the Seminar Internacional Relations, Social Policy and Health, Bogota, 1998.

ARRIAGA, IRMA. "El debate actual de las políticas sociales en América Latina." *Nueva Sociedad* journal (Caracas), no. 144 (1995).

BARREIRO, GEORGINA. "Presentación a la Asamblea Nacional del Poder Popular del Proyecto de Presupuesto del Estado para el 2004." *Granma* daily, 26 December 2003.

BELL LARA, JOSÉ and DELIA LUISA LÓPEZ GARCÍA. "La novísima dependencia." In *La Nueva América Latina*. Madrid: Ediciones FLACSO-SODEPAZ, 1993.

CASTRO, FIDEL "Speech Given by President Fidel Castro Ruz, First Secretary of the Central Committee of the Communist Party of Cuba, at the Main Ceremony for the 45th Anniversary of the Attacks on the Moncada and Carlos Manuel de Céspedes Garrisons." *Cuba.cu*. http://www.cuba.cu/gobierno/discursos/1998/ing/f260798i.html. Accessed July 23, 2004.

CENTRAL DE TRABAJADORES DE CUBA. *Sistema de seguridad social*. Havana: n.p., 1980.

CIEM and UNDP. *Investigación sobre el desarrollo humano en Cuba*. Havana: Editora Caguayo, 1997.

DÍAZ, BEATRIZ. "Cuba: modelo de desarrollo equitativo." In ALAS/CEA, *Sistemas políticos, poder y sociedad (Estudios de casos en América Latina)*. Caracas: Editorial Nueva Sociedad, 1992.

DÍAZ, ELENA. "Calidad de la vida en Cuba: efectos de la política norteamericana." *Cuadernos de África y América Latina* journal, no. 16 (1994).

DÍAZ, ELENA and BEATRIZ DÍAZ. "Cuba y los siete países capitalistas más desarrollados. Working Document at FLACSO, University of Havana. 1990.

ECLAC. *La economía cubana. Reformas estructurales y desempeño en los noventa*. Mexico City: CEPAL and FCE, 1999.

———. *Estilos de desarrollo y política sociales*. Mexico City: Siglo XX, 1980.

"Informe de Cuba a la Cumbre Mundial de Desarrollo Social." World Summit for Social Development, Copenhague, 1995.

LÓPEZ GARCÍA, DELIA LUISA. "Crisis económica, ajuste y democracia." Working Document no. 3 at FLACSO, University of Havana, 1994. Typescript.

MARTÍNEZ PUENTES, SILVIA. *Cuba Beyond Our Dreams*. Havana: Editorial José Martí, 2004.

MINISTRY OF HEALTH. *Anuario estadístico de salud, 2002*. Havana: MINSAP, 2003.

———. *Situación de la salud en Cuba. Indicadores básicos, 1999*. Havana: MINSAP, 1999.

———. *Situación de la salud en Cuba. Indicadores básicos, 2002*. Havana: MINSAP, 2002.

MORALES, ALFREDO. "Batalla de ideas, empleo y seguridad social." *Granma* daily, 5 and 6 March 2004.

NATIONAL OFFICE OF STATISTICS. *Cuba en cifras, 1999*. Havana: n.p., 2000.

———. *Estadísticas seleccionadas, 1997*. Havana: n.p., June 1998.

———. *Estadísticas seleccionadas, 1999*. Havana: n.p., 2000.

RODRÍGUEZ, ÁUREA. *La seguridad y asistencia social en Cuba*. Havana: Editora Política, 2000.

RODRÍGUEZ, JOSÉ LUIS. "El desarrollo económico y social en Cuba: resultado de treinta años de revolución." *Cuba Socialista* journal, no. 39 (1989).

————. "Informe sobre los resultados económicos del 2003 y el Plan Económico Social para el 2004." *Granma* daily, 25 December 2003.

Rojas, M. and A. Delgado (Compilers). *Política social: desafíos y utopías.* Bogota: Pontificia Universidad Javeriana, 1997.

Stahl, Karin. "Política social en América Latina. La privatización de la crisis." *Nueva Sociedad* (Caracas), no. 131, 1994.

Vilas, Carlos (Coordinator). *Estado y políticas sociales después del ajuste.* Caracas: Editorial Nueva Sociedad, 1995.

The Transition to Sustainable Agriculture and Rural Development in Cuba

BEATRIZ DÍAZ GONZÁLEZ

Beatriz Díaz González

Ph.D. in Psychology. She has conducted various studies on Cuban quality of life and is an expert on problems of infant development, agriculture cooperatives, coastal communities and sustainable development. She is a senior researcher and the Director of the FLACSO-Cuba Program.

The Concept of Sustainable Development

It would be an error to assume that the concept of "sustainable development" has a fixed and precise definition. In reality, this notion connotes a wide range of positions, some of which are even contradictory. One of the most frequently cited definitions appeared in the Brundtland report made by the World Commission on Environment and Development in 1987. Published under the name *Our Common Future*, it was expressed that: "Sustainable development is that which satisfies the needs of present generations without compromising the capacity of future generations to satisfy their own needs."[1]

In general, however, more precise formulations that could better contextualize the definition were missing in that report. For example:

> Needs are understood particularly as essential needs of the world's poor, to whom absolute priority should be given. . . . Sustainable development requires the promotion of values that stimulate consumption patterns that are within ecologically possible limits and to which all can reasonably aspire. . . .

> Sustainable development requires that societies satisfy the human needs by increasing productive potentials and assuring equitable opportunities for all. . . . At a minimum, sustainable development must not endanger the natural systems that support life on Earth: the atmosphere, the waters, the soils and the living beings. . . . The majority of renewable resources are part of a complex and interrelated ecosystem, and in order to define the maximum yield that is sustainable, the effects that exploitation has upon the entire system should be taken into account. . . .

> Sustainable development demands that the rhythm of exhausting non-renewable resources should be reduced to the most minimal possible levels.[2]

In a general sense, this report that did so much to popularize and contribute to raising consciousness about the need for sustainable development, expressed progressive as well as moderate positions with respect to the issue. Although it advocates for greater equity in the distribution of wealth and for assisting the development of the poorest countries, it did not analyze in any profound way the causal structures of persistent inequality and underdevelopment. In a similar manner, it calls for protecting and conserving both renewable and non-renewable natural resources as well as for promoting reasonable patterns of consumption on the one hand, but without managing to establish the relationship between the exhaustion of resources, consumerist patterns and the economic rationality of capitalist accumulation.

A rather similar approach appeared in the publications of the World Resources Institute. In *1992-93 World Resources,* different definitions of sustainable development were summarized, emphasizing the physical (use of renewable and natural resources), economic (maximizing the net benefits of economic development while maintaining the services and quality of natural resources), and human developmental aspects (improving health, education, and social welfare services), including the participation of local inhabitants in the decisions that affect their residential habitat as well as showing that equity is an important component of practically all definitions of sustainable development.[3]

How is it possible that notions as diverse as these remain grouped together under the same conceptual referent? As James O'Connor so brilliantly expressed:

> There are few expressions as ambiguous as sustainable capitalism and their derivative concepts of "sustainable agriculture," "sustainable resource use," and "sustainable development." This ambiguity pervades all of the most important notions concerning the economy and environment that appear in government reports and UN documents, academic research, popular journalism and ecological political thinking. It is precisely this lack of clarity that leads to so many people having spoken and written for so long about sustainability: the term can be used in practically whatever sense of meaning that one wishes to give to it, which is precisely what is so attractive about it. This signifies that sustainability is an ideological and political question, and not so much an ecological and economic question.[4]

Thus, the first contribution we can make from a social scientific point of view is to comprehend this diversity of positions along with all of their determinants and various interconnections. Of greatest relevance would probably be the ties between economic globalization and global environmental problems. The possibility of contextualizing ecological concerns from a North-South perspective also seems promising, i.e., which are the main concerns and priorities of the developing and more developed countries with respect to environmental questions? Why do such marked differences exist between them and what precisely determines these differences?

There exists an important group of researchers, almost all of whom are to some degree influenced by Marxism, that conduct studies in this area. Political ecology, economic ecology, and eco-Marxism are some of the labels associated with such thinkers. Among the most distinguished of these include James O'Connor (cited above), who since 1988 has been editing the journal *Capitalism, Nature and Socialism*, his son Martin, both U.S. academics, as well as Joan Martínez Alier of Spain and Enrique Leff of Mexico. The two following citations illustrate the value of these approaches; Lori Ann Thrupp states:

> In the perspective of political ecology, the goals of "sustainable develop-ment" emphasize or call for social equity and the respect for human rights as well as ecological sensitivity and economic productivity. This does not refer solely to the rights of future generations (as was emphasized in the Brundtland Commission report) but indeed, these propositions are urgent for present day societies and intragenerational rights. This requires a diver-gence with respect to the purely ecological and conservationist areas (for example, protected park and wildlife areas), and implies a critique of op-portunistic "green investors" on the part of some large companies such as the electricity and energy firms, that are making superficial technical changes or donations to environmental causes while continuing exploitation prac-tices that operate in their own interests of accumulation. In place of this, the implications of a political ecology perspective support the notion of social justice and human rights as essential factors for resolving the dilem-mas related to natural resources. The means for reaching these ends in-clude wide reaching political changes, challenging power relations, protect-ing the interests of marginalized persons, including women, the poor and racial and ethnic minorities, supporting cultural and epistemological diver-sity, and legitimating local bases of knowledge that have been displaced by the hegemony of Western, scientific reductionism. In this way, an alternative vision can help challenge the dominant paradigm that continues to perpetu-ate socially and environmentally unsustainable conditions.[5]

With even greater theoretical sophistication, Enrique Leff has developed ideas in his book *Green Production: Toward an Environmental Rationality* where he argues the necessity of "a theory that is . . . capable of constructing an environmental rationality based on the principles of eco-technological produc-tivity and participatory management of environmental resources that could pro-vide a foundation for ecological sustainability and social equity in the process of development."[6] These proposals offered by Leff constitute a notable advance towards a theory of sustainability as an alternative to the destructive course being charted by contemporary capitalism when viewed from the economic, social and ecological points of view. Leff considers that

> . . . materialism should move towards building an economic environmental policy, for which Marxism should re-elaborate the categories of nature and culture so as to situate them at the center of the productive process. This new theory of production, "ecoMarxism," beyond considering the environment as an externality or as just another element in the general conditions of production, actively incorporates the environment as a potentiality in the productive process. An ecoMarxist theory would give a new orientation and grounding to the development of the productive forces by integrating ecological, technological and cultural processes into more solid, equitable and sustainable productive processes. EcoMarxism puts forward a field that articulates economic ecology and political ecology, capable of integrating the ecological conditions of production, the environmental potential of sustainable development and the political power of the ecological movement towards the end of constructing an environmental rationality.[7]

It can therefore be concluded that the study and further elaboration of these social scientific contributions being made to environmental issues constitute both an indispensable requirement and a distinct potential for facilitating a possible transition towards sustainable development in Cuba. In this, there are many obstacles that will need to be overcome, including the lack of a current bibliography, sparse availability and the lack of means for their reproduction and distribution, and the high level of complexity in some texts. Last but not least is the fact that fairly rigid conceptions of Marxism had prevailed during the years of philosophic training of many of our specialists. This legacy promotes a certain prejudice that expresses itself in the aspiration towards maintaining a better known orthodoxy rather than engaging in more novel but less well known theoretical approaches.

Sustainable Agriculture and Rural Development

If we limit ourselves to the sphere of agricultural and livestock production in rural areas, a great diversity of positions can be observed concerning sustainable development. In the first place, we should distinguish between the positions related to the technological-productive process proper. "Sustainable agriculture," "organic agriculture," "permaculture," "low input sustainable agriculture (LISA)," and "agroecology" are some of the most frequently encountered concepts found in this specialized literature. Although differences exist in approaches and procedures, they all share a common status of being alternatives that became formed in opposition to the so-called "green revolution" whose negative environmental consequences have been amply documented, above all beginning when Rachel Carson published her famous 1962 book *Silent Spring*.

Today, it is known that these technologies result in biodiversity losses because they are based on a monocrop approach to just a few "improved" varieties of agricultural products. These practices promote among other things the disappearance of species and varieties resulting from the use of petroleum-based products and the destruction of the natural environment through the violent modification of existing ecosystems. Also associated is the creation of bio-resistant plagues, extensive soil and water contamination, erosion and salinization of soils, deforestation, and ultimately severe harm to human health. But we will not focus here on those issues, but rather on the approaches and research studies in the social sciences that have made a contribution to the deeper understanding of the "green revolution" and its generalized practice around the world.

In the first place, it should be pointed out that the "green revolution" constituted the expression of the modernization model of development in the agricultural and livestock sectors. This model was based upon orthodox economic theory that understood development as a historical process in which societies evolve in a natural manner and pass through predictable stages towards industrialization, a greater availability of goods and services, and mass consumption, with a predominance of private enterprise and "representative democracy."[8] For that, it was supposed that all nations must pass through five stages of development: 1) traditional stage; 2) establishment of the pre-conditions for an economic "take-off" through the construction of a political and technical infrastructure; 3) "take-off" stage (formation of capital); 4) the drive to maturity (of the economy); and 5) the age of mass consumption.[9]

It is well known that the "improved" varieties of the "green revolution" reached high levels of agricultural yield when employed in an intensive manner, using such inputs as machinery, irrigation, fertilizers, and chemical herbicides and pesticides. Much less well known is that the transnational corporations that produce and sell these inputs actively financed the research that led to the development and utilization of these special crop varieties (principally wheat, corn and rice). Put another way, these corporations invested in research characterized by a marked blindness to the problems associated with this development, since in the final analysis, it was an investment in the creation and expansion of new markets for seeds, tractors, harvesters, irrigation equipment, and petro-leum byproducts.[10]

The social and economic consequences of agricultural modernization have also been studied, particularly with respect to the distribution of wealth. The more unequal the pattern of land ownership and access to credits and other mechanisms that could protect small producers, the more severe are the nega-tive social consequences of agrarian modernization.[11] Such is the case in Latin America where "the productivity per person employed in agriculture grew 2.3% annually during the 1960s and 1970s, while agrarian production grew at an average of almost 4% annually. At the same time, poverty and rural immiseration, rural-urban migration, and urban poverty grew rapidly while the dependence upon imported foodstuffs likewise intensified."[12] It could be concluded that

> The capitalization of agriculture associated with the green revolution gener-ated an overproduction and under-consumption of foodstuffs, leaving be-hind a devastating legacy of socio-environmental degradation . . . generated by the intensive use of water, agrochemical and energy inputs. Recent stud-ies have demonstrated the impact that modernization in the countryside had upon expropriation, expulsion and marginalization of the rural popula-tion, in uprooting peoples from their land and tradition, and on intensifying impoverishment and increased malnutrition.[13]

New fields of socioeconomic research deserve greater attention. The first relates to a current phase of agricultural modernization, i.e., the development of agrarian biotechnology. Certain aspects have been revealed such as private sector control over research and its resulting blinders, the production of substi-tutes for primary goods that the underdevelopment countries are busily export-ing, and above all, the relationship that exists between biodiversity and phyloge-netic resources possessed by the countries of the South and the development needs of the biotechnological industries of the North. This explains why the developed countries, especially the United States, have imposed policies that reinforce the rights of intellectual property over genetically modified organisms.[14] It also explains why the Global Plan of Action agreed upon in 1996 at the Fourth International Technical Conference on Plant Genetic Resources in Leipzig did not recognize the property rights of the countries of origin to their phylogenetic resources, but rather only those who already possessed them in their collections abroad.[15]

The creation, introduction into production, and commercialization of ge-netically modified organisms (GMO) appears at present to be uncontainable, in spite of a growing preoccupation about their possible ecological, socioeconomic, and human health related effects. From the ecological point of view, the release of these organisms constitutes a serious threat to genetic diversity. Nonetheless, global concern over these risks, above all in the European countries, has been gradually giving way in the face of the tremendous power of the transnational foodstuff corporations. As a result, the barriers to importing genetically modified foodstuffs have been disappearing along with the means by which to protect consumers, such as the obligation to adequately label commercial food products so as to inform consumers that they contain GMO.

In the same manner that occurred with the introduction of the "green revolution," this process is presented as the possible path towards the elimination of world hunger, a miraculous technological solution that will permit the production of more food for all. The fallacy in these declarations are described in numerous studies dedicated towards deepening our comprehension of the causes and socioeconomic consequences of the actions being taken by transnational corporations mentioned earlier. One of the most cited cases is that of the Monsanto Corporation who has produced genetically modified seeds as well as the herbicide Roundup to which their seeds are resistant. In selling this technological package to agricultural producers, the producers become completely subordinated to Monsanto's designs. Not only must producers buy all of the seeds that they sow from Monsanto when using this pesticide, but they are also obligated to strictly follow the company's instructions throughout all aspects of the productive process.

Little is known with respect to the possible effects of GMO upon human health. It does not appear that any country in the world or any individual citizen (unless they produce all of their own foodstuffs) can consider themselves free of this potential threat. In Cuba, for example, there are strict norms in place on biosecurity insofar as GMO goes, but we are a food importer country. Goods such as powdered milk are imported, involving livestock that was possibly fed with transgenetic soy and other cereals. We have also imported chicken meat from the United States that are fed not only with transgenetic cereals but also with hormones that are designed to stimulate their rapid growth. All of this indicates the need to continue researching and disseminating information about the introduction of GMO in the global production of foodstuffs.

Other directions in this literature have worked on the sociodemographic and socioeconomic analyses of rural life, especially with regard to rural poverty, as well as on development project design and implementation, including participatory management of natural resources by rural communities and the recognition of local knowledge bases.[16]

The vast collection of studies briefly summarized above attests to the economic, social and ecological aspects that should be considered in their interaction and mutual determination. More than just thinking in terms of "sustainable agriculture," the conceptually appropriate thing to do would be to integrally consider agrarian development and rural sustainability in their totality. That is how the United Nations Food and Agricultural Organization (FAO) formulated its approach in "The Den Bosch Declaration on Sustainable Agriculture and Rural Development" when it reported to the 1991 Conference on Agriculture and the Environment in the Netherlands. That report considered that the essential goals of sustainable agriculture and rural development (SARD) are: a) food security by ensuring an appropriate and sustainable balance between self-sufficiency and self-reliance; b) employment and income generation in rural areas, particularly in order to eradicate poverty; and c) natural resource conservation and environmental protection.[17]

At the same time, the report showed that

The fundamental changes and adjustments to promote SARD should include:

1. active involvement and participation of rural people through their organizations such as farmers organizations, cooperatives and informal groups in the research and development of integrated farm management systems compatible with maintaining the essential biological processes and related training activities;

2. decentralization by devolving more decision-making authority and responsibility down to the local level, by providing incentives and resources for initiatives by local communities, by enhancing their status and management capacity, including that of women, rather than relying on top-down administrative mechanisms;

3. allocating clear and fair legal rights and obligations with regard to the use of land and other natural resources, including land reforms where necessary, and particular attention should be paid to the important role of rural women as decision-makers, food producers and food providers;

4. relieving pressure on natural resources by investing in improvement, rehabilitation and conservation of natural resources so that they can be used intensively and safely;

5. adjusting macro-economic and agricultural policies and instruments to promote production systems and technologies that can help to attain the objectives of SARD;

6. encouraging demand and providing incentives favoring the crops and animals which can be produced and processed sustainably;

7. promoting agronomic practices, production and processing systems that pay particular attention to safeguarding human health and environmental quality, especially in relation to the use of dangerous pesticides;

8. promoting alternative off-farm livelihood opportunities in rural areas, such as food processing and other industries, and, where necessary, facilitating the accommodation of migrating populations in better-endowed areas.[18]

In examining these goals and proposed changes, it can be concluded that this approach encompasses issues ranging from the socioeconomic aspects relative to rural development to the ecological aspects tied to the technologies of agricultural production and the management of agro-ecosystems. The extensive citation is useful for us since we frequently speak of the technical-productive aspects (organic agriculture or sustainable agriculture) while the social aspects relative to rural development and the active participation of people as the protagonists of this process in the countryside tends to be forgotten.

Sustainable Agriculture and Rural Development in Cuba

Cuba presently has favorable conditions for sustainable agricultural and rural development from the sociological (decentralization, participation) as well as the technical-productive (introduction of environmentally appropriate alternative technologies) points of view. In both categories, the social sciences can and should make an important contribution. For a better understanding and evaluation of the present situation, it would be useful to briefly explore the recent historical evolution in both directions.

Democratization of the Rural World

As in the rest of Latin America, Cuba had once possessed a bimodal structure[19] in the distribution of landed property. According to the 1945 Agricultural National Census, 8% of farms and ranches had controlled 71% of the land, while 92% of all farms and ranches composed the remaining 29% of land. Only 21.7% of arable land was actually cultivated. The large sugar and cattle ranches made up 87% of the national areas.[20]

Poverty was most concentrated in the rural areas. In the 1950s, the rural population was made up of 600,000 rural workers, 100,000 sugar workers, and 200,000 campesino families, all of whom were subject to seasonal unemployment and underemployment, and were poorly fed on the whole. Only 8% received state organized, free medical attention and 40% of those older than 15 years of age were illiterate while only 10% of rural homes had electricity.[21]

The rural poor constituted a priority objective for the projects of social justice and redistribution of wealth that marked the profound social transformations initiated in 1959. The Agrarian Reform Laws (1959 and 1963) transferred the control of landed property (up to 67 hectares) to those who worked the land. More than 100,000 campesino families were beneficiaries of these expropriations of the large landowners. Programs designed to generate employment were put into practice in the agricultural and livestock sectors and social services were instituted so as to provide education, health, electricity and communications to the countryside, thus producing a radical democratization of the Cuban rural sector.

By the middle of the 1980s, Cuba achieved social development indicators that were comparable and in some cases higher than that of the developed countries, without leaving behind appreciable regional differences or a large inequality in rural-urban quality of life.[22] The strong upward social mobility that characterized the decades of the 1960s and 1970s especially involved the inhabitants of rural zones, above all, the children of campesino families.

As Rodríguez argued, "the preferable solution for the development of Cuban agriculture, in view of earlier cases of socialist development, was considered to be the agrarian management by the State of large confiscated properties that were already organized in a capitalist style or maintained largely vacant by the previous large landowners,"[23] a policy that in Cuba was seen as favorable due to the former predominance of the large landowning class and agrarian wage-earning class prior to 1959. After 1959, this permitted "the construction of socialism in agriculture by virtue of having 40% of cultivated lands already in the most advanced form of agrarian socialization, socialist people's property. In the conditions that existed in Cuba, the socialist transformation of agriculture consisted in the first instance of working to incorporate 70% of agrarian lands into state people's property, which included 60% of all of the workable land on the island.[24]

The participation of the State in landed property grew still further in subsequent years and came to include more than 82% of the total land by 1989.[25] State agricultural production was organized in the form of large enterprises of which 385 existed by 1988, with 146 of them dedicated to sugar cane agriculture.[26] It has been recognized that the "gigantic" size of these enterprises become one of the obstacles preventing their efficient economic functioning.

According to Figueroa, "the average size of agrarian enterprises extended to 13,413 hectares in the sugar cane sector, 28,000 in the cattle sector, 27,200 in rice production, 17,400 in citric and fruit groves, 4300 in assorted farm produces, and 3100 in tobacco fields."[27] The so-called "diseconomies of scale" in management reduced the benefits of large scale agriculture due to the increase in management costs at the same time that efficiency decreased. The problem rested in the increased distancing of management links, the vertical structuring and time delays in implementing the dynamic decision making necessary in agricultural production along with other difficulties associated with decision making.[28]

This hierarchal, centralized and vertical conception that had been put into practice throughout the agricultural sphere notably limited the real possibilities of participation among the agrarian workers, and thus the development of a sense of participation. To this can be added the scant material and moral incentives offered to the state agricultural workers (almost 79% of the rural sector). The average monthly salary in the state agricultural sector was the lowest of the 16 economic sectors in 1975-80; in 1981-84, it remained among the lowest and only beginning in 1985 did agrarian salaries substantially close the gap with the average of the overall productive sphere. The construction of housing constituted one of the strongest incentives for campesinos that since 1976 became organized by the Agricultural Production Cooperatives (CPA), something that did not exist for the state agricultural workers.[29]

In search of greater economic efficiency and providing better incentives for work, various organizational reforms were enacted in state agriculture during the course of the 1980s. An attempt was made to reduce the number of persons working in administration as well as to produce a stable relationship between the workers and the areas or crops in which they worked. To facilitate that, the enterprises were subdivided into farms, basic production units, and ranches.

Nevertheless, it was not until 1993, a time when the crisis that began in 1989 had become strongly felt that a process some consider to be the third agrarian reform was initiated. The state lands began to be handed over in permanent usufruct to those workers that wished to join up in cooperatives known as the Basic Units of Cooperative Production (UBPC – Unidades Básicas de Producción Cooperativa).

Each UBPC functions as an economic unit that receives a permanent usufruct of land and is able to assure its harvest through purchasing its means of production and other inputs through credits from the National Bank. The principal inputs are provided by state enterprises that operate under the direction of the ministries of sugar or agriculture (depending on the economic activity involved) to whom their product is also sold.

The UBPCs function according to the principle of one person, one vote and the members of the general assembly of each UBPC is the maximum authority for all of its decisions and should meet once every month. Each assembly elects from its own an administrative board whose members can be recalled at any time by the assembly.

Given that the creation and operation of the UBPCs represent a transformation of such great scope and since they are intimately linked to sensitive aspects like the production of food, sugar and other export crops such as tobacco, it has attracted the interest of wide sectors of Cuban society, including social researchers. During their first year of operation in 1993, the Scientific Pole for the Humanities sponsored a research project on these new cooperatives in collaboration with the FLACSO-Cuba Program, designed to bring together researchers from different scientific centers around the country to study the first three years of the UBPCs' operation.

The studies took as their objective diverse aspects of the economic and productive functioning of the UBPCs, the stability of the work force, the principal motivations of its members and other issues.[30] The lack of autonomy, basically due to the persistence of hierarchical ties and methods of administrative management on the part of the state enterprises as well as the absence of a "sense of ownership" on the part of the members of the new cooperatives have been two of the themes most debated by researchers. Some have even thought that the only way to adequately resolve both of these limitations would be to privatize the lands involved.

In our judgment, this would constitute a grave error because it would represent an attack on the nation's patrimony and because the present level of urbanization of the Cuban population (at 80%) signifies that there no longer exists a rural population of campesino traditions and culture that would be apt for the conversion of small inheritances of land into productive and well-cared for plots. We consider that the creation of the UBPC constitutes a moment of greater democratization in the process of Cuban agricultural production because it "implies an accelerated step of the transition from a centralied and hierarchical, statist system of production to one that is more democratic and participatory."[31] Considering that the core of the concept of social participation consists of the participation in decision-making, the evolution of this process within the UBPC has constituted a fundamental object of our research efforts. In that regard, two levels can be distinguished: the elected members of the administrative board and the general assembly of cooperative members.

The first involves a small group that makes decisions on a daily basis (although those decisions of greatest importance should be approved by the assembly) and which has greater possibilities of exercising participation and thus to develop a sense of participation and ownership within the cooperative. This notion was confirmed by two case studies of UBPC dedicated to the cultivation of "varied crops." In these studies, the following profiles emerged of cooperative members:

A. S. has served as an UBPC administrator for one year. He was initially proposed to the assembly by the state agricultural enterprise to which this cooperative is affiliated following a period of growing productive and labor disorganization within the unit. The evolution of his attitudes and behaviors has been rapid. His growing interest in exercising leadership can be observed towards the end of creating a more efficient collective. His aspiration for greater autonomy of the cooperative from the state enterprise, something practically non-existent at the onset, has become notably accentuated. He feels increasingly more like an active participant and works towards developing more long term projects.

J. D. is the economist of a UBPC, a post that he has occupied for three years or since the unit was first created. Before that time, he had worked another three years as an economist on a state farm out of which this UBPC was created. He believes that there exists a big difference between his work then and now. On the state farm, he was limited to writing reports and sending them up the chain of command, but he never knew if they were being taken into account for anything, although he tended to think not. This is because "up above," they always said everything that they were in a hurry to accomplish. Now, everything is different. Each calculation that he makes has a direct utility and it helps the cooperative to know how they are working and to better know what they should do.

The participation of cooperative workers in the decision-making of general assemblies was the object of a separate case study carried out between June, 1994 and June, 1995.[32] In its conclusions, it was found that the cooperative members of the UBPC studied had advanced a significant portion of the way towards constructing a real, participatory democracy. Nevertheless, it was learned that:

> As these meetings have conclusively shown, the road to greater participation is not smooth or linear. Social attitudes and behaviors accumulated over a period of years do not change overnight and it will take time to shape

new and more cooperative attitudes, including a new self-perception. Such changes imply multiple transitions, i.e., from "receiving orientations," to making decisions; from being a salary worker striving to get more money, to postponing immediate gratification and remaining austere so as to "advance payments" in order to obtain greater revenues at the end of the year; from being receptive and demanding more from an overprotective state, to assuming greater responsibility and giving priority to the best areas of investment. Great importance must be placed upon the "operational" aspects of cooperative organization. . . . Today, everybody accepts that the general assembly is the "highest decision-making body" in the cooperative. But the key question is how to best exercise this democracy; how to stimulate the adoption of elaborate yet clear proposals; in short, how to avoid the anarchic operation and inefficiency of the assembly. . . .[33]

It can thus be concluded that the creation of the UBPC constituted a step forward in the process of democratization of the Cuban countryside that was initiated with the first Agrarian Reform Law of 1959. It has created greater potential for a transition towards a sustainable rural and agrarian development in Cuba by making possible a greater and more direct form of direct participation of the producers themselves in decision-making, making them protagonists in their own process of development. Nonetheless, this is only a potential to which very diverse kinds of obstacles stand in opposition, structural impediments that are both external and internal to the Cuban economy as well as conceptions, habits and customs. Cuban social sciences can make an important contribution in helping to characterize these obstacles as well as searching for ways to overcome them.

From the "Green Revolution" to Sustainable Agriculture

Agricultural modernization or the "green revolution" was the model adopted by Cuban agrarian development during 1959-89. More precisely, it meant the possibility of applying science and technology with an economy of scale, leading to the organization of extensive state enterprises basically dedicated to specialized, monocrop production or cattle raising (bovine, pork and poultry). Of course, monocrop production was not initiated in Cuba during that period but on the contrary had been established since the 18th century with the expansion of sugar cane destined for the refined sugar industry. Indeed, the cattle grazing that existed in the 1950s had its distant origins in the patterns that became established even earlier than sugar cane during the era of the Spanish conquest.

The change in social conditions brought about by the revolutionary triumph contributed to increasing the necessity for mechanization, above all for the sugar cane harvest. The sugar cane cutters found new work opportunities that were better paid and the aspirations for humanizing this extremely arduous work began to unfold. But there was also a certain installation of firm beliefs that machinery, irrigation, fertilizers and pesticides constituted the most advanced scientific and technological means of developing agrarian production. In much the same manner that took place in other branches of the economy, the agricultural sector has come to totally accept the modernization model. This tendency was accentuated with the entry of Cuba into the Council of Mutual Economic Assistance (CMEA) in 1972 and the subsequent integration of the Cuban economy into the economy of the former Eastern European socialist countries and the former Soviet Union in particular. Modernization was basically the model of development that had been adopted by that country.

Some figures might better illustrate the magnitude of efforts realized under that model. During the 1960-90 period, agriculture absorbed 25% of national investments, for a total of 15,677 million pesos, with 56% of that amount made during the final decade. Almost one fourth of the basic productive means of the country were utilized in this sphere. The 40 scientific research centers connected to agricultural production represented a third of all existing scientific resources. One out of every 10 agricultural workers possessed a technical-professional or university degree. In 30 years, the amount of land under cultivation had doubled and agricultural production grew by 70%.[34]

During the ten year period between 1975-77 and 1985-87, the percentage of land under irrigation relative to that which was cultivated went from 21% to 26%, while the average annual use of fertilizers grew from 118 to 192 kilograms per hectare. The annual average use of pesticides went from 7817 to 9567 metric tons of ingredients. The number of tractors increased by 11% to reach a total of 62,462 while harvester combines increased by 71%, reaching a total of 4212. In 1989, 1,374,000 tons of fertilizers and ingredients were imported along with 17,151 tons of herbicides and 9740 tons of other pesticides.[35]

In spite of these tremendous efforts, numerous shortcomings persisted in this sector where extensive growth predominated, low agricultural yields persisted, poor productive efficiency was widespread, and the application of scientific results to production was generally slow. Meanwhile, 57% of land under cultivation was dedicated to exports and 43% to domestic consumption or what amounts to 0.14 hectares per inhabitant. By the end of the 1980s, imports were still providing 55% of calories being consumed, 50% of proteins, and more than 90% of dietary fats.[36]

Among the causes of this undesirable situation, beyond that which has already been mentioned with respect to the lack of incentives for agricultural workers, was the growing influence of the Soviet model during the 1975-85 period. This needs to be taken into account because it accentuated the formation of rigidly centralized and vertical tendencies along with the bureaucratization of society. Consequently, the whole process of agricultural production was centrally planned and vertically directed, issuing "technical instructives" which called for mandatory compliance, while the observations of numerous specialists that worked in farms and enterprises were not at all taken into account and indeed, local decision-making was not at all encouraged.

The economic crisis that unfolded in 1989 rendered the modernization of the Cuban agricultural system non-viable. With the disappearance of the former Socialist Bloc and the Soviet Union, a substantial decline in oil imports made it impossible to import steel for the mechanical equipment industry that had earlier made notable achievements. Mechanical spare parts became ever scarcer as were fertilizers, herbicides and pesticides. By 1993, the worst year of the crisis where the national product was now 35% less than it was in 1989, the nation's food security had become seriously affected.[37]

The magnitude of the impact forced a search for alternative solutions, creating a kind of favorable "niche" for generalizing the results of various experimental practices that has been developed over the years by the agricultural research institutes. The novel character of these alternative approaches, and above all, their massive extension into agricultural production, captured the interest of numerous scientists, especially in the United States. Professor Richard Levins who had maintained close ties to Cuban scientists ever since the 1960s wrote:

Cuba is the first country in the world that has restructured its society in accordance with ecological principles. This decision was in part the result of urgent necessity, in part the result of conviction, and in part the retrospective result of that which had been developing for various short term reasons. . . . The development of science and Cuban policies . . . made it possible for ecologists to have an important impact on policy when the so-called "Special Period" made it impossible to continue the old ways of doing things.[38]

In 1992, a group of U.S. scientists organized what they called an international scientific delegation with the mission to search for data on low input, sustainable agriculture in Cuba. The report prepared by this mission, edited by Peter Rosset and Medea Benjamin, was first published in 1993 under the title "Two Steps Backward, One Step Forward" and then later as a book by Ocean Press under the title *The Greening of the Revolution: Cuba's Experiment with Organic Agriculture.* In that same year, a group of articles edited by the participants of that mission was published in the journal *Agriculture and Human Values* (vol. 10, no. 3).

A good synthesis of the changes that were taking place in Cuban agriculture was published by Vandermeer, et al.:

> The alternative model incorporated virtually all of the programs imagined by agricultural specialists with an alternative approach in the developed countries, plus numerous characteristics that are specifically Cuban. The alternative model included: 1) the use of organic fertilizers (commonly called biofertilizers in Cuba); 2) biological control of pests; 3) crop adjustments according to local ecological conditions; 4) animal traction and other forms of alternative energy; 5) diversification of crops and intercrops, especially with the use of local and native crop varieties; 6) an increase in the use of local workforces and reinvigorated forms of community participation in decision-making; 7) soil conservation, reforestation, and attention to degraded lands; 8) exploration of local knowledge as a base for alternative technologies; and 9) an inversion of the rural-urban migration so as to increase the number of people dedicated to agriculture.[39]

Many of these programs had an accelerated development, such as the use of animal traction, while others like intercropping developed more slowly. Nevertheless, the contribution that probably most stood out in Cuba in this experience was the development, production, and use of biopreparations for the control of pests and plant diseases. Based upon experiments that were carried out by the Instituto de Investigaciones en Sanidad Vegetal (Institute of Research on Plant Health) and other research centers, the "biopesticides" were produced through procedures developed out of the so-called second generation biotechnology, i.e., through techniques of fermentation, microbiological and continuous processes (although not by genetic engineering). These biopreparations can be produced locally in an artisanal manner in centers for reproduction of entomophagous and entomopathogenic species of which more than 200 are operating in the country, as well as industrially in three existing factories.

For their ecological and economic potential, the capacity of tropical ecosystems to generate biomass and to advantageously utilize harvest remains and other agricultural waste, Cuba's experience in the production of biopreparations by means of second-generation biotechnological techniques can have important applications in other tropical, underdevelopment countries. The development of alternative agricultural programs in Cuba has not come up short on encountering obstacles. As was the case for some biofertilizers such as ozobacter and azosperillum, for example, the rhythm of their extension into production overtook the amount of experience accumulated earlier and the practical conditions to guarantee their effective utilization.[40]

But it is important to take obstacles of another sort into account. The fact is that the majority of engineers and technical experts involved in agricultural production had been trained in accordance with the conception of the green revolution. For them, agrarian modernization is tantamount to the use of science and technology for obtaining high agricultural yields as the only means to guarantee "food for all." In this manner, alternative technologies tended to be perceived not for what they are, an expression of highly refined scientific application and a fusion of local and traditional knowledge, but rather as temporary solutions imposed by the crisis which can be abandoned once the crisis has passed over.

In reality, much of this has changed since the application of the alternative model first became initiated. New generations of agricultural technicians have been formed in accordance with conceptions that are more in tune with sustainable agriculture. In addition, many of those specialists that were trained earlier have been undergoing retraining through agro-ecology courses that have been organized in the country's agrarian universities. Another important change, in my judgment, has been the revalorization of campesino knowledge and the lessening of the distance between researchers and the agricultural sphere of the producers.

Nevertheless, the permanence of these changes cannot yet be guaranteed. The recovery of the Cuban economy began in 1994 and has had a sustained, albeit somewhat unstable, rhythm of growth over the 1994-2004 period. What will happen to the alternative programs of agricultural development and ecological agriculture in Cuba as the economic recovery takes hold? Above all, how can the social sciences contribute to the consolidation of the transition to a sustainable rural and agrarian model of development?

For some years now, we in FLACSO-Cuba have worked on a research project whose principal areas include:

- General socio-economics, i.e., theoretical development around the concept of sustainable development and study of the socioeconomic deter-

minants that favor or obstruct it in the rural sector and agricultural production.

- Sociological-participative, i.e., study of the agrarian cooperativization
process in Cuba as a way of increasing social participation in decision-
making and the administration of material resources.
- Environmental education, i.e., utilization of the methods of popular education for community-based, environmental education and particularly
for promoting the acceptance of alternative environmental technologies
that have been successfully adapted to agricultural production.

We hope in this way to contribute, along with other Cuban research collectives, to the process in our country where an already notable degree of social
equity, the indispensable prerequisite for sustainable development, can consolidate its experience and move forward on the path to more integral transformations towards sustainability in agricultural production and rural development.

Notes

1. World Commission on Environment and Development, *Our Common Future*, 43.
(The full facts of publication of all the sources are found in the Bibliography, at the
end of the essay. *Ed.)*

2. Ibid., 43-46.

3. World Resources Institute, *1992-93 World Resources*, 3.

4. James O'Connor, "Is Sustainable Capitalism Possible?," in Martin O'Connor (ed.),
Is Capitalism Sustainable?, 152-175.

5. Lori Ann Thrupp, "Political Ecology of Sustainable Rural Development: Dynamics of
Social and Natural Resource Degradation," in Patricia Allen (ed.), *Food for the
Future: Conditions and Contradictions of Sustainability*, 47-73.

6. Enrique Leff, *Green Production: Toward an Environmental Rationality*.

7. Ibid.

8. Edward McCoughan, *Competing Approaches to Studies of Development*.

9. Walter Rostow, *The Stages of Economic Growth: A Non-Communist Manifesto*.

10. Susan George, *Les Stratèges de la Faim*.

11. Andrew Pearse, *Seeds of Plenty, Seeds of Want: Social and Economic Implications of the Green Revolution.*

12. Solon Barraclough, *An End to Hunger? The Social Origins of Food Strategies,* 7.

13. Enrique Leff, "Pobreza y medio ambiente" [Poverty and Environment], in *Ecología Política,* 127-128.

14. Beatriz Díaz, "La biotecnología y los países subdesarrollados" [Biotechnology and the Underdeveloped Countries] and "Biotecnología moderna y conservación de la biodiversidad" [Modern Biotechnology and Preservation of Biodiversity], in *Cuadernos de África y América Latina,* 55-63.

15. Gabriel Nemoga Soto, "The Effects of 'Leipzig' on Latin America and the Caribbean," in *Biotechnology and Development Monitor,* 2-5.

16. Miguel Altieri, *Agroecology. The Scientific Basis of Alternative Agriculture;* Enrique Leff, "Pobreza y medio ambiente"; Enrique Leff and Julia Carabias, *Cultura y manejo sustentable de los recursos naturales* [Culture and Sustainable Management of Natural Resources]; Victor Toledo et al., *Plan Pátzcuaro 2000. Investigación multidisciplinaria para el desarrollo sostenido* [Pátzcuaro 2000. Multidisciplinary Research for Sustained Development]; and Lori Ann Thrupp, "La legitimación del conocimiento local: de la marginación al fortalecimiento de los pueblos del Tercer Mundo" [The Legitimation of Local Knowhow: From Marginilizing to Strengthening Third World Peoples] in Enrique Leff and Julia Carabias, op. cit.

17. FAO, "The Den Bosch Declaration and Agenda for Action on Sustainable Agriculture and Rural Development," 5.

18. Ibid., 5-6.

19. Solon Barraclough, op. cit.

20. Beatriz Díaz, "Desarrollo social y políticas públicas: el caso de Cuba" [Social Development and Public Policies: The Case of Cuba].

21. Ibid.

22. Beatriz Díaz, "Cuba: modelo de desarrollo equitativo" [Cuba: A Model of Equitable Development], in ALAS/CEA, *Sistemas políticos, poder y sociedad (Estudios de casos en América Latina)* [Political Systems, Power and Society. Case Studies in Latin America].

23. Carlos Rafael Rodríguez, "Una nota sobre las peculiaridades de la transformación socialista de la agricultura en Cuba [A Note on the Peculiarities of Socialist Transformation of Agriculture in Cuba], in *Cuba en el tránsito al socialismo 1959-1963* [Cuba in the Transition to Socialism], 153.

24. Ibid., 155.

25. Beatriz Díaz and Marta R. Muñoz, "Biotecnología agrícola y medio ambiente en el período especial cubano" [Agricultural Biotechnology and Environment in the Cuban Special Period], in *Cuadernos de África y América Latina*, 77-90.

26. Ibid., 79.

27. Víctor Figueroa, "El nuevo modelo agrario en Cuba bajo los marcos de la reforma económica" [The New Agrarian Model in Cuba under the Economic Reform], in *Desarrollo rural y participación* [Rural Development and Participation], 8.

28. Ibid., 9.

29. Beatriz Díaz, "Cooperativización agrícola reciente: estudio de caso en Cuba" [Recent Agrarian Cooperativization: A Case Study in Cuba].

30. Prisco Barroso, Lázaro Romero and Ramón Díaz, "Vías para el perfeccionamiento de la actividad socioeconómica de la UBPC 9 de Abril" [Ways for Improving the Socioeconomic Activity of the "9 de Abril UBPC], in *Resúmenes e investigaciones sobre las UBPC* [Abstracts and Research on the UBPCs], 42-43; Ángel Bú, et al., "Las UBPC y su necesario perfeccionamiento" [The UBPCs and Their Necessary Improvement]; Beatriz Díaz and Marta R. Muñoz, op. cit.; Beatriz Díaz, R. Almaguer, et al., "Cooperativización agrícola: retos y alternativas" [Agricultural Cooperativization: Challenges and Alternatives], in *Resúmenes e investigaciones sobre las UBPC*, op. cit., 31-36; Víctor Figueroa, op. cit.; Miguel Limia, "Las UBPC cañeras como forma embrionaria de nuevo tipo de colectivo laboral en Cuba" [The Sugar Cane UBPCs as an Embryonic New Form of Work Collectives in Cuba], in *Resúmenes e investigaciones sobre las UBPC*, op. cit, 17-19.

31. Beatriz Díaz and Marta R. Muñoz, op. cit., 88.

32. Beatriz Díaz, "Cooperativización agrícola reciente," op. cit.

33. Ibid., 16-17.

34. Miguel Figueras, *Aspectos estructurales de la economía cubana* [Structural Aspects of the Cuban Economy], 50-78.

35. Beatriz Díaz and Marta R. Muñoz, op. cit., 81.

36. Miguel Figueras, op. cit., 53.

37. Beatriz Díaz, "Desarrollo social y políticas públicas," op. cit., 20-21.

38. Richard Levins, "The Ecological Transformation of Cuba," in *Agriculture and Human Values*, 52, 54.

39. John Vandermeer, et al., "Cuba and the Dilemma of Modern Agriculture," in *Agriculture and Human Values, 5*.

40. Beatriz Díaz, "Biotecnología agrícola: estudio de caso en Cuba" [Agricultural Biotechnology: A Case Study in Cuba].

Bibliography

ALTIERI, MIGUEL. *Agroecology. The Scientific Basis of Alternative Agriculture.* Berkeley: University of California, 1983.

BARRACLOUGH, SOLON. *An End to Hunger? The Social Origins of Food Strategies.* London: Zed Books, 1991.

————. "Food Security and Modernization of the Agricultural Sector." Paper submitted for the G-77 Sectorial Review Meeting on Food and Agriculture, Guyana, 15-19 January 1996.

BARROSO, PRISCO, LÁZARO ROMERO and RAMÓN DÍAZ. "Vías para el perfeccionamiento de la actividad socioeconómica de la UBPC 9 de abril." In *Resúmenes e investigaciones sobre las UBPC.* Havana: Polo Científico de Humanidades and FLACSO, 1995.

BÚ, ÁNGEL, PABLO FERNÁNDEZ, ARMANDO NOVA, et al. "Las UBPC y su necesario perfeccionamiento." *Cuba: investigación económica* journal, year 2, no. 2 (1996).

CARSON, RACHEL. *Silent Spring.* New York: Houghton Mifflin Co., 1962.

DÍAZ, BEATRIZ. "Biotecnología agrícola: estudio de caso en Cuba." Paper presented at the 19th LASA International Congress, Washington, D.C., September 28-30 1995.

————. "Biotecnología moderna y conservación de la biodiversidad." *Cuadernos de África y América Latina* journal, no. 11 (1993).

————. "La biotecnología y los países subdesarrollados." Working Document at FLACSO, University of Havana, 1989. Typescript.

————. "Cooperativización agrícola reciente: estudio de caso en Cuba." Paper presented at the 19th LASA International Congress, Washington, D.C., September 28-30 1995.

————. "Cuba: modelo de desarrollo equitativo." In ALAS/CEA, *Sistemas políticos, poder y sociedad (Estudios de casos en América Latina).* Caracas: Editorial Nueva Sociedad, 1992.

————. "Desarrollo social y políticas públicas: el caso de Cuba." Study prepared for UNRISD, Geneva, at FLACSO, University of Havana, 1996. Typescript.

Díaz, Beatriz, María E. Solé and Elena Díaz. "Caracterización sociopsicológica del joven campesino" (Research report of the "Juventud" Scientific-Technical Program), FLACSO, University of Havana, 1996. Typescript.

Díaz, Beatriz and Marta R. Muñoz. "Biotecnología agrícola y medio ambiente en el período especial cubano." *Cuadernos de África y América Latina* journal, no. 16 (1994).

Díaz, Beatriz, R. Almaguer, J. Bell Lara, et al. "Cooperativización agrícola: retos y alternativas." In *Resúmenes e investigaciones sobre las UBPC*. Havana: Polo Científico de Humanidades and FLACSO, 1995.

FAO. "The Den Bosch Declaration and Agenda for Action on Sustainable Agriculture and Rural Development." *Food and Agriculture Organization of the UN*. http://www.fao.rog/sd/epdirect/EPre0024.htm. Accessed July 29, 2004.

Figueras, Miguel. *Aspectos estructurales de la economía cubana*. Havana. Editorial de Ciencias Sociales, 1994.

Figueroa, Víctor. "El nuevo modelo agrario en Cuba bajo los marcos de la reforma económica." In *Desarrollo rural y participación*. Havana: Sociology Department, University of Havana, 1996.

George, Susan. *Les Stratèges de la Faim*. Geneva: Editions Grounauer, 1978.

Kathen, André de. "The Impact of Transgenic Crop Releases on Biodiversity in Developing Countries." *Biotechnology and Development Monitor* journal, no. 28, 1996. It is also available in http://www.biotech-monitor.nlo/2805.htm.

Leff, Enrique. *Green Production: Toward an Environmental Rationality.* New York: Guilford Press, 1995.

―――. "Pobreza y medio ambiente." *Ecología Política* journal (Barcelona), no. 8 (1994).

Leff, Enrique and Julia Carabias (Coordinators). *Cultura y manejo sustentable de los recursos naturales.* 2 vols. Mexico City: Centro de Investigaciones Interdisciplinarias en Humanidades, UNAM, 1993.

Levins, Richard. "The Ecological Transformation of Cuba." *Agriculture and Human Values* journal, vol. 10, no. 3 (Summer 1993).

Limia, Miguel. "Las UBPC cañeras como forma embrionaria de nuevo tipo de colectivo laboral en Cuba." In *Resúmenes e investigaciones sobre las UBPC*. Havana: Polo Científico de Humanidades and FLACSO, 1995.

McCoughan, Edward. *Competing Approaches to Studies of Development.* Santa Cruz: University of California, 1992.

National Office of Statistics. *Estadísticas agropecuarias de 1995*. Havana: n.p., 1996.

NEMOGA SOTO, GABRIEL. "The Effects of 'Leipzig' on Latin America and the Caribbean." *Biotechnology and Development Monitor* journal, no. 28 (1996).

O'CONNOR, JAMES. "Is Sustainable Capitalism Possible?" In *Is Capitalism Sustainable?: Political Economy & the Politics of Ecology.* Edited by Martin O'Connor. New York: Guilford Press, 1994.

PEARSE, ANDREW. *Seeds of Plenty, Seeds of Want: Social and Economic Implications of the Green Revolution.* Geneva: UNRISD, Oxford: Clarendon Press, 1980.

RODRÍGUEZ, CARLOS RAFAEL. *Cuba en el tránsito al socialismo 1959-1963.* Havana: Editora Política, 1979.

ROSSET, PETER and MEDEA BENJAMIN, eds. *The Greening of the Revolution: Cuba's Experiment with Organic Agriculture.* Sydney: Ocean Press, 1995.

ROSTOW, WALTER. *The Stages of Economic Growth: A Non-Communist Manifesto.* Cambridge: Cambridge University Press, 1971.

THRUPP, LORI ANN. "Political Ecology of Sustainable Rural Development: Dynamics of Social and Natural Resource Degradation." In *Food for the Future: Conditions and Contradictions of Sustainability.* Edited by Patricia Allen. New York: John Wiley and Sons, 1993.

TOLEDO, VICTOR, P. ÁLVAREZ ICAZA and P. ÁVILA, eds. *Plan Pátzcuaro 2000. Investigación multidisciplinaria para el desarrollo sostenido.* Mexico City: Fundación Friederich Ebert, 1993.

VANDERMEER, JOHN, JUDITH CARNEZ, PAUL GESPER, et al. "Cuba and the Dilemma of Modern Agriculture." *Agriculture and Human Values* journal, vol. 10, no. 3 (Summer 1993).

WORLD COMMISSION ON ENVIRONMENT AND DEVELOPMENT. *Our Common Future.* Oxford: Oxford University Press, 1987.

WORLD RESOURCES INSTITUTE. *1992-93 World Resources.* Oxford: Oxford University Press, 1993.

Science and Biotechnology in Cuban Development

MARINA MAJOLI VIANI

M<small>ARINA</small> M<small>AJOLI</small> V<small>IANI</small> (1939-2004)

Ph.D. in Educational Sciences. She was professor at the University of Havana and researcher in the FLACSO-Cuba Program. Her research focused on issues related to the impact of science and technology upon Cuban society and development.

The profound disparity that exists across social and economic sectors world-wide is even more pronounced in the sphere of science and technology. Around 95% of the world's research and development is carried out in the so-called "developed" countries. It should therefore be of little surprise that 90% of patents and 80% of Internet users worldwide are concentrated in those countries. Meanwhile, the underdeveloped world falls ever further behind with increasing financial debts and economic stagnation. Can a poor, Third World country display real possibilities for success in one or another of existing state of the art technologies? This is the central question to be addressed in the present essay.[1]

I wish to explore the possibilities for the appropriation of scientific knowledge within the limitations imposed by underdevelopment. Why is it so important for a developing country to actively engage in efforts to produce and apply its own scientific knowledge base? Cuba's experience with biotechnology will serve as an example to show how a revolutionary society can create the conditions for consolidating an authentic, national program for scientific development and for placing it at the service of social and economic development. I will also set out to identify some of the main constraints on biotechnological development, both internal and external, and discuss how major advances were made in spite of the pervasive economic crisis that affected Cuba during the final decade of the 20th century.

My underlying premise is that knowledge-intensive, technologically driven industries constitute an essential component of economic expansion in the long run. It is becoming increasingly evident that if a nation is to emerge from underdevelopment in the context of a rapidly globalizing market, it must be in control of at least one of five key technologies, namely, computer science, biotechnology, space technology, new generation energy sources, or synthetic materials. Many experts now argue that biotechnology may actually be the most important of these.[2]

Defining Biotechnology in the Context of Scientific Development

What exactly is biotechnology? Quintero Ramírez understands it as a multi-disciplinary endeavor whose objective is the cultivation and application of micro-organisms in the service of producing goods and services capable of generating economic profit and social benefits.[3] This means that it broadly spans six scientific fields that interact with each other: chemistry, biochemistry, microbiology, genetics, engineering, and economics. It is widely believed that biotechnology became consolidated as a result of two important events: the need to produce penicillin in large quantities during the Second World War period (1938-45) and the publication of the first manual on biochemical engineering that took place in England in 1958.

Albert Sasson recalls that in the decade of the seventies, there was much talk about a "new biology," capable of changing the manufacturing processes of chemical and pharmaceutical substances.[4] It was a period in which knowledge and techniques of genetic engineering were being collected and improved, spurred on by a sharp increase in breakthroughs within the fields of biochemistry, genetics, and molecular as well as cellular biology. All of this was particularly observable with regard to work around enzymes in the processes of industrial production and investigations in molecular genetics where discoveries concerning the techniques of alteration and transfer between organisms were constantly occurring.

From Sasson's point of view, biotechnological practice consists of the use of bacteria, yeasts, and animal and vegetable cells in cultures, all of whose metabolism and capacity for biosynthesis are directed toward the manufacturing of specific substances. When the European Federation of Biotechnology was founded in 1978, it adopted a definition that was based on the integrated application of know-how and techniques of biochemistry, microbiology, genetics, and chemical engineering, viewing biotechnological development as that which makes it possible to utilize the properties and possibilities of microorganisms and cellular cultures at a higher technological level. Through the use of renewable and readily available resources, the possibility was envisioned of producing substances and compounds that are essential for human life and for improving the human condition. When applied on an industrial scale, these biotechnologies became the foundations for a bio-industry.

Rodrigues Pereira picks up on a definition worked out by Bull, et al., for the OECD according to which "biotechnology is the application of scientific principles and engineering to the processing of materials by biological agents in order to provide goods and services."[5] He adds that biotechnology harnesses the catalytic power of biological systems, both in the direct use of enzymes and in the application of a complex biochemistry of complete cells and microorganisms. His emphasis was placed on the incipient commercial opportunities that opened up in the 1970s with the development of new products and techniques based upon the progress achieved in genetic engineering and other innovative ways of transforming biological organisms.

Rodrigues Pereira explains that enhanced application of traditional biology has existed for centuries, such as in the fermentation of alcohol or the manufacturing of bread and cheese. It is understood that "the first biotechnological revolution" owes its existence to Pasteur on account of his revolutionary treatment and prevention of infectious human and animal diseases through immunization back in the second half of the 1800s. The "new biotechnology" (or "second biotechnological revolution") was in turn embodied in more recent advances in genetic engineering and in the technology of enzymes and fermentation. There are numerous other definitions concerning biotechnology which make it clear that scientific and technological knowledge within this field takes the form of multiple applications that cover a wide spectrum of human, veterinary, and industrial needs, often by resorting to renewable resources and cleaner, "non-smokestack" processes. The possibilities of developing and offering a multitude of new products and services that can result in improvements of the quality of life for all human beings and their environment also opened up a tremendous margin of commercial potential. It is estimated that by the year 2000, the world biopharmaceutical market now hovered around 300 billion dollars, with one-half of this under the control of the United States.[6]

Biotechnology in Cuba

In Cuba, the first signs of interest in biotechnology could be seen around 1981 when a group of six physicians became devoted to working out a method of producing interferon. Their goal was achieved in forty-two days, providing the impetus for a variety of subsequent efforts. By 1986, the Centro de Ingeniería Genética y Biotecnología (Center for Genetic Engineering and Biotechnology) was inaugurated with up-to-date facilities and equipment, staffed with a group of capable and highly motivated young scientists.

From the mid-eighties until the mid-nineties, there was an accelerated growth in the fields of biotechnology, genetic engineering, pharmaceutical development, and medical equipment design. It resulted in part from the global evolution of science, but also on account of conditions already established in Cuba in these fields. There was a long medical tradition in Cuba as well as a strong educational background in the sphere of biological and chemical sciences. These were areas of scientific and technological development for which the country had created favorable conditions and had acquired a solid reputation. Thus, it was possible to make progress based upon a blend of skill, intelligence, integrity, and dedication, rather than just huge amounts of strategic raw materials. Cuba had begun to seriously consider the new comparative advantages of products deriving from a high scientific and technological level. It was clearly becoming understood that such products were something which if adequately developed could significantly contribute to the island's economic development.

Certain internal, structural factors existed which made the advanced development of biological sciences viable in Cuba. In addition to high educational levels that were well-qualified for research and development, there was a favorable environment for promoting the application of such technologies. This was due in large part to the wide range of health services practiced throughout the country as well as the ongoing need for improved technical levels within agriculture, cattle raising, and food production.

One of the many factors that promoted investment in biotechnology was its significance for agriculture and its potential contribution for feeding the country and well as assisting other nations. Improvements in agricultural production have been attempted through tissue culture, the transfer of genes from one cell to another, and through the search for new crop varieties that are more productive and resistant to plagues, ailments, and other environmental challenges. The use of biopesticides and biofertilizers was first contemplated during the 1980s as an option that offered economic and environmental advantages. By the 1990s, it turned into an urgent necessity due to the limited possibility of sustaining previous levels of chemical imports used in agriculture. Although problems continue to be encountered in their extensive application, all signs seem to indicate that biopesticides and biofertilizers hold an important place in the future.

It should also be noted that Cuba found it necessary to develop its own protection against possible biological threats, as was the case with hemorrhagic dengue, African swine fever, and others diseases. The most recent case involved the plague *Thrips palmi*, an illness apparently introduced in Cuba at the end of 1996. This disease, unknown in Cuba prior to that time, had already wrought devastating effects elsewhere. Perhaps the most influential factor in accelerating biotechnological research and production lies in the extremely important role it has played in the prevention, diagnosis, and treatment of illnesses. It is precisely here that some of the greatest achievements have been registered.

The impact that the development, production and application of biotechnology and genetic engineering has had on the Cuban public health system may be summarized as follows:

- Availability of vaccines.- Cuba produces twelve vaccines that insure full coverage of the whole population.

- Programs of prenatal and neonatal diagnoses.- This includes early detection of defects of the neural stem, Down Syndrome, and metabolic diseases.
- Availability of new medications.- These include interferon, used to control viral diseases; streptoquinase, a medication used in hospitals to significantly improve the survivability of a heart attack; monoclonal antibodies, particularly MoAb-73, used in the organ transplant program; PPG or ateromixol, a product derived from sugar cane which reduces the level of blood cholesterol, in addition to being a blood platelet blocking agent and other, more secondary beneficial effects on the human organism, especially among the elderly; and blood derivatives and nuclear medicinal products.

Nearly 20 biopharmaceutical products, including interferons, monoclonal antibodies, blood derivatives, vaccines and others have already been registered in Cuba. Over a relatively brief period, Cuba has developed more than 200 biotechnological products that represent substantial economic potential in view of their high aggregate value. In addition, they can help satisfy the country's needs in the areas of diagnoses, analyses, vaccine application, and development of additional high-technology products. Commercial activities related to these products have been growing steadily and have become substantially more diversified with specialized applications in the health care area, resulting in exports to several continents.

Overall, health products and services related to biotechnology contributed more than $100 million to the country by 1994. This amount continued to grow as progress was steadily made in consolidating the institutions involved in their research, development and production, while at the same time gaining the commercial experience necessary for successfully marketing them. All of this had to be accomplished in the context of serious shortages of certain resources that were due mostly to the tough economic restrictions imposed by the United States. The key element which permitted success in many of these efforts rested in the organization of the entire industry, beginning with its technical and scientific foundations. In this, the particular model chosen to govern the organization of science and industry is something of critical importance for developing countries.

Organizational Prototypes for a Dynamic Scientific Infrastructure

Castells and Hall, scientific advisors to the project Cartuja 93 in Sevilla, Spain, and the Multi-function Polis (MFP) in Adelaide, Australia, are experts in the process of creating innovative industrial methods that lead to dynamic economic growth. They define *technopolis* in general terms as the "specific forms of territorial concentration of technological innovation with a potential to generate scientific synergism and economic productivity."[7] Their proposed profiles for the *technopolis* are as follows: a first type would consist of industrial complexes of high technology enterprises, connecting research and development with manufacturing. This type can be seen in the case of the Silicon Valley complex in California as well as in other cases that were more the result of economic reorganization and reindustrialization processes such as in Highway 128 area of Boston, Massachusetts.

Another type of *technopolis* can be considered a kind of city of science, or as individual scientific complexes without an immediate, territorial relationship to production. Their purpose is to achieve scientific excellence per se. Some prominent examples would include the Siberian city of Akademgorodok, near Novosibirsk, or the Japanese experiment of Tsukuba, near Tokyo, Taedok in South Korea, and Kansai, the multinuclear city of science located in Japan.

A third type of *technopolis* is that of the technological parks, defined as areas that might act as magnets for attracting companies that produce high technology, but without specific innovative functions besides those specifically related to economic development. The basic objective of the technological park is industrial competitiveness rather than scientific quality. Examples with varied characteristics can include Hsinchu in Taiwan, Sophia Antipolis in France, and Cambridge, England.

The model that was ultimately adopted in Cuba was designed to achieve scientific excellence in addition to technological excellence in production. To establish the context for describing the Cuban case, I will by way of contrast briefly expound a bit further on the experience of previously existing industrial complexes of high technology enterprises. Here, I will make again reference to the three well known cases of Silicon Valley in California, Highway 128 in Boston, as well as one city of science, namely, that of Novosibirsk.

Silicon Valley can be described as a complex of technological excellence in the area of microelectronics. It is regarded as an original industrial nucleus in computer technology, employing more than 300,000 high technology workers, including 6000 doctors in engineering and the sciences. Spanning an area measuring 70 km x 15 km on the peninsula just south of San Francisco, descending from Palo Alto down to San José, this area contained around 3000 companies engaged in electronic manufacturing during the 1980s. About 85% of them employ less than 50 workers. An additional 3000 companies were engaged in production services while 2000 were engaged in high technology. This amounted to approximately 8000 companies in the overall complex which came to be considered an exemplary display of managerial organization, symbiotic relations between scientific and economic development, and of the collaboration between universities and competitive research and production. The valley's strong ties with universities such as Stanford University, San José State University, University of Santa Clara, and University of California at Berkeley were supported financially by private sources as well as by the U.S. military establishment and the aerospace program.

In contrast to Silicon Valley, the scientific-industrial complex located in the Commonwealth of Massachusetts specialized in the production of microcomputers. Known as "Boston's Highway 128," this area is an example of reindustrialization based on high technology. This suburban belt connects 20 smaller cities which prior to 1950 had traditional industries such as textiles, and which subsequently experienced two waves of reindustrialization. By 1980, about 900 high technology enterprises, with more than 250,000 employees had become concentrated in the greater Boston area, in addition to 700 companies offering high technology consulting. This concentration transformed the area into the third largest high technology complex in the United States, after the multinuclear *technopolis* located in Southern California and the above-mentioned Silicon Valley. The location of this complex is largely due to its direct access to academic centers represented by scientists and engineers from 65 universities of the Great Boston area, including the Massachusetts Institute of Technology (MIT), Harvard University, University of Massachusetts, Tufts University, and Brandeis University. Its rapid progress was partly due to the evolution of the late Cold War era when strong support was forthcoming from the Pentagon with the aim of assuring provision of precision instruments, aviation electronics, missiles, and electric machinery.

Some common features of these complexes include: their size in terms of the number of companies involved and of their highly qualified personnel; their close ties with sources of industrial production and with universities; their high scientific, technological and productive qualities; and their assured viability via an internal market, mainly through military and aerospace demands, during a time when such markets were subject to fluctuations.

Another place of special interest is the scientific city of Akademgorodok, better known in Cuba by the name of Novosibirsk. This project was conceived of at the end of the 1950s by Khrushchev and one of his scientific advisors, the mathematician Mijail Alekseevich Lavrentiev, as a means of scientific innovation to serve industrial development in Siberia and the former Soviet Union at large. For a time, there was a dream of creating a favorable environment for productive exchanges between scientists and research institutions, between institutions and industrial enterprises, between institutions and universities, all of them open to national and international scientific cooperation, with a steady flow of new and famous researchers designed to enrich the whole complex.

The dream failed for several reasons, however, beginning with the bureaucratic methods imposed by the Academy of Sciences. Coupled with a failure on the part of industry to participate, Novosibirsk instead became a symbol of one of the great contradictions which helped to undermine the former USSR, namely, an extremely high scientific level on the one hand and technological and organizational backwardness on the other. In retrospect, it can be argued that Cuba was wise in its determination to avoid these pitfalls.

The Development of a Biotechnological and Medical-Pharmaceutical Industry in Cuba

The scientific-productive Poles that were developed in Cuba resemble other complexes of accelerated technical innovation formed over recent years. The so-called *technopolis* or planned centers for the promotion of high technology industry, including biotechnology, can be applied not only to technological parks and cities, but also to national *technopolis* development and technological belts. Some analysts associate them with a type of production and economic management viewed as purely informational. This is due to the fact that productivity and competitiveness are increasingly based on generating new knowledge and on developing access to the processing of pertinent information. In the case of Cuba's scientific Poles as elsewhere, there is a shared consensus that the decisive element is not the total number of institutional parts but rather the interchange of the institutional factors involved.[8]

An important characteristic of Cuba's biotechnological and pharmaceutical sectors is found in the presence of a large number of scientific centers, each of which displays different technical profiles and specific work objectives. The institutional interdependence of each center varies in that some participate in the general structure of Cuba's national health services while others serve to enhance the island's pharmaceutical industry. Another group of centers may relate more closely to research institutions or ministries such as those of Agriculture, of Sugar, of Foodstuffs, and so on.

These interrelated centers were made more effective as they became organized into scientific and productive "Poles." This idea was first expressed by

176

President Fidel Castro in 1990 who expressed the idea that such institutions should become instruments for mutual cooperation and support. Their organizational design and practice became geared towards achieving a multiplier effect in the optimal utilization and assimilation of scientific and technological potential. The Ministry of Science, Technology and Environment (CITMA) suggested the following definition: "The Poles are the organized constellations of institutions and entities which by embracing the latest approaches to scientific and technological efficiency will integrally cooperate in the solution of problems associated with those programs of social and economic development that hold the highest importance for the country."[9]

By 1997, the country had 15 scientific-productive Poles, consisting of 455 institutions, entities, and other work groups, with 23,743 people participating. Forty-three percent of the work force in that year (or 10,223 staff members) were university graduates and 5932 were middle-level technicians. Approximately one-half of the staff employed in the Poles at that time were women (11,437). The complexity involved with coordinating the work within and between Poles was heightened by the fact that these 455 scientific-pole institutions were spread out over the 14 provinces of the country, located in 24 cities.[10]

Cuban scientific Poles with their biotechnological and pharmaceutical industries remain highly active in the process of their development. For example, the "West Scientific Pole" refers to a scientific complex in the city of Havana that involves science, production, instruction, and services. Most of its component institutions such as the Centro Nacional de Investigaciones Científicas (National Center for Scientific Research), the Instituto de Ingeniería Genética y Biotecnología (Institute for Genetic Engineering and Biotechnology), the Instituto Carlos Finlay (Carlos Finlay Institute), the Centro de Inmunoensayo (Center of Immunoassays), the Centro de Ingeniería Molecular (Center for Molecular Engineering), and the Centro Internacional de Restauración Neurológica (CIREN – International Center for Neurological Restoration), are physically concentrated over an extensive area near the western limits of Havana. Due to a special affinity in their activities, however, it also includes important centers elsewhere such as the Instituto de Ciencia Animal (Animal Science Institute) to the southeast and the Instituto de Medicina Tropical Pedro Kourí (Pedro Kouri Institute for Tropical Medicine) at a distance of some 70 kilometers to the west of the city.

Thirty-eight institutions belonging to 13 state agencies are integrated within this Pole. It has a labor force of 11,292, of whom more than one half (6933) are women. Of the total force, 4046 are university graduates, with 45 of them holding the scientific degree of Doctors and 445 the title of Doctor of Sciences, that is to say, 4% of the total labor force. The 1440 researchers represent another 12% portion of the total with the number of middle technicians totaling up to 3089. Of the 38 institutions or entities with ties to the West Scientific Pole, 23 regard research as their basic activity, 4 are defined as production, 1 as information services, 9 oriented towards health, and 1 oriented towards teaching. Another 9 centers guarantee the essential services which are provided by the Pole.

The centers associated with the biotechnological field are developing a series of activities that give them a sense of integration and of work performed in complete cycles.

- Research and development are the basic activities geared towards the uninterrupted flow of improvement, the renewal of present results, and future projection in the field.
- Production and quality control transforms the results of the research effort, either within or outside the laboratory, into a product ready for the market on a massive scale. This activity requires a highly rigorous quality control of each operation.
- Marketing is essential so the product may become known and be used, and so that it yields the necessary economic benefits for subsequent development.
- Operation and maintenance of all kinds cannot fail in an industry working with biological products, with specific requirements that cannot be violated. It is not only a question of efficiency in the process of production, but also of insuring that the conditions essential for its existence continue to be met.
- A fifth activity, of vital importance for each center, is the organization of teams, the dispensing of special attention to the technical and scientific development of the participants, as well as providing for their integrity not only as science workers but as human beings.

An integral part of continuing research work is made up of certain activities that are required of all institutions:

- Investments for the creation of centers, either complete or partial, as required to complete or renew ongoing processes.
- Economics, financing, and control.

- The growing importance of legal requirements pertaining to intellectual property, contracts, associations and sales, among others.

The most overarching objective in these areas has been the integration both inside each center with respect to the chain represented by research-development-production-marketing as well as the external integration of institutions for purposes of cooperation, reciprocal assistance, and the development of common objectives among the various institutions. The Scientific Poles to which all centers belong have a mission of organizing the analysis of common problems in order to further promote integration, cooperation, and most especially the productive and social life of the country in view of the connection between biological sciences and the economy. The Poles are regional and although the largest one is located in Havana, there are fifteen of them distributed across the island. From a developmental perspective, it should be apparent by now that it is not sufficient for a national economy and its underlying technical infrastructure to simply aspire to assimilate new technologies. Rather, it is of fundamental importance to cultivate the capacity to generate new technologies via the expanding application of scientific knowledge. In this sense, the link that exists between Cuba's Scientific Poles and the nation's universities has been a vital one and constitutes an essential component in demarcating the continuing potential for the island's technological, economic and social development.

Cuban Universities in Service of the Scientific Infrastructure

As we have seen, the Scientific Poles assemble together a heterogeneous set of scientific institutions with their diverse relations to different state agencies. In common, they share a dedication to the production of advances in scientific knowledge, the development and application of new technologies, particularly in the elaboration of new products under strict conditions of production and quality control. Their work is a function of the satisfaction of the nation's needs along with the economic imperative to commercially develop goods for export. The latter requires the Poles to compete with large transnational enterprises who command tremendous resources in their pursuit of scientific research and development.

Fulfilling this challenging task implies the necessity for a constant assimilation and production of knowledge which in turn generates the need to carefully supervise each investment and to ensure the optimal utilization of each available resource. In this process, an ongoing exchange with the universities constitutes a permanent and essential feature. It means that there is a continuing need to create, nurture and update a scientific and technological culture among students and professors linked to the Scientific Poles. Through this culture, a deepening awareness of the characteristics and advantages of high technology and its employment in the specialized activities of the Poles can be disseminated to the remaining faculties and university students alike.

This critical linkage of the universities with scientific activities of the Poles goes back to the application of the Cuban concept of education, namely, in the unity of study-work-research, adapted in varying proportions and with specific characteristics in each sector of social and technical preparation and training. Indeed, this formed part of the principle of universalizing the whole process of teaching in service of developing the intelligence of the entire population. It aspired to motivate all individuals to study by means of an increasing comprehension of applications, thereby showing the unity of theory and practice. At the same time, it stressed a deepening of the knowledge base of professors and all professionals involved with teaching at some level.

The Cuban vision of the universalization of teaching permitted the creation of a broad educational base. It was this foundation that made possible a cultural, scientific and technological "take-off" that can be associated with a new phase involving the universalization of scientific thinking as a basic instrument of work. We can see how this concretely evolved in the university sector. The first great research and development institution created in 1965 was the National Scientific Research Center (CNIC) that was part of the University of Havana and subsequently came under the direction of the Ministry of Higher Education. It was in CNIC that all of the present directors of the Scientific Poles were trained and where students have always carried out their scientific labor beginning in their third year of study on through graduation.

In various provinces, the universities have constituted the lynchpin of scientific activity and where the principle research centers have been directed. This can clearly be seen in the case of biotechnology. For example, the province of Villa Clara is home to both the Instituto de Biotecnología de las Plantas (Institute for Plant Biotechnology) and the Centro de Bioactivos Químicos (CBQ – Center for Bioactive Chemicals), two important research institutions directly tied to universities. In the province of Camagüey, the Centro de Ingeniería Genética y Biotecnología (Center for Biotechnology and Genetic Engineering) is located which likewise shares a constant interchange with the university.

In the specific case of the University of Havana, it is linked to the Havana's Western Scientific Pole principally through the Faculties of Chemistry and Biology as well as through the Instituto de Farmacia y Alimentos (IFAL – Institute of Pharmacy and Foodstuffs). The University's Rector is a permanent invitee to the

Pole's work sessions. Since the University of Havana participates in the training of professionals, it links up with specialists through graduate level education, the development of highly rigorous, scientific research studies tied to the main interests of the country, and through the scientific and technical services it offers in support of the priority projects developed by the Pole. As noted earlier, professionals employed in the Pole participate in university instruction and students are permitted to carry out their practicum within the institutions of the Pole, all of which helps to elevate the quality of higher education and help to compensate for some of the material resource shortages within the university.

The University of Havana offers graduate programs, including Doctor in Sciences degrees in various areas of specialization. In recent years, just the Faculties of Chemistry, Biology and the IFAL are producing more than three thousand professionals per year within various graduate degree programs. Recent university graduates have played an important role in the achievements registered in the area of research studies carried out by the University of Havana and serve as a national reserve of scientists and guest teachers who can in turn count on further improvement of their skills and qualifications.

Examples of the kind of work carried out jointly by the University and the Pole would be laser development as utilized in the application of ophthalmology, studies on the effect of magnetized water in the cultivation of live organisms, the elaboration of ultrasound plates for medical applications, the optimization of diets for laboratory animals, and so on. Results with considerable repercussions can be observed in the areas of vaccine development. It is worth noting that the research studies carried out in the Laboratorio de Antígenos Sintéticos (LAGS – Laboratory of Synthetic Antigens) under the direction of Dr. Vicente Vérez, University of Havana Professor of Chemistry, have made important advances in vaccinations for *Haemophilus influenzae*[11] and in cancer prevention. Another notable result was achieved in the formulation of the synthetic adhesive skin tissue product Tisuacryl which is useful in sealing accidental or surgical wounds. Tisuacryl is now patented in Europe thanks to the work of Dr. Rubén Álvarez at the Centro de Biomateriales (Center for Biomaterials).

As we have seen earlier, these close ties of high-tech production with universities are not unique to Cuba. Rather, they are a necessary and vital characteristic of the latest generation of industrial parks, technological belts and cities of science. With an ever more rapid rhythm of obsolescence among products, the competition for productive innovations in a global economy is increasingly based upon information and instantaneous knowledge operations. This demands a workforce that is more educated, coordinated, integrated and more deeply infused with scientific awareness. Cuba possesses a tremendous human potential in its social infrastructure, one that has been created through a concerted effort over four and a half decades.

We have seen how Cuba's Scientific Poles represent the formation of integrated centers of science and production. Traditional institutions of research tend to be more exclusively dedicated to furthering knowledge and generally fall short in displaying a fundamental consideration of the existing needs of development. In contrast, the Poles performed research and development in close cooperation with the country's academic institutions and eventually through agreements with foreign companies or institutions. As priority projects, the Scientific Poles have enjoyed the unconditional support of the Cuban State and have carried out their activities with a minimum of bureaucracy, with dedication and flexibility in their decisions, and with the regulation of their activities achieved via signed contracts. The complex interrelationships that became formed between the various institutions in the Scientific Poles favor the integration and multiplication of the country's human and material potential.

We have also seen that the formula adopted by Cuba favored the national consolidation of the Poles during an extended period of economic crisis. The scientific-technological culture that has been reached now displays the capacity not only to assimilate technologies but to produce them and to transfer them to production processes, all in compliance with strict requirements for quality control. The prospects for further development will depend upon the nation's ability to effectively capitalize upon the appropriation of scientific knowledge being generated and in expanding the existing capacities for applying it.

The biotechnological branch of knowledge has been pursued for over two decades in Cuba with the twofold aim of improving the population's overall quality of life and to create a dynamic component of the national economy in accordance with larger trends in the global economy. The specialized products and services that grow out of this high-tech, industrial branch have been integrated into the island's health care system. The initial investment of resources has since been recovered and the institutions making up this field are now making net contributions to the Cuban State budget via the export of high value-added products.

Cuba's strategy of prioritizing education, health and scientific research in conjunction with the total array of efforts directed towards the solution of concrete problems confronting the nation have resulted in a considerable knowledge base. The country's scientific infrastructure became further consolidated despite the enormous difficulties and limitations experienced during the period immediately following the collapse of the former Socialist Bloc. The resulting social accumulation and educational infrastructure today offers Cuba, a Third World country subjected to a more than forty-year long economic blockade, the possibility to achieve impressive results in state-of-the-art technologies such as in the case of biotechnology.

We have also stressed that the relationships between the university and the institutions of advanced science and technology, and of both with the production of high-tech goods and services, is indispensable and should be the object of constant enhancement. In this regard, the method utilized in university level instruction is a key link in teaching how to think and confront concrete problems in a creative manner. It is no longer sufficient to simply learn knowledge; rather, it is necessary to learn the process for obtaining new knowledge and to universalize scientific thinking throughout the larger society.

As part of its revolutionary heritage, Cuba feels an obligation towards the hungry and disunited Third World to which it belongs. At the same time, its struggle for survival has obligated the country to learn how to compete in a global economy in which the rules of commerce and finance are dictated by more developed nations obsessed with war. To realize its aspirations, the country will need to rely upon its good sense and ultimately upon all of its accumulated intelligence as its principal asset.

Notes

1. This essay is based on an earlier study entitled "El impacto social de la ciencia y la tecnología en Cuba: el caso del Centro de Inmunoensayo" [The Social Impact of Science and Technology in Cuba: The Case of the Immunoassay Center]. (This essay was updated not long before the author died, at the beginning of 2004. *Ed.)*

2. Heinz Dietrich Steffan, "La Escuela Cubana de Biotecnología: la posibilidad de salir del subdesarrollo" [The Cuban School of Biotechnology: The Possibility of Leaving Underdevelopment], in *Proceso*, 52. (The full facts of publication of all the sources are found in the Bibliography, at the end of the essay. *Ed.)*

3. Rodolfo Quintero Ramírez, "Biotecnología contemporánea" [Contemporary Biotechnology], in A. Peña (comp.), *La Biología Contemporánea*, 207-209.

4. Albert Sasson, *Las biotecnologías: desafíos y promesas* [Biotechnologies: Challenges and Promises], 11.

5. Paulo Rodrigues Pereira, "New Technologies: Opportunities and Threats," in *The Uncertain Quest: Science, Technology and Development*, 466-467.

183

6. Heinz Dietrich, op.cit., 12.

7. Ibid.

8. Manuel Castells and Peter Hall, *Tecnópolis científico-productivos. La formación de los complejos industriales del siglo xxi* [Scientific-productive Technopolis. The Formation of Industrial Complexes in the 21st Century], 17 and 22.

9. Science and Technology Agency, CITMA, "Polos científico-productivos" [Scientific-productive Poles], 3.

10. Ibid., 3, 61 and 68.

11. As of 2002, Cuba spent U.S.$2.5 million in acquiring this vaccination, the application of which has reduced by 34% the number of serious cases of meningitis and pneumonitis in children.

Bibliography

CASTELLS, MANUEL and PETER HALL. *Tecnópolis científico-productivas. La formación de los complejos industriales del siglo xxi*. Madrid: Alianza Editorial, 1994.

DIETRICH STEFFAN, HEINZ. "La Escuela Cubana de Biotecnología: la posibilidad de salir del subdesarrollo." *Proceso* journal (April 25, 1994).

MAJOLI, MARINA. "El impacto social de la ciencia y la tecnología en Cuba: el caso del Centro de Inmunoensayo." M.Sc. diss., University of Havana, 1997.

QUINTERO RAMÍREZ, RODOLFO. "Biotecnología contemporánea." In A. Peña (comp.), *La Biología contemporánea*. Mexico City: UNAM, 1983.

RODRIGUES PEREIRA, PAULO. "New Technologies: Opportunities and Threats." In *The Uncertain Quest: Science, Technology and Development*, edited by Jean-Jacques Salomon, Francisco R. Sagasti, and Céline Sachs-Jeantet. Tokio, New York, Paris: United Nations University Press, 1994. It is also available in http://www.unu.edu.unupress/unupbooks/uu09ue/uu09ue00.htm.

SASSON, ALBERT. *Las biotecnologías: desafíos y promesas*. UNESCO, 1984.

SCIENCE AND TECHNOLOGY AGENCY, CITMA. "Polos científico-productivos." Paper presented at the 2nd National Workshop of the Scientific-Productive Poles, Havana, March, 1997.

Family and Social Security in Cuba

MARÍA DEL CARMEN ZABALA ARGÜELLES

María del Carmen Zabala Argüelles

Ph.D. in Psychology. As professor at the University of Havana and researcher in the FLACSO-Cuba Program, she has conducted studies on family, poverty, social development, community programs and the methodology of social research.

Introduction

As the 21st century began amidst complex social, economic, political, and cultural transformations, the process of globalization constituted an ever more important factor influencing all spheres of social development. The effects of globalization on the family touch upon various aspects: social, educational, health, work, housing and social security, among others. Taken together, these areas make up the living conditions in which families develop and reverberate in their existence, quality of life, and social projection.

In spite of the unquestionable advances in the fields of information, communications, and technology that ultimately have positive implications for families, one of the most heinous results growing out of the process of neoliberal globalization has been the tendency towards increasing poverty and social exclusion around the world.

In Latin America, this situation has been clearly manifested. According to the United Nations Development Program,[1] 61.8% of the people from this region, or 270 million, are poor while even the most conservative estimates minimally place this figure at 165 million.[2] In addition to the significant increase of poverty, a growing zone of social and economic vulnerability is observable with ever more heterogeneous and complex situations of poverty and social exclusion.[3] Latin America is the region with the most acute contrasts between rich and poor anywhere, the product of the world's highest inequality and inequity in income distribution.[4]

It is necessary to unite our efforts and convictions in order to make this region one in which "all have their place," this is, to contribute to the building of more just societies with strong ties of solidarity and free of social exclusion. To this end, it is necessary to reflect upon and actively discuss questions like the following:

What challenges and impacts does the globalization process pose to the families of the region?

Given this scenario, how can we help to create a social environment that guarantees the satisfaction of family needs?

What new challenges does the social protection of families face in this context, particularly in terms of their social security?

How can we combat the poverty and social exclusion that affect millions of families?

Finally, how can the efforts of states, local governments, communities, and social organizations work together around this objective?

This essay has as its main purpose the task to reflect upon the issue of poverty and social security in Cuba. Specifically, I pursue the following objectives:

- To identify some of the main challenges to social security with respect to the protection of families in Cuba.
- To deepen our analysis concerning the characteristics, problems, and necessities of poor families who require greater social protection.
- To propose an integral strategy of assistance for such families, in which social policies are coherently articulated, specifically those related to social security and community empowerment.

In taking on the first objective, I will present a macro-social analysis of Cuba's present social reality based on documentary analysis of secondary sources (census data and statistics, reports of organizations and government institutions, and other research reports).

The second objective will be addressed by presenting a summary of a study that was conducted with selected families from a specific community in the country's capital. This study created a diagnostic profile about living conditions, characteristics and configurations in poverty contexts, emphasizing the transformations of the family life cycle that take place as well as the condition of women.

Consideration of the third objective will lead us to analyze a fieldwork experience that was carried out in a Cuban community with the support of local government and community organizations. The analysis that evolved incorporated elements of action-participation research and popular education.

Challenges for Social Security and Ensuring Family Protection in Cuba

In most countries around the world, the social security system is conceived of as a set of services and benefits that the individual enjoys by virtue of being a salaried worker. These benefits serve as a mechanism to deal with the risks of sickness, disability, and to guarantee a retirement pension during old age, or in case of injury or permanent disability, or death. It also usually implies supplementary services for specific populations like the elderly and the handicapped as well as for people in transitory situations like unemployment, the death of a spouse or a child's primary caretakers, among others. Under the criteria of "focused support," social security also includes the development of "social safety nets," i.e., social programs destined to support the most vulnerable groups of a society that require special consideration.

In Cuba, the social security system is situated in the ensemble of social policies that have been developed during the revolutionary process. This system is predicated on a conception of integral development that considers the economic and social aspects of society in an interconnected manner; the application of a comprehensive social policy through the State; and broad popular participation in the implementation of the designed policies; all of this with the main purpose of systematically elevating living standards through increased consumption and better social services, with a preferential treatment towards children, women, and the rural population.[5]

The above-mentioned principles have been applied in a concrete manner through specific social policies enacted by the Revolution. These policies can be characterized as having been systematic, coherent and integral. Among the policies applied, those related to health, education and employment have been fundamental, and thus need to be taken into account when analyzing the Cuban system of social security.

The emphasis in universal policies and social programs that cover health, education, employment, and housing, all with an essentially preventive character, makes the Cuban situation a unique one. While it is true that the family has not always been considered as the unit of analysis for all of these policies, their impact as a whole has very positively influenced the institution of the family.

The scope and efficiency of this social policy as developed by the Cuban State can be summarized in the following results:

- The maintenance of high levels of employment and guaranteed salary, even during economic crises and the ongoing restructuring of the domestic economy, by utilizing mechanisms of work relocation and retraining, subsidies, and the broadening of employment alternatives through the authorization of self-employed work.
- Universal free access to health services, expansion of the primary care system, and the development of preventive medicine, specific health programs and medical science capacities. All these have made possible the achievement of health indicators that correspond more to developed countries. Among the programs developed, it is worth singling out the impact that the Child and Maternal Care Program and the Family Physician Program have had upon the wellbeing of families.

- Universal free access to education, the almost total elimination of illiteracy, high skill levels throughout the labor force, a high level of schooling for the general population, and the advanced development of scientific-technical capacities.

Specifically, the Cuban system of social security, non-contributive and with free universal coverage, has been broadened and improved over time. The beneficiaries of social security have increased to 1.3 million, or more than 10% of the population, while expenditures on social programs have increased to 1.6 million pesos.[6]

Law 1100 of 1963 first guaranteed social security to all workers and their families by establishing the general character of the system, i.e., a benefit applicable to all workers and 100% paid for by the employer. Law 24 of 1979 improved this system and expanded the coverage offered workers and their families to further include the portion of the overall population that required assistance in fulfilling its basic needs.

The present system provides social assistance and protection benefits to those who are sick, engaged in maternity, injured at work, permanently disabled, and to workers who become ill in carrying out their profession, who retire, and to their survivors in the event of the worker's death. The benefits contemplate not only monetary payments (direct income in the form of salaries, subsidies or pensions) additional to the usual benefits available to all under the universal regime of social protection, but also include additional support in the form of services and goods in kind.[7]

For its part, expenditures on social assistance have also increased in terms of the number of families and beneficiaries under protection. They now include elderly people who lack adequate family support, single mothers, and families of the incarcerated. The assistance includes temporary and continuous monetary payments, the provision of services and goods in kind, and access to diverse social programs, including comprehensive care for the unsupported elderly, social workers for single mothers as well as for troubled youths, and social support services for the handicapped.

While highly significant successes have been achieved, Cuba's social security system must confront several challenges relative to the protection of families. First, the efforts to maintain the present level of social protection are enormous for a developing country like Cuba. In the middle of a complex and difficult economic situation, a highly substantial amount of resources are being spent on social security in both direct payments and indirectly through the provision of basic social services. During the last several years, the expenses of social security have increased as a result of the increased number of persons covered[8] and the increase of average annual expenditure per capita. To maintain and broaden still further this level of social protection constitutes both a difficult economic challenge and an urgent necessity from the political point of view.

A second challenge relates to the very conception of social policy with respect to the family. Although a broad consensus exists about the important need for public policies that target the family as the integral recipient of such policies, in our case, there is also a need to move towards new forms of direct engagement with the family based upon a greater level of their participation as active subjects in the solution of their problems.

The third challenge involves acknowledging the specific characteristics, problems, and needs of the diverse kinds of families found in Cuban society. While the nuclear family continues to predominate in Cuba like in many countries of the region,[9] there exists a substantial diversity of family types including those headed by a single parent, reconstructed or reconstituted families, multigenerational, multiple shared living arrangements, etc., with heterogeneous socioeconomic conditions shaped by their social class and territorial location that all have their particular characteristics, needs and demands.

The fourth challenge relates to the sustained increase of households headed by women,[10] necessitating that priority attention be given to this type of family and to the situation of these women who bear the responsibility of economically sustaining the entire household as well as providing educational and emotional support to her children. Special consideration should be given to situations involving single and/or adolescent mothers, families abandoned by the father, and those who become separated from their work.

The fifth challenge arises as a consequence of the aging of the Cuban population.[11] On the one hand, this requires continual improvements of services and protection for single person households, mostly made up of elderly persons living alone. On the other hand, an expansion and diversification is needed of those institutions that support the family in targeting the aging population, guaranteeing the preservation of their family ties, and assisting the ongoing support efforts being made by families, especially women, with greater social activities.

The sixth and final challenge I will mention involves the need to combine the universal character of existing social policies and programs, whose effect is essentially preventive, with the focusing of specific actions targeted to the needs of those families living in poverty.

The existence of poverty as a social phenomenon manifests *sui generis* characteristics in Cuba. Insofar as its magnitude is concerned, a minority sector of the population suffers from poverty. In terms of its intensity, there is a total absence of extreme poverty or critical poverty that is typically associated with malnutrition, widespread illness, illiteracy, lack of security, lack of protection, and social exclusion. Even the sector with the least resources in this society is guaranteed access to basic social services.

On the other hand, the social policies implemented throughout the country, and the measures of social protection around work, salaries, nutrition, health care, and education, together impede the extension and intensification of poverty. The development of these policies have allowed Cuba to achieve or surpass the goals that were established in 1990 at the Second Regional Conference on Poverty in Latin America and the Caribbean held in Quito, with the goal of reducing poverty.[12]

The particularly advantageous situation which Cuba has in the Latin American context becomes evident when one contrasts its rate of poverty, 4.7%—as established in the UN Human Poverty Index—, making it one of the lowest five in the world.[13] It is also evident in terms of the broader social development indicators where the Cuban population compares with those of the most developed countries.

In summary, Cuba exhibits indisputable achievements in the area of social security, specifically in the social protection of families. The preservation of this social protection requires us to confront difficult challenges given the prevailing socioeconomic conditions and the tendencies that characterize the social development of the population and their families.

A Profile of Families Living in Conditions of Poverty

As mentioned above, one of the challenges facing the Cuban social security system is the protection of families in conditions of poverty. A diagnostic analysis based on a case study of families living in conditions of poverty has helped to reveal a set of characteristics that should be carefully considered in order to develop a more effective social security system in Cuba.

Regarding their composition, these families are characterized for having a large number of members on the average, mostly young in age, with somewhat lower levels of education and a lower rate of employment than the rest of the country. The heads of most of these families are predominantly young and female, and are not economically active.

The material living conditions of these families are very unfavorable. Their housing situation is particularly critical, located predominantly in tenement houses and shantytowns with the physical home being in a poor to bad structural state, typified by small amounts of living space and ambient conditions of overcrowding and heightened promiscuity. The hygienic and sanitary conditions pose serious problems insofar as the water supply and sanitation services are of poor quality, and the overall state of domestic appliances is inadequate and badly deteriorated.

The economic situation of these families is likewise unfavorable, with a per capita income that is below the poverty line in Cuba. This reality is conditioned by a low average number of workers per household, lower salaries than the average worker due to the type of work being performed by those with employment, high economic dependence due to the high number of children living in the household and the low level of employment, and by parents failing to fulfill their full capacities as caregivers.

In relation to the family structure, these families are classified as nuclear and extended, with a slight predominance of the latter (extended). In both types of families (nuclear and extended), the restructured family and the single parent family (female head) predominate.

The role structure of these families is characterized by the maternal role in all the spheres of family life: affective, educative and material. This maternal-centered pattern is reinforced in the norms and cultural patterns reproduced across generations. The distribution of authority gives high levels of decision-making to the women as mothers and heads of household. Another characteristic of the structure of these family systems is the heterogeneity that conditions the delimitation of its boundaries. Inside the family, the boundaries between the parental and the conjugal system are too unstable. This is the effect of the absence of specific spaces to support a more healthy nuclear differentiation and of the instability of marital unions, while the boundaries between generations are well-delineated. The boundary limits of the family with its immediate social environment seem excessively permeable when the family lives in such close proximity to others.

Regarding the functioning of the family, the development of the biological-reproductive function is characterized by a pattern of early motherhood and of the high fertility rate of women. These patterns are reproduced across generations through an accumulating set of norms and values. In the realization of the economic function, there is an overemphasis on achieving subsistence as well as differences relating to the organization of the family's income, consumption, and domestic work. These dimensions are also related to the type of family structure, the domestic workload of the household, and with the employment condition of the women in the family. Regarding the cultural-spiritual functions, one can distinguish the limitations of the educational role of the family, and its consequences in different kinds of schooling issues and behavioral problems on the part of the young children and adolescents.

The dynamics of the family is characterized by high cohesion, an adaptive response that is flexible to the circumstances, and by a relatively low level of communication among its members. These low levels of communication are suggested in the reduced amplitude of topics that are discussed, in the selective handling of everyday problem solving, and by the imbalance existent between the regulatory and affective functions of the family.

Everyday problems identified by the families basically include the unfavorable living conditions, the precarious economic situation in the household, difficulties with the water supply, the situation of the children, the condition of single women, shoes and clothing needs, insufficient food availability, and other family problems. Generally, these families do not seem to develop a deeper grasp of the causes behind their family problems. Overall, there was a high grade of consistency among the families with respect to the main difficulties that they identified.

Families generally developed a set of strategies for the solution of these problems. These strategies were basically directed towards generating additional revenues and increasing their income and taking better advantage of their family resources. Some of these practices involved private paid work, sale of food products, obtaining benefits through gaining employment, prioritization of family spending on food, changing the family's food consumption patterns, handing off their children to other family members, hooking up with social support networks, and making diverse appeals for support from official institutions.

The analysis of family projects revealed that these families tended to have a high level of cooperation. The projects included improvement of their economic situation, seeking the upward social mobility of their children, improving their housing, and resorting to emigration. In all cases, however, the level of elaboration in these projects was low, due to the lack of a clear and coherent articulation of objectives, content, time frame, and division of responsibilities among family members. Also, the projects tended to be characterized by a short-term vision, thus limiting the possibilities for mobilizing these families.

With regard to social integration and participation, there is an imbalance between the level of social integration which was high, except for employment, and the level of social participation which was low. The families' perception of the quality of relations with social organizations and institutions vary. In some cases a strong bond is expressed. In other cases, a certain level of conflict and distance was perceptible, which can turn into dysfunctional relations between the families and the broader society and limit the possibilities of influence over the families.

The families tended to self-identify as being poor, the product of unfavorable living conditions and characteristics of their family, which in turn created conditions for a low level of self-esteem. A few families identified themselves as non-poor, citing the transient conditions of their present shortages but the guarantee of basic social services and the possibility of work. In some families, there was no consensus at all about whether their position was poor or non-poor.

The particular configurations of these families based on how they confronted their situation of poverty, show the different forms in which family networks interact with the larger society, exhibiting a greater or lesser connection with social organizations and institutions, and in participation in social activities.

From a structural perspective, the incorporation of gender into the analysis allows us to understand some peculiarities of the organization of these families and to focus in a deeper way upon the socially constructed differences between men and women in families living in poverty. There was an acute contrast between the preeminent role of women in virtually all spheres of family life and their limited level of social participation, especially in the workforce. The low level of women's work, together with the instability of their conjugal unions and the limitations of paternal care giving, tended to put them in a vulnerable and dependent economic situation. This in general meant that households headed by single women remain in an unfavorable position.

For the development and sequential analysis of the situations of these families living in conditions of poverty, the notion of a family life cycle was used. The family cycle is based on two dimensions: individual growth of family members[14] and the systemic maturation of the family unit.[15] Both dimensions of the life cycle reveal that the household's poverty tends to increase in accordance with the increase in family size, the increased presence of minors/children, and an imbalance in the complex tasks of family development. These dimensions do not permit the optimizing and regulation of the resources available in the family structure.

There are several unfavorable conditions that must be considered in the social security system developed for these families. These include the large number of families with low levels of employment, high economic dependency, relatively inferior level of schooling, high proportions of households headed by women, low levels of technical skills, unfavorable housing conditions, low per capita income, absent father, family instability, early motherhood, and multiple social, cultural and educational problems.

The tendency towards the generational reproduction of poverty makes it necessary to articulate the services of social security with the tasks of prevention and social treatment. This can be accomplished through better articulation with the work of the community and in the educational sphere, given special attention to problems of a social, cultural and educational character that are present in these families, thus integrating a preventive type of treatment with the remedial kinds of services that are already in place.

These families have skills and resources that, if utilized wisely, can provide important dynamics to resolve their problems and improve their life conditions. Among these skills and resources, we can mention the following: family cohesiveness and support, adequate mother protection, participation in support networks, an adequate level of health and education, social integration, among others. Thus, it is a human and socially important task to find the ways that can make it possible to maximize these capacities for developing the skills needed to enjoy an integral family and social life.

A Proposed Strategy of Integral Assistance to These Families

The social protection of poor families must articulate the coverage of basic social services that allow for the satisfaction of the family's essential needs with a social security policy that guarantees assistance and security during specific times of need. Efforts being made in both directions must harmoniously combine the elements of universality and targeted policies as well as both integral and sectorial approaches. However, it is also necessary to supplement the social protection of poor families with community strategies that can promote the participation and active role of families as protagonists in the problem-solving process.

In Cuban society, communities constitute a privileged space for providing assistance to those sectors of the population with unfavorable socioeconomic conditions. This is the result of the human resources that are available to them, the overall absence of social exclusion, the favorable social and territorial organization of the country, and the prevalent values of solidarity and social justice that predominates in the broader society. These resources can be maximized and concretized in community strategies that promote greater participation and initiative from the different actors making up the community.

As a result of a profound social transformation that has been carried out in Cuba with popular support, the broad fulfillment of the minimal basic needs of the general population and a fundamental redistribution of wealth has been achieved. This has allowed for a high level of social integration and broad spaces of active community participation. These characteristics against the backdrop of strong values of solidarity have to be further built upon in the search for solutions to existing problems.

Taking these values of solidarity as the point of departure, the following proposal to enhance the social integration and participation of families living under unfavorable socioeconomic conditions seeks a better coordination of efforts and the increased participation of different agents, organizations and community institutions. Cuba has a microsocial infrastructure that enables the systematic development of community work. This infrastructure is composed of mass organizations that function at the level of the neighborhood, local government, social prevention and treatment commissions, as well as various other social institutions inclined towards social welfare.

There are some weaknesses, however, that limit the effectiveness of results from this infrastructure. This makes it necessary to develop new substantive tasks in accordance with the present circumstances. Among these are the need for new working methods and styles; greater initiative and creativity in the solution of problems; greater integration and cooperation between actions, plans and programs of all involved institutions and organizations; and greater technical training of those activists working in a voluntary manner in this area, perhaps moving towards the professionalization of some of these tasks so as to better attend to their complexity.

Given the characteristics of those families that are experiencing unfavorable socioeconomic conditions, it can be shown that the level of scope and effectiveness of existing programs is limited when these families only partially avail themselves to the opportunities that already exist.[16] For that reason, the integral assistance given to these families should include more differentiated and focused interventions so as to help to maintain the overall levels of equity and social justice that has been achieved by our society.

The general principles for the proposed strategy include the following:

- A systemic focus that situates the family as the unit of analysis and intervention, instead of the traditional focus on individual beneficiaries (children, women, elderly, handicapped, etc.). This is not meant to disregard the gender and intergenerational differences within the family.
- A participatory focus, giving an active protagonist role to those families living in precarious conditions, and to the community associations and institutions in the identification and solutions of existing problems.

- Recognition of the importance of community work. This will promote taking better advantage of the existing community infrastructure, its material and human resources, and the coordination of actions and efforts among all the organizations working for the empowerment of the bonds between the family and the community.
- An integral and holistic character in the interventions and mechanisms used for solving the complex, heterogeneous, and multifaceted problems being targeted.
- A focused approach to the most vulnerable families, with attention given to their specific resource scarcities.
- Emphasis on the early targeting and prevention of families at risk and in precarious situations, while strengthening the relevant factors of social protection.

The proposal takes different cues from the methodologies of popular education and from action-participation research and group work. The methodology of popular education privileges the participation of people in the process of sharing knowledge, predicated on mutual respect and acceptance of all those involved. This process strengthens group cohesion and cooperation, individual and collective growth, and above all facilitates the analysis and the transformation of social reality on a continual basis. The action-participation research model permits the formation of collective knowledge for the transformation of a specific social reality context. Due to its participatory and collective character, this research model allows the participants to acquire high levels of responsibility and social commitment.

Group work is an aspect that characterizes popular education as well as action-participation research. As a basic element, the group provides the space for reflection and analysis of the everyday social reality, thus allowing for learning as well as personal and social activism in the solution of existing problems.

Upon the foundation that these contributions can provide, it is proposed that a set of actions, articulated in the community with the participation of different actors, organizations and local institutions, be carried out to provide for the integral assistance of families living in unfavorable socioeconomic conditions.

The strategy includes two basic components:

- Design and development of a community program for offering integral assistance to families living in unfavorable socioeconomic conditions with the coordinated efforts and participation of different community agents.

• Training for all people involved in the program: social activists, teachers, physicians, social workers, and cultural workers, among others.

The participants with respect to the first component are: presidents, vice-presidents and other members of the Popular Councils (health, education, culture, sports, labor, and social security), prevention and social assistance commissions, prevention groups at the neighborhood level, elementary schools, family physician consultation offices, political and social organizations, orientation houses for women and family, and various other social institutions.

In the experience that was gained by working together with the local government between 1998 and 2000 in the Catedral Popular Council of the Habana Vieja Municipality in the nation's capital, some objectives have been achieved with regard to the first component of this strategy. Various group sessions have been conducted with the participation of the local government representatives and the social organizations of that locality, which utilized according to the proposed objectives, diverse participatory techniques (animation, analysis, organization, planning, and evaluation).

A participatory diagnostic analysis regarding the characteristics and problems of families living in unfavorable socioeconomic conditions and better knowledge of the situation in the community has been gathered. The diagnostic suggested two limitations: first, these families are seen negatively, suggesting stigmatization in the connection between poverty and social marginality; and second, the emphasis that people place upon their family's own actions in explaining the causes for their poverty. This indicates the need to consider the self-perceptions of these families when carrying out the participatory diagnostic process.

However, motivations and expectations for the task at hand could be observed among group members, with a certain disposition and capacity for developing the strategy. This was based on motivations of solidarity and humanism, particularly inspired by the notion of helping to secure the future of the children and youth of these families. One of the most important aspects revealed in the process is that these families must come to feel that they are being understood and helped by their society rather than being excluded. They must perceive the possibility to participate in their communities and society.

The methods of this work are diverse and are applied pragmatically, including the use of individual conversation, calling attention to issues, control, the allocation of simple social tasks, a need for better organization and the development of cultural activities, among others. The deepening of analysis into the causes that promote the existence of these families managed to identify and deepen into social and economic factors as well as those related to the efficiency of prevention and social assistance on the part of the community organizations and institutions.

The areas of intervention defined by the group were the following:

- Economic situation (employment, training).
- Housing situation (constructive, hygiene-sanitary).
- Security and social assistance (benefits, assistance, pensions).
- Schooling situation of minors.
- Family health.
- Social prevention.
- Social participation.
- Legal assistance (paternity support).

Presently, the work around the identification of actions that can be done in the community, the first part of the strategy, continues. This also entails the training of the different groups participating and the definition of criteria for the evaluation of the strategy.

The results of this work with the group composed of the Popular Councils and their representatives have a multiplying effect in that the results are replicated in similar activities at other levels with the purpose of reaching consensus and support for the strategy. At this level, the work of the prevention groups in the neighborhood is added. Those groups are made up of the delegate, a representative of the mass organizations, a teacher, and a family physician that lives in the area.

The second component of the strategy is to train the community members involved in the program. This strategy develops parallel with the first component and has as its basic objective the development of skills and advising for community work with families living in unfavorable socioeconomic conditions.

For the training, family physicians and teachers have been selected for the first stage. Different work groups will be formed with each of them. Each group will focus discussions on different themes through group dynamics and workshops. The common themes to be considered include the importance of the family, family and society, family and community relations, community work, families living in unfavorable socioeconomic conditions and their main problems and needs.

The basic objective of the work with the teachers group is to train them in educational orientation for families living in unfavorable socioeconomic conditions. In the group session with the teachers, the main themes discussed revolved around the school-family-community relationship; the role of the teacher;

200

the educative role of the family; the training of adults; characteristics of socially disadvantaged children; and assistance strategies.

The objective of the work with the family physicians is to train them for the health orientation of families living in unfavorable socioeconomic conditions. Beginning with the fact that their medical training involves the holistic treatment of the family, themes of a more social nature will be developed such as quality of life, human welfare, family health, working with groups at social risk, family planning, health and environment issues, among others.

The training of teachers and family physicians will not only help to strengthen the effectiveness of their treatment of families in unfavorable socioeconomic conditions, but should also prepare them to be able to better identify at-risk families at an earlier stage, with an eye towards helping to promote their social integration.

Alongside of these two strategic components, the existing spaces of social participation in the community such as electoral meetings, neighborhood councils, parents' councils, grandparents' circles, and others, should be used effectively. It is also important to create new spaces of social participation where the family has a central role based in mutual cooperation and solidarity networks.

By developing this overall strategy, a higher stage involving more direct work with the families and their social engagement will be necessary. It should be clear that the particular details of these advanced strategies must emerge in the process of practicing these dynamics in their specific contexts. It is important to point out that what we have presented above only refers to general principles and the main components of a proposed strategy. Its complete elaboration should be carried out during its own accumulating experience under concrete and specific social conditions. Once this experience is carried out, the analysis of its most general aspects will serve as a basis for the extension of the strategy to other communities, attending to their problems, resources and specific potentials.

In the context of a global and regional scenario in which globalization and its devastating effects of poverty and social exclusion are affecting millions of families, the social protection of these families aimed at guaranteeing the satisfaction of its basic needs is a task of the highest order.

It is necessary to consider in an integral manner, the complex problems that are affecting families, to analyze them against the social reality in which they are conditioned, and to systemically interpret them. The solutions to these problems must go beyond the sectorial level and shift towards a more universal and holistic framework, not remaining confined to inter-institutional efforts but instead emphasizing the participation of families as active subjects, and with a more decentralized management that involves different agents and community organizations in the effort.

With respect to social security in the protection of families, Cuba represents a favorable situation in the region as the result of its social policies developed over the last several decades. Even though the achievements made in this area are impressive, the country must confront difficult challenges that have emerged in the 21st century. These challenges exhibit specific characteristics related to the Cuban family and its particular development as well as to the new economic situation in which it is immersed.

The social protection of families living in poverty constitutes a particularly important issue from the political and human point of view. Cuba represents a very special case in the present world system. It is a small country with limited resources that has developed for over four decades under an alternative social model in the context of difficult external and internal conditions. In such circumstances, the concrete manifestation of poverty in Cuba exhibits characteristics that are *sui generis*, especially given the comprehensive coverage of basic social services and the absence of extreme poverty and critical social exclusion.

The bases of the Cuban social project—social participation, justice and equality—and the existent social infrastructure, allow for the possibility of community strategies guided by human solidarity to assist those families living in poverty. The further development of such a strategy should contribute not only to strengthening the integration and social participation of these sectors of the population but also to a greater social empowerment of the community environment in finding collective solutions for existing problems. The aim is a harmonious development of a broad set of social policies with universal coverage that promotes social security and the central role of communities, a social environment that provides adequate family protection, and the satisfaction of basic needs and the fullest possible human development.

Starting in the year 2001, the Cuban Government developed a broad set of social programs that had very direct repercussions upon the living conditions and welfare of different sectors of the population and their families. These included the training of social workers whose mission is to work directly in the communities, detecting and attending to specific social situations. In addition, there was an integral improvement in the creation of new work options for young Cubans, new programs for special attention to the handicapped and their families, and other related initiatives. Without any doubt, the strategy to eradicate poverty will have to consolidate all of the various achievements which our country has made in social security.

Notes

1. UNDP, "Proyecto regional para la superación de la pobreza" [Regional Project for Overcoming Poverty]. (The full facts of publication of all the sources are found in the Bibliography, at the end of the essay. *Ed.)*

2. Juan Luis Londoño de la Cuesta, *Poverty, Inequality and Human Capital Development in Latin America,* 1950-2025.

3. Eduardo Bustelo and Alberto Minujin, "La política social esquiva" [The Elusive Social Policy] in *Pobreza, exclusión y política social* [Poverty, Exclusión and Social Policy].

4. World Bank, *World Development Report 1990.*

5. José Luis Rodríguez y George Carriazo, *Erradicación de la pobreza en Cuba* [Eradication of Poverty in Cuba].

6. Ángela Ferriol, "El reto de la equidad en Cuba" [The Challenge of Equity in Cuba]; José Bell, *Cambios mundiales y perspectivas de la Revolución Cubana* [World Changes and Future Prospects of the Cuban Revolution].

7. Services include medical assistance as well as physical, psychological, and work rehabilitation. Goods distributed for free include medicines and foodstuffs during hospitalization, orthopaedic devices or prosthetics in the event of accidents or professional illnesses, and medicines for those accidents or work illnesses that do not require hospitalization.

8. Today, one out of ten Cubans receives a pension (José Bell, op. cit.) and the figure is expected to increase due to the aging of the population.

9. In Cuba, 50.9% of family households are nuclear, 31.5% are extended, 10.7% consist of a single person, and 7% involve combined living arrangements Data taken from "Encuesta nacional de migraciones internas" [National Survey of Internal Migrations].

10. By the mid-1990s, these households represented 36% of the national total with 50% of those in the capital city. Data taken from "Encuesta nacional de migraciones internas," op. cit.

11. In 1994, 12% of the Cuban population was over the age of 60. By 2000, it had grown to 13.4% and it is projected that by 2025, it will reach 20.1%. To this must be added the growth in life expectancy that has already reached 75 years, creating a 20.5 year period of geriatric life expectancy (Raúl Hernández, *El envejecimiento de la población en Cuba* [The Aging of the Cuban Population]).

12. The goals included the following: reduction of child malnutrition under the age of five, reduction of infant and maternal mortality, reduction of underweight newborns, elimination of neonatal tetanus, 85% coverage of child immunizations, reduction of illiteracy, guarantee of universal education, extension of health coverage to the entire population, and creation of jobs at decent salaries.

13. UNDP, *Informe sobre el desarrollo humano* [Report on Human Development].

14. Evelyn Duvall, *Family Development*.

15. Peter Steinglass, Linda A. Bennett, Steven J. Wolin, *The Alcoholic Family*. (The author consulted the Spanish version, *La familia alcohólica*, published by Gedisa Editorial, Barcelona, 1996. *Ed.)*

16. María del Carmen Zabala, "Aproximación al estudio de la relación entre familia y pobreza en Cuba" [Studying the Relationship between Family and Poverty in Cuba].

Bibliography

BELL LARA, JOSÉ. *Cambios mundiales y perspectivas de la Revolución Cubana*. Havana: Editorial de Ciencias Sociales, 1999.

BUSTELO, EDUARDO and ALBERTO MINUJIN. "La política social esquiva." In *Pobreza, exclusión y política social*, edited by Rafael Menjívar Larín, Dirk Kruijt and Lieteke van Vucht Tijssen. San José, Costa Rica: FLACSO, Utrecht University and UNESCO – MOST Program, 1997. The Table of Contents of the book is available in http://www.unesco.org/most/povpobre.htm.

DUVALL, EVELYN. *Family Development*. 4th edition. Philadelphia, New York, Toronto: J. B. Lippincott, 1971.

"Encuesta nacional de migraciones internas." Report at National Office of Statistics and Center for Demographic Studies, 1995.

FERRIOL, ÁNGELA. "El reto de la equidad en Cuba." *Cuadernos de África y América Latina* journal, no. 36, 1999.

HERNÁNDEZ, RAÚL. *El envejecimiento de la población en Cuba*. Havana: CEDEM, 1994.

LONDOÑO DE LA CUESTA, JUAN LUIS. *Poverty, Inequality and Human Capital Development in Latin America*. Washington, D.C.: World Bank Latin American and Caribbean Study, 1996.

RODRÍGUEZ, JOSÉ LUIS and GEORGE CARRIAZO. *La erradicación de la pobreza en Cuba*. Havana: Editorial de Ciencias Sociales, 1987.

STEINGLASS, METER, LINDA A. BENNETT and STEVEN J. WOLIN. *The Alcoholic Family*. New York: The Perseus Books Group, 1987.

UNDP. *Informe sobre el desarrollo humano.* Madrid: Ediciones Mundiprensa, 1999.

————. "Proyecto regional para la superación de la pobreza." *Comercio Exterior* journal (Mexico), vol. 42, no. 4 (April, 1992).

WORLD BANK. *World Development Report 1990.* Washington D.C.: World Bank, August 1990.

ZABALA, MARÍA DEL CARMEN. "Aproximación al estudio de la relación entre familia y pobreza en Cuba." Ph.D. diss., University of Havana, 1999.

Women's Empowerment in Cuba

Tania Caram León

TANIA CARAM LEÓN

Ph.D. in Educational Sciences. A linguist by training, she has researched issues of social development, specifically as they relate to women. She is a professor and researcher in the FLACSO-Cuba Progam, and an expert in empowerment thematic.

To analyze the present situation of women in Cuban society, this study utilizes the concept of *empowerment* as defined by UNICEF,[1] although adapted for application to Cuba's social reality. There are four cumulative levels associated with empowerment, including wellbeing, access, consciousness, and finally, participation and control. Following this scheme, the study examines each level and presents an overall reflection in view of the factual information available. In addition, comparisons will be made with other studies carried out in Cuba on this topic. The aim is to form an evaluative portrait of the level of women's empowerment in Cuban society.

Women's Wellbeing in Cuba

At the level of wellbeing are basically included health, nutrition and social security. Wellbeing as such reached a high level of satisfaction during the initial thirty years of socialist transformation by virtue of the overall elevation of the population's quality of life and a dramatic redistribution of wealth. Various authors have pointed towards the characteristic of equity as one of the most distinctive and important characteristics of Cuban society to be considered in this regard. This becomes particularly evident when analyzing Cuba's social indicators and comparing them with other underdeveloped countries, or even to the most developed ones.[2]

Within this context, we can see that the situation of women has developed in a particularly favorable way. Women were recipients of the social policies implemented on behalf of the entire population, including various policies designed especially for them as a special category of beneficiaries. But here, it must be noted that there is insufficient data disaggregated by gender with which to perform a deeper and more reliable analysis.

With regard to health, indicators show a highly favorable evolution for women. The ultimate proof of this can be found in the decline of fertility and in infant mortality rates.

Fertility declined from a peak of 4.7 children per woman in 1963 to 1.9 in 1978 (a reduction by more than a half in just 15 years). From that point forward, fertility has oscillated around and below the replacement rate, descending to a low point of 1.5 in 1992. Among the main determinants surrounding this decline would include generalized access and the use of birth contraception methods as well as an increase in the number of abortions. Likewise, child mortality registered a sustained fall from between 46.7 in 1969 to 10.2 in 1992, a reduction of close to one-fifth of that reported towards the end of the 1960s.[3]

In the following decade, the rate continued to decline in spite of the economic crisis, so that by 2002 it was recorded at 6.5 per 1000 live births.[4]

These indicators are in large measure attributable to the extension of community medicine where 99.2% of the population is attended to by a family physician[5] as part of a fundamentally prevention oriented system of medical care. As evidence of this, it can be seen that 98.2% of Cuban children have been immunized against 12 key diseases by the age of two.[6]

The achievement of lowering infant mortality helped to influence in a decisive manner the social policy and cultural accumulation of users, principally women, by converting them into active participants. As involved social actors, they could guarantee the implementation of these policies within their nuclear families and communities. Back in the 1960s, when the healthcare system was not yet fully structured, mass vaccinations of children were carried out utilizing popular participation vis-à-vis the Cuban Women's Federation (FMC) and the Committees for the Defense of the Revolution (CDRs). In this way, for example, polio was eradicated and Cuban women played a decisive role in this great achievement.[7] By moving forward with this kind of social integration as expressed in multiple experiences, it can be perceived that the situation of Cuban women does not merely consist of being passive recipients of an advancing welfare system. Rather, they have played and continue to play an active role in carrying out these policies which directly benefit them.

Certain indicators exemplify the development that has been achieved in health: 99.9% of births are delivered within institutions of healthcare;[8] the rate of direct maternal mortality, although with discrete oscillations, has evolved favorably, from 3.2 per 10 thousand live births in 1990, to 4.3 in 1994, down to 2.4 in 1996, and then to 2.2 in 1997.[9] Overall life expectancy in 1997 reached 75.7 years.[10]

Despite this highly successful scenario regarding health, there were nevertheless several years in which some disequilibrium occurred. This was expressed by increases in the number of teenage pregnancies as well as in the erroneous use of abortion as a means of birth control and family planning. This notwithstanding, the figure for pregnancies for mothers under the age of 20 subsequently declined, basically due to the interventions of the family physicians. The percentage of births by mothers in that age group was recorded at 13% in 1997.[11]

Abortion was often utilized excessively due to its high reliability and to the fact that it was available upon demand, without charge, and with seldom any problems reported. Eventually the use of abortion began to diminish in keeping with the priorities set by family planning healthcare policies. "The greatest number of abortions per live births ever recorded (9.7 abortions per 10 live births) occurred in 1986. Beginning in 1987, a marked decline was observed in the number of abortions."[12] By 2002, this indicator had been reduced by almost one-half.[13]

The capacity to decide about childbearing is a social fact that implies a certain level of dominion over women's sexuality. It translates into greater freedom and a high level in the conscious appropriation of their bodies. This dimension of wellbeing that has been reached by Cuban women in such massive proportions is not often publicized and nor are Cuban women themselves sufficiently aware of it.

Another aspect that contributes to the overall panorama of heightened female wellbeing as an important part of their empowerment relates to social security. Cuban women enjoy the benefits of favorable legislation, both in terms of the stipulated retirement age of 55 as well as by the laws that protect their retirement. Since the social security system supports all retired and pensioned individuals, 1878 million pesos were spent in 2001 so as to satisfy the needs of 1.4 million citizens who were beneficiaries of the system, making up 13% of the population.[14] One further protection of great importance to working women is that of maternity leave, guaranteeing 12 months of leave with full salary paid during the 1.5 months prior to giving birth up through 3 months afterwards. It also includes the right of prolongation up to one full year at a 60% rate of salary.

We have briefly characterized the favorable panorama of women's wellbeing as achieved in Cuba. It is also necessary to consider some of the effects resulting from the economic crisis that afflicted the country during the 1990s. The country's economy suffered a devastating impact following the disappearance of the former Socialist Bloc and the intensification of the U.S. blockade. The compounding effect of this was felt upon the Gross Domestic Product (GDP): "In 1990, the GDP fell 3.6%, followed in 1991 by a contraction of 24% and in 1992 by an additional 15% decline."[15]

In spite of the fact that the crisis did not result in a neoliberal style of structural adjustment,[16] the parameters of Cuba's quality of life shifted downwards under this impact. Nevertheless, Bell Lara argues that "the collective support of the majority of the historic paradigms of the Revolution amounted to a material force for resistance and overcoming the crisis."[17] Following a process of gradual recovery, the country's economy grew by 6.7% in 1999, revealing an evident upturn, but one still short of reversing sufficiently the unfavorable effects on everyday life caused by the crisis.

In the sphere of health care, the crisis resulted in shortages of medicines and in the deterioration of some services. The negative effects of the blockade, among others, included increasing the prices of medicines paid by the Cuban State due to the need to resort to more distant markets, and this influenced availability of some specific medicines. It has been calculated that between the years 1991 and 1999, the blockade cost Cuba 1.2 billion dollars in the sphere of health care alone.[18]

One of the negative effects of the crisis was the increase in low birth weight babies. This tendency was reversed following social policies that were applied at the community level, especially a concerted effort to treat pregnant women, working or not, for any noted nutritional deficiencies by utilizing cafeterias in the closest production centers near to where pregnant women live. The trend in numbers of children with low birth weight was as follows: 7.3% in 1989; 8.9% in 1994; and 8% in 1995, followed by a process of gradual improvement after that year, reaching 5.9% in 2002.[19]

The public health budget was not reduced, reaching the amount of 1732 million pesos by the year 2000. In that year, there was one physician for every 168 inhabitants and an oral health physician for every 1123 inhabitants, distributed across the country in 283 hospitals, 440 polyclinics and 14,622 physician's consultation offices.[20]

With respect to food consumption, an area in which the Revolution had made important advances and had achieved considerable equity in distribution, the crisis had a strong impact which could be seen in the following statistics. During the years 1993-1995, the average per capita kilocalories consumed per day fell under 2000, down from 2300 in 1998. By 1999, the figure was back up to 2369 with 59.4 grams of protein consumed daily.[21] Unfortunately, disaggregated figures on food consumption by sex are unavailable. Although the selection and processing of these data have improved relative to other periods in the past, they continue to be insufficient. While we know about the relative recovery of consumption per capita in terms of calories, we cannot be totally certain that there is gender equity at this level.

Other negative effects resulting from the crisis are still having repercussions upon everyday life, with notable shortages in such areas as transportation, the scarce availability of consumer goods, and the deterioration of household items that help to facilitate domestic tasks, presently without any possibility of repair or replacement, given that most of this equipment had been imported from Eastern Europe and the former Soviet Union. All of these adversities wear upon the wellbeing of Cubans and women are the first to be directly affected.

The bulk of housework and the main responsibility for domestic and family tasks continue to be placed on their shoulders.

Nevertheless, the results of studies point to a relative compensation regarding this situation. In the first place, Cuba does not experience the kind of social exclusion found in many other countries. Those families that live in a situation of social disadvantage nonetheless remain socially articulated, receiving the general benefits of education, health care and social security. The various modalities of social differentiation do not impede their access to the social platform of welfare that has been constructed in Cuba over the last three decades and which has been maintained in spite of all the difficulties and the limited reintroduction of market dynamics. This has been possible due to the effective commitment expressed by the country's top leadership.

Measures have been adopted to help to impede social polarization such as the strengthening of the national currency relative to the dollar, the taxation system, and the creation of programs oriented towards the most socially disadvantaged sectors. Nevertheless, if there is one thing that conspires against the wellbeing of women, it is the continuing burden placed upon her by domestic and family tasks, this in spite of their active role in the larger society. This characteristic continues to persist in spite of the Cuban Family Code that went into effect in 1975. The Code, which was massively discussed all across the island, establishes the equality of rights and duties among men and women with respect to family responsibilities and the upbringing of children.

In this area, two tendencies essentially developed, one operating in a fleeting, short-term manner while the other is more permanent and medium term in character. The former was linked to the immediate impact of the crisis during its most severe phase (1990-94) upon the day-to-day operation of family life, something that necessitated the assistance of all family members, including husbands and children, to complete basic household tasks.[22] Although this had the positive effect of making visible the burden that domestic work signified for women, the tendency abated when the most serious of these economic problems began to subside.

The latter tendency arose among the most recent generations where according to research studies, the youngest of new couples cannot necessarily count on the support of older adults, something that during other periods they had been more willing to assume as a kind of "rearguard" backup for essential tasks.[23] This displacement demands that other family members assume responsibility for such tasks on a rotating or at least temporary basis.

The situation becomes further complicated by the economic tensions referred to earlier, which means that many women do not have the option of exclusively dedicating themselves to household tasks since they are performing important social functions outside the home. While this favors the situation of the woman insofar as her personal self-actualization is involved, it simultaneously demands a high quota of sacrifice from her in the form of what is commonly known as the "double-day workload."

Nevertheless, we should point out that over the latter half of the 1990s, a slow process of economic recovery began that has been sustained into the current decade. By 2003, the economy was growing at a 2.6% rate.[24] In spite of the impediments discussed above, the wellbeing experienced by Cuban women can be distinguished by its basic homogeneity and for the essential services that are received which serve to guarantee their quality of life.

Cuban Women's Access

The second level of empowerment, access, refers to employment, to the legal protections that are conferred upon women so as to enhance their capacity for participation in society, to the resources at their disposal, and to the ability to acquire skill levels necessary for engaging in paid labor. Also important in this regard is their access to the resources of their household.

The FMC carried out an extremely important effort so as to favor the incorporation of women, using the combined methods of persuasion as well as the force of social obligation and compulsion. In 1975, more than 20,000 women worked in construction brigades and many others joined in the sugar harvests, helping to break down the traditional barriers that had previously demarcated traditional female work. Increasingly, the FMC pushed for women's incorporation into the areas of technical training, advocating for women's participation in more skilled areas of employment. By 2003, women made up 44.7% of those employed in the state civil sector, but even more significant was the change in their profile. By that same year, women accounted for 66.4% of the country's technicians and professionals.[25] Although their participation in this area was largely found in the service sector, they did not remain confined to only minor or auxiliary positions, but on the contrary made up 60% of physicians and 60.8% of oral health physicians. Even in the specialty areas of medicine, women reached the level of 60% of immunologists, dermatologists and psychiatrists, and 70% of neurologists and nutritionists.

The principal limitations to this explosive transformation in labor force participation were twofold. Already mentioned was the tendency for women to maintain a traditional profile in terms of the domestic sphere and to carry primary responsibility for family duties. Additionally, there was a weak female presence in leadership positions with access to decision making with women comprising 29.8% of leaders in 1990, then reaching only 31% in 2001, but still with much less representation in the highest levels of leadership.

After 3 decades of sustaining full employment, the level of unemployment began to grow in the 1990s. From 4% in 1994, it reached 8% in 1996, then dipped back down to 6.9% in 1997 and continued to decrease to 6% in 1999. By 2004, the unemployment rate was back down to 2.3%, approaching the situation of full employment.[26]

In the state sphere that continues to make up the principal source of work for the country, female participation grew to 42.5% in the 1990s, at a time when the number of men left without work due to the crisis was higher than that of women.[27] The fact that women who participated in the labor force during this first stage of the crisis were not as greatly affected by unemployment could be explained by their relatively higher skill level and their lesser presence in the blue-collar sector (19.5%). By February 1994, women were becoming incorporated into the newly authorized sphere of private or self-employment. Data concerning these groups indicate that in 1995, women made up 25% of the private or self-employed total, with 13% of them being housewives. By the end of 1997, the total amounted to 26.9% of which 16% were housewives. Thus, at the neighborhood level, it was predominantly women who were employed in the service types of work that flourished in this sector, basically in the food services sphere of mini-cafeterias or in small, private restaurants that became popularly known as *paladares.*

Although it is mostly women who have retired from their former state sector jobs that pursue this kind of work, their increasing presence may possibly relate to the necessity to augment or supplement their family earnings as well to the gradual increase of female head of families, estimated several years ago to be at around 35% of the total.[28]

While this tendency resembles what has come to prevail in the rest of Latin America, where female employment in the informal sector is growing, it is also necessary to point out the important difference that in Cuba, the female presence has been maintained in the most advanced sectors of the economy as well. For example, women constitute 60% of those working in the medical pharmaceutical industry and 50% of those working in scientific research centers.[29]

In general, women represent 66.4% of all professional and technical workers at the medium and higher end of that labor force segment, 72% of the educational labor force and 67% of the health care sector.[30] It is significant to note that in spite of the existent amount of unemployment, there remain spheres

215

where a labor shortage persists, especially in agriculture. It happens that these unfilled positions do not correspond either to the skill levels reached by the majority of idled workers nor to their expectations which have accumulated over the previous decades.

With respect to salaries, Cuban law provides for equal compensation for work without distinction between men and women. Moreover, the maximum distance between the highest and lowest salaries within the state sector is not all that significant.

Although I have identified earlier the lack of correspondence between this high rate of social and labor force participation and the amount of leadership responsibilities being exercised by women, 30% of the country's leadership posts are held by females. While it is true that within the larger pyramid of responsibilities, women's access to the very highest levels diminishes proportionally as they approach the apex, this can be explained by various factors. Over and above the weight of tradition in selecting leaders, one of the elements that impinge with greatest force is the burden of domestic and family responsibilities, something which demands an overwhelming amount of sacrifice in the exercise of leadership roles. Another influential factor is the type of high ranking leader that tends to prevail in the country, namely, people exceptionally dedicated to their work. This is something that requires the investment of a lot of time and effort so as to reach the level that is required for their leadership role.

In the analysis of access, it seems that the changes that have occurred in the sphere of education have been extremely valuable. Women are incorporated to a notable extent in the process of training that is being promoted throughout the country. In the decade of the 1960s, an important process of retraining women was carried out along with an accumulation of a wide range of knowledge that helped to expand their social participation. There were courses of instruction on how to sew, organized by the FMC, acting as points of social reinsertion as well as cultural extension for young rural women who were the beneficiaries. In 1986, there were 99,392 housewives who had achieved a ninth grade education and 18,048 that were studying towards that end. The FMC also organized schools for the advancement of women, dedicated to retraining former domestic servants and prostitutes so as to subsequently reposition them in society.

From the very beginning of the revolutionary process, the Literacy Campaign of 1961 benefited large numbers of Cubans, with women making up 55% of the beneficiaries, and 59% of the literacy workers. This process moreover signified a dialectic of interaction between generations of literacy workers and their families, that transcended this educational labor.[31]

The process for changing the gendered compartmentalization of skills begins in primary schooling when traditional roles that are associated with aspirations and the socially differentiated role behaviors of boys and girls can be eradicated or substantially reduced. As girls began to remain in school and experience an increased rate of promotion, this encouraged a more privileged position of women at the primary and secondary levels of schooling. At present, the Cuban population possesses an average educational attainment at the ninth grade level. One item worth mentioning with respect to Cuban education is that of special education, which in 1997 involved 425 schools with 57,348 children experiencing varied behavioral irregularities, mental retardation, psychiatric disturbance, deafness and hyper acoustic problems, blindness and visually impairments, and a variety of other physical disorders and impaired physio-motor functions.[32] What is significant about this attention is that it offers a potent boost to the quality of life of its beneficiaries as well as to their otherwise overwhelmed mothers.

In an accelerated manner, women achieve a level of training that offers the potential of participating under conditions of equity. Their participation at the tertiary level of teaching is occurring in an increasing and qualitatively differentiated way, enabling them to break into fields traditionally reserved for men. For example women make up more than 40% of the enrollment in fields such as electronics, automation, and biology, among others.

The crisis that the country suffered throughout the 1990s did not substantially change this situation. Although there existed and still exists a negative impact upon the availability of school materials and at other levels of teaching in terms of the availability of specialized bibliographies, laboratory reagents for experimental work, and other shortages, an extraordinary effort was made to maintain the quality of teaching and the participation of females at all levels throughout the crisis. Evidence of this can be found in a recent research study carried out by UNESCO in Latin America, dedicated towards students at the primary level, where Cuba obtained first place in terms of female participation. In this regard, female teachers who are a majority at this level have played an important role.

In spite of the crisis, scientific development became further integrated into teaching, with significant advances in areas such as the increased availability of computer equipment per capita within higher learning. The participation of women in higher education is progressively relevant,[33] whereas of the more than 64,000 Cuban workers deployed in science and technology, 52% are women.[34]

While the negative effects of the crisis prevailed throughout the 1990s, Cuban women had a greater presence in the sphere of higher education. Of the total population reported graduated in higher education during the academic year 1996-97, 56.4% were women. For the following academic year, females made up 60.6% of the total enrollment.[35] They also accounted for 46% of the faculty, the highest percentage in Latin America.[36]

It must be said however that serious limitations remain due to the reproduction of the traditional models of behavior of both men and women which become transmitted through both formal and informal mechanisms. Despite the advances made in the curriculum of teaching in biology and sex education, the higher education system at the undergraduate level has not yet managed to systematically incorporate issues of gender. Indeed, even at the graduate level, progress remains limited. One factor contributing to this insufficient progress rests in the instructors themselves as transmitters of values. Since they have not managed to sufficiently develop their own expertise in this area, they are consequently unable to rapidly generate the needed changes. Meanwhile, traditions at the informal level remain in place and become expressed in everyday social relations alongside of the new patterns being presently generated in Cuban society. It could be said that a gradual process of access, albeit with significant limitations, is underway and continues to display a favorable trend overall.

Women's Consciousness in Empowerment

In terms of the third level of empowerment, i.e., raising the consciousness of women, there has been a significant change in the overall way of thinking on the part of both women and men in Cuba. Behavior in this regard can be evaluated in terms of the changing codes that govern the relations between the two genders and in their larger social projection. This is closely related to the larger social structure, with the first relevant change having to do with the elimination of structural barriers that impede female participation. In a study carried out by FLACSO-Cuba base in an industrial electronics setting as well as in a center of higher education, it was shown that Cuban women do not feel discriminated against in terms of their social integration or for being a woman.[37]

These same results were found in other studies.[38] Nevertheless, a neatly formed ideology with respect to the issue does not exist and although the majority of women openly respond if they are questioned, the fact of non-discrimination does not yet form part of the cultural accumulation that implies a certain level of consciousness.

Another aspect to be considered involves those changes that include women and men as social actors. The construction of such an egalitarian society, with an emphasis on values such as solidarity and social justice became a way of life and thinking that has uplifted human dignity. These values continue being rooted in the population in spite of the limitations and emergent contrasts that have arisen in the 1990s, and they form part of women's consciousness and their self-esteem.

The FMC has promoted increased women's consciousness at all levels and has created Departments on Women in various universities as well as multiple Orientation Houses on Women and Family in communities. Currently, there are 175 such Houses located in all of the municipalities, where 4338 people work in concert, including psychologists, sociologists, lawyers, pedagogical specialists and others who offer consulting services and carry out educational activities in communities on a voluntary and unpaid basis.[39]

Yet, the dissemination of ideas about gender still remains insufficient in a society that has in practice broken with the ties of the past. It thus seems paradoxical that a subtle difference persists between the assimilation of actual behavior and the predominant self-image of women, and in this regard, we feel the effects of a continuing deficit of familiarity with feminist theory.

Another way of observing the level of women's consciousness is through the imagery depicting women in the mass media as well as in school textbooks. In Cuba, work has been done in the area of altering the portrayal of family life in existing textbooks towards the aim of presenting more positive images of women and to encourage the sharing of housework and childrearing tasks on the part of men and women. There still prevails a perception on the part of children about the predominant role which mothers must play in carrying out the bulk of domestic tasks, consistent with that which occurs in reality. An interesting study, carried out by Patricia Arés, illustrated this situation by looking at gendered family roles through the use of children' sketches that depicted their respective families.[40] The sketches vividly portrayed the male-female dichotomy insofar as domestic work tasks are concerned.

All of this involves the beginning of a deconstructive process both of the prototypical male model of being and of knowing as well as the female model, towards the end of constructing a third representation that is based upon the contributions of both.[41]

The images of women in the mass media have been gradually modified, in radio, cinema, television and the printed press. Although the focus often remains traditional in character, the FMC has struggled to modify this situation and it is increasingly the case that a larger proportion of female figures appear in more active roles, reflecting the increased participation of women. A positive role in this sense has been played by the program "Para la vida" (For Life), promoted by the Ministry of Education with support by UNICEF. The program has touched upon gender issues in a delicate and sensitive manner, some errors notwithstanding. Meanwhile, another battle led by the FMC has taken aim at the use of inappropriate imagery that utilizes Cuban women to commercialize Cuban products abroad, something that will require consistent attention in order to eradicate.

It can be seen that the net product of all these processes has resulted in a female identity that exhibits high self-esteem and feelings of deeply rooted dignity that encourage a positive valorization of women in Cuba. Continuing to increase women's consciousness in this positive way will definitely require still further changes in the educational sphere.

Women's Participation in Cuba

In the sphere of social participation, the fourth level of empowerment that we have considered, a significant amount of change has been produced. According to the available figures, it is possible to appreciate a notable alteration in the representation of women with an increase in their participation. Within the organs of People's Power, women make up 23.37% of municipal delegates, 31% of delegates at the provincial level and 35.96% of the deputies to the National Assembly,[42] figures that are very favorable even though they could stand to be even more representative of the real level of women's participation in Cuban society.

The figures are promising, especially since the worldwide average of women's participation in parliaments remains at 10%. Perhaps even more important is the connotation of a subjective change in women with respect to participation. In this regard, one of the explicit results of the increased educational level of Cuban women, a product of revolutionary educational policies, is the creation of progressive forms of empowerment. "In terms of women parliamentarians, Cuba is only surpassed by Sweden, Denmark, Finland and Norway. The United States occupies the sixtieth place."[43]

In a national study carried out by the FMC, it was shown that the majority of women that were interviewed about their feelings on becoming a delegate to the People's Power responded affirmatively. Between their expectations and their actual nomination, however, a process occurs that reduces the actual number of women participating and this is something that cannot be reduced to mere self-exclusion. The low percentage of women who decline their nominations further demonstrates that the problem does not rest in a reluctance to assume responsibilities, but rather in the lack of their being nominated. The majority of those that accept their nomination result in their becoming candidates for delegate posts, something that allows us to infer that if the number of women being proposed were to increase, so too would the overall female representation at all levels of People's Power, including among the existing number of local women delegates in the Parliament that has already reached 50%.[44]

The study carried out by the FMC that included a total of 6224 People's Power assemblies throughout the country showed that out of 4507 women proposed as candidates, only 334 (or just over 7%) turned down the opportunity. Likewise analyzed was the process by which the number of women proposed tended to decrease after being studied by the candidacy commissions at the municipal and provincial levels. In the case of the national level, representation on the part of the mass organizations tended to see a lower number of females ascending to candidacies which corresponds to their lower overall presence at those levels.

The author of that study argued that "the persistence of *machismo* upon attitudes in the form of biases and stereotypes, whose content undervalues women on account of considering that they are not sufficiently capable nor adequately prepared for such tasks and are less able to manage and exercise power, and above all, nurtured the generalized fear that their leadership responsibilities would not be compatible with their maternity and obligation to carry out domestic tasks."[45]

This fact carries considerable significance for the analysis of participation. It means that in spite of the elimination of structural barriers that confront women in the assimilation of their empowerment, other obstacles of a subjective nature continue to exist for both women and men and they constitute a braking effect on real gender integration. This could be associated with two generalized perceptions, namely: the tendency to underestimate the capacity of women to manage public affairs when compared against the hegemonic male role of leader; and the generalized feeling of compassion and/or identification with the overburdened task load that women routinely assume. Of course, both perceptions are directly challenged by the practice of successful women, with a particular style of management emerging that enables them to alternate their responsibilities with those of the home and family.

Another, more positive reading of the results of the FMC study could consider that the potential of women's participation in managing public affairs is greater than that which currently exists. This fact arrests the supposition of self-resignation on the part of women and enriches our analysis of the level of empowerment previously discussed, that of increased consciousness. But the balance insofar as parliamentary representation goes is consistent with a changing reality that is trending towards even better results.

Indeed, other spheres of representation help to complement this image. In the Council of State, elected from among deputies, the female presence has grown from 13.6% to 16.1%. Likewise in the Communist Party of Cuba, women now constitute 30.1% of militants, 22% of the membership of municipal party committees, 23% of provincial party committees and 13.3% of the Central Committee, although within the Political Bureau, only 8% of its members are female.[46]

It can be observed in these figures that there is a tendency of strong participation at the base levels while the proportion shrinks at the higher levels. Within the Youth Communist League (UJC), the percentage at the higher levels of leadership is also generally lower—there is only 1 first secretary at the provincial level—, although 19.2% of the National Bureau members and at the municipal level are women. In the Cuban Workers Union (CTC), women make up 52.5% of union section leaders and 48.2% of bureau members as well as 24% of the National Committee. In the Committees for the Defense of the Revolution (CDRs), 34.7% of the municipal secretariats are held by women, as are 33% of the provincial level secretariats, and 32.8% of the national secretariat. In the National Association of Small Farmers (ANAP), women constitute 14.5% of the associate members, 15.3% of the municipal bureaus, 18.7% of the provincial bureaus and 18.1% of the national bureau.

In the Cuban Ministry of Foreign Affairs (MINREX), 50% of vice-ministers are women, with 14 female ambassadors or mission chiefs, 11 consuls along with 133 women serving in other diplomatic posts. In the administration of justice, women make up 49% of professional judges at all levels and 61% of the prosecutors,[47] and these figures remain current as of 2004. It could be pointed out here that in these last two spheres, the level of training necessary to carry out such tasks plays an important role and favors an enhanced presence of women. Nevertheless, this is not the same in the political sphere where a stricter requirement to have such qualifications could play the same role in promoting women's participation.

It is evident that the growing level of women's participation is being produced in a pyramidal form. Their representation is partially limited by their scarce presence at the very highest levels, by their strong burden of responsibilities in the domestic and family sphere, and by the hegemonic content of male leadership roles.

It can be shown that there is a lack of correspondence between the qualitative growth of female education and their actual level of participation. But it is in this educational sphere where the possibilities are found for a greater representation on the part of women, this due to the effect of ideological changes weighing upon the behavior of both genders.

Control as Empowerment

Control, the last and highest sphere of empowerment, is the most complex and difficult to analyze. It expands upon the preceding levels and simultaneously embraces various dimensions. Control refers to the exercise of power, including that which involves decision-making and access to resources, in spheres that reach up into the highest leadership levels of the country and down to the more intimate family and domestic levels.

At the very highest level of government leadership, female participation remains low. Nonetheless, there are currently six female ministers, only two of which carry out duties in spheres traditionally considered to be female (domestic commerce and light industry) while the others work in spheres in which control constitutes an important factor. These include the Ministry of Science, Technology and Environment (CITMA),* the Ministry of Investment and International Cooperation (MINVEC), the Ministry of Audit and Control, and the Ministry of Finance and Pricing. In a certain sense, it would seem that those ministries reflect the polarized tendencies within women's empowerment with regard to control. This notwithstanding, to evaluate with precision the entry of Cuban women into leadership roles, their presence at the levels of mid-range management must be seriously taken into account. It is there that a high representation of women can be found, especially prevalent in the most innovative areas. Moreover, women are serving as vice-ministers in almost all of the ministries.

Meanwhile, control at the family level can be initially associated with the right of divorce. In Cuba, the divorce rate has grown from 0.6 per thousand inhabitants in 1961, to 3.6 in 1989, 4.1 in 1991 and 6 in 1993. According to Rojas: "In a general way, the statistical figures from the last decades show that 1 out of every 3 marriages end in divorce."[48]

In 1997, the divorce rate was 5.5 per 1000 inhabitants. These figures respond to multiple causes (intense social dynamics for each partner, adverse housing conditions, difficulties in everyday tasks, among others) as well as expressing a certain grade of female independence. In past generations, divorce was considered a terrible failure for the woman involved as well as posing the

---

*. While this book was preparing for publication, Dr. Rosa Elena Simeón, Work Hero of the Republic of Cuba, Minister of CITMA, died. *Ed.*

threat of her increased vulnerability and symbolically constituting a synonym for her licentiousness. But in the contemporary era, women are not forced to put up with an unhappy marriage for economic reasons of survival, infidelity or mistreatment, something that they had to endure with humiliation in the past.

Further emancipatory changes in these behaviors will not be immediate. The family suffers from the impact of a model that presupposed women's subordination and oppression. The rate of dissolution or divorce index is one consequence of the evolving changes. It is certainly true that this index has more than one reading. One the one hand, it can signify the capacity for women's economic independence, high self-esteem, and a relatively high level of expectations with respect to men as a consequence of a well-developed, personal pride. But it likewise can be evaluated as a dysfunction within the family model that results in pain and instability for both parts of a couple as well as their offspring.

It is necessary to comprehend the specificity within the ways of seeing life by women, something that implies specific spiritual needs that are identified with the family, children and their emotional ties. It is part of the difference between the genders, in a subjective sense, and recognition of its importance will require greater attention.

It has been seen that the complexity in the quality of participation in social relations on the part of both genders is imprinted upon the relations of couples, and as the dynamics generated in this sphere give rise to a dimension of stress and the need for constant adjustment, greater analysis at deeper levels must be pursued. Another reading of this data could suggest the contradictions generated by a more active attitude on the part of female "protagonists" with respect to the amorous relations of couples and a prevailing incapacity of males to tolerate the "rising star" of women.

In any case, other factors that influence divorces would have to be taken into account, such as that of young couples that married early, unprepared for developing a life project in common with another, but heavily pressured to formalize a relationship that should have remained temporary so that the two can live together with one or another of the parents. In other countries, these experimental kinds of relationships do not normally become included in the marriage indexes or in the divorce rates, essentially because they do not result in ties of formal marriage. In Cuba, however, these relations often become legally formalized for reasons of a material nature.

Within the interior of families constituted by more traditional patterns, the woman tends to exercise an important part of control. Generally, she decides or participates in decisions of considerable importance regarding the family budget and income, schooling for children, interpersonal relations and their dynamics, and so on. In the end, she is a main actor within the domestic sphere. Even conflictual dynamics relate to decisions and control that express her hegemonic role. Nevertheless, there exist definite situations that present a divergent context, such as in the rural sector, where the women's role in decision-making can be decidedly inferior.

One aspect already mentioned earlier but worthy of emphasis is that decision-making power about reproductive capacity and sexuality is of considerable importance to women's empowerment. The family planning program and the security offered by the possibility of interrupting an unwanted pregnancy offers women a capacity for exerting control over their own bodies. This characteristic along with a break with the most reactionary traditions concerning sexuality constitutes a favorable scenario that has brought with it the development of new and more genuine values.

At the same time, an observable tendency towards certain forms of promiscuity (including sexual commodification) can constitute a negative element in the balance sheet regarding this acquired liberty, particularly if it reaches significant weight in the existing framework of social relations. Studies have shown that prostitution in Cuba acquires very specific characteristics in the way that it is not motivated by a desperate need for survival, not socially organized as an industry, or institutionally associated with tourism. Young women who dedicate themselves to this activity tend to possess a medium level of schooling, with many not at all self-identifying as "professionals" in this activity or seeing it as a form of work, but rather entering into the world of foreign tourists in search of their own "fair prince." In short, most do not consider themselves to be engaging in prostitution.[49] To combat these trends, laws have been placed into effect and are particularly severe against those serving as pimps, with priority given towards the prevention of exploitation of children by way of sexual abuse or pornography.

This issue has also been progressively extended into education, beginning at the day care level up through middle school, where important information about sexual education is being provided. A greater development of specific educational policies could help to contribute to preventing these unwanted behaviors, both at the community level as well as in the incorporation of these topics into children's literature, for example. But true prevention ultimately rests in assimilating a deeper knowledge of gender theory with respect to exercising sexuality.

A general evaluation of this gendered process of social integration could conclude that Cuban women have achieved significant successes, although important limitations still persist. With respect to the remaining obstacles, it is essential to develop a strategy that includes the strengthening of educational factors, with the explicit objective of promoting a social, ideological and structural transformation on behalf of women.

Women's empowerment envisions an eventual utopia of gender equality. The progressive pursuit of this goal forms part of the larger process of social transformation in creating a more just society, one where new forms of living and thinking can be constructed on a daily basis.

Notes

1. UNICEF, "El marco conceptual de igualdad y empoderamiento de las mujeres" [The conceptual Framework of Equality and Women's Empowerment], in Magdalena León, *Poder y empoderamiento de mujeres* [Women's Power and Empowerment]. (The full facts of publication of all the sources are found in the Bibliography, at the end of the essay. *Ed.)*

2. Beatriz Díaz, "Cuba: modelo de desarrollo equitativo" [Cuba: A Model of Equitable Development], in *Sistemas políticos, poder y sociedad. Estudios de casos en América Latina* [Political Systems, Power and Society: Case Studies on Latin America]; and "Desarrollo social y políticas públicas. El caso de Cuba" [Social Development and Public Policies: The Case of Cuba].

3. *Cuba, transición de la fecundidad. Cambio social y conducta reproductiva* [Cuba, Transition to Fertility. Social Change and Reproductive Behavior], 20. This study was carried out by experts from the Center for Demographic Studies (CEDEM), National Office of Statistics, Ministry of Health, FNUAP and UNICEF.

4. Ministry of Health, *Anuario estadístico de salud, 2002.* [By 2004 it was recorded at 5.8 per 1000 live birth. *Ed.]*

5. Ibid.

6. *Programa Nacional de Acción,* 58. This is the 6th report of follow-up and evaluation presented at the World Summit in favor of the Childhood, held on September 20-29, 1990.

7. Beatriz Díaz, "Políticas sociales y justicia social: el caso de Cuba" [Social Policies and Social Justice: The Case of Cuba].

8. Ministry of Health, Pan-American Health Organization, World Health Organization, et al., *Health Care Situation in Cuba. Basic Indicators, 2003.*

9. *Programa Nacional de Acción,* op. cit.

10. UNDP, *Informe sobre el desarrollo humano* [Report on Human Development].

11. *Programa Nacional de Acción,* op. cit., 44.

12. Luisa Álvarez, *El aborto en Cuba* [Abortion in Cuba].

13. Ministry of Health, op. cit.

14. Silvia Martínez, *Cuba Beyond Our Dreams.*

15. Eugenio Espinosa, "La economía cubana en 1989-1995: crisis, reformas y relanzamiento, vulnerabilidades y perspectivas estratégicas" [The Cuban Economy during 1989-95: Crisis, Reforms and Operation, Vulnerabilities and Strategic Perspectives], 15.

16. Delia López, "Período especial y democracia en Cuba" [The Special Period and Democracy in Cuba].

17. José Bell, "Cuba: perspectivas objetivas para superar el período especial" [Cuba: Objective Prospects for Overcoming the Special Period], 45.

18. José de la Osa, "En los últimos ocho años ascendió a 1 200 millones de dólares el costo del bloqueo a la salud pública" [In the Last Eight Years the Cost of the Blockade to Public Health Grew to 1200 Million U.S. Dollars].

19. Ministry of Health, Pan-American Health Organization, World Health Organization, et al., *Annual Health Statistics Report, 2003,* 76. [In 2003 percentage of all live births was 5.5%. *Ed.]*

20. María Julia Mayoral and Sara Más, "Realidades para aquilatar la capacidad de nuestro pueblo" [Realities for Valuing the Capacity of Our People].

21. "Carlos Lage al resumir la Reunión Nacional de Presidentes Municipales del Poder Popular."

22. Carolina Aguilar, Perla Popowski and Mercedes Verdeses, "Mujer, período especial y vida cotidiana" [Woman, the Special Period and Daily Life].

23. Tania Caram, "La mujer cubana y la participación social: educación y ciencia. Un estudio de caso" [The Cuban Woman and Social Participation: Education and Science. A Case Study].

24. José Luis Rodríguez, "Informe sobre los resultados económicos de 2003 y el Plan Económico Social para el 2004" [Report on Economic Results of 2003 and the Economic and Social Plan for 2004].

25. Sara Más, "Crece empleo femenino" [Women's Employment Grows].

26. Alfredo Morales, "Batalla de ideas, empleo y seguridad social (I)" [Battle of Ideas, Employment and Social Security (I)].

27. Cuban Women's Federation, *Mujer, economía y desarrollo sostenible* [Woman, Economy and Sustainable Development]. Paper presented at the International Meeting of Solidarity among Women, April 13-16, 1998.

28. María Elena Benítez, "Panorama sociodemográfico de la familia cubana" [Sociodemographic Panorama of the Cuban Family].

29. Marina Majoli, "Ciencia, tecnología y desarrollo social. La industria biotecnológica cubana: una aproximación" [Science, Technology and Social Development. Understanding the Cuban Biotechnology Industry].

30. Silvia Martínez, op. cit., 262.

31. Lino Borroto, "Education and Development. Cuba, Challenges for the Second Millenium," in *Cuba in the 1990s*, 179-202.

32. *Programa Nacional de Acción*, op. cit., 94.

33. Soledad Díaz, et al., "El caso de Cuba" [The Case of Cuba].

34. Silvia Martínez, op. cit., 123.

35. National Office of Statistics, *Indicadores sociales y demográficos de Cuba por territorios* [Cuba's Social and Demographic Indicators by Territorios], 20.

36. Teresa Valdés and Enrique Gomáriz (coordinators), *Mujeres latinoamericanas en cifras* [Latin American Women in Figures].

37. Elena Díaz, "Economic Crisis: Employment and Quality of Life in Cuba."

38. Tania Caram, "La mujer cubana y la participación social: educación y ciencia" [The Cuban Woman and Social Participation: Education and Science].

39. Mayda Álvarez, "Políticas, programas y proyectos de familia en Cuba" [Family Policies, Programs and Projects in Cuba].

40. Patricia Arés Mucio, *Mi familia es así* [My Family is Like That].

41. Tania Caram, "La mujer cubana y la participación social: educación y ciencia," op. cit.

42. Silvia Martínez, op. cit., 263.

43. Ibid., 263.

44. Mayda Álvarez and Perla Popowski, *Mujer y poder, las cubanas en el gobierno popular. ¿Dónde se pierden las mujeres?* [Woman and Power, Cuban Women in the Popular Government. Where Do the Women Lose?], 15.

45. Mayda Álvarez, "Mujer y poder en Cuba" [Woman and Power in Cuba], in *Lectura sobre género* [Reading on Gender], no. 2, 25.

46. Cuban Women's Federation, *Participación política y acceso a la toma de decisiones* [Political Participation and Access to Decision-Making], 17. Paper presented at the International Meeting of Solidarity among Women, April 13-16, 1998.

47. Ibid., 15-18.

48. Reynaldo Rojas, "¿Qué tipo de pareja queremos y para qué pareja nos preparamos? [What Kind of Couple Do We Want and for What Couple are We Preparing?], in *Diversidad y complejidad familiar en Cuba* [Diversity and Family Complexity in Cuba], 160.

49. Elena Díaz, Tania Caram and Esperanza Fernández, "Turismo y prostitución en Cuba" [Tourism and Prostitution in Cuba], part of "Cuba: impacto de la crisis en grupos vulnerables: mujer, familia e infancia" [Cuba: Impact of the Crisis on Vulnerable Groups: Woman, Family and Children].

Bibliography

AGUILAR, CAROLINA, PERLA POPOWSKI and MERCEDES VERDESES. "Mujer, período especial y vida cotidiana." *Temas* journal, no. 5, 1996.

ÁLVAREZ, LUISA. *El aborto en Cuba*. Havana: Editorial de Ciencias Sociales, 1994.

ÁLVAREZ, MAYDA. "Mujer y poder en Cuba." In *Lectura sobre género*, no. 2, Havana: FMC-UNICEF, Center for Studies on Woman, 1999.

―――. "Políticas, programas y proyectos de familia en Cuba." In *Diversidad y complejidad familiar en Cuba*. Havana: Center for Demographic Studies (CEDEM), University of Havana, 1999.

ÁLVAREZ, MAYDA and PERLA POPOWSKI. *Mujer y poder, las cubanas en el gobierno popular. ¿Dónde se pierden las mujeres?* Havana: n.p., 1999.

ARÉS MUCIO, PATRICIA. *Mi familia es así*. Havana: Editorial de Ciencias Sociales, 1990.

BELL LARA, JOSÉ. "Cuba: perspectivas objetivas para superar el período especial." *Cuadernos de África y América Latina* journal, no. 16, 1994.

BENÍTEZ, MARÍA ELENA. "Panorama sociodemográfico de la familia cubana." Research report at CEDEM, Havana, 1997.

BORROTO, LINO. "Education and Development. Cuba, Challenges for the Second Millenium." In José Bell Lara (Coordinator), *Cuba in the 1990s*. Havana: Editorial José Martí, 1999.

CARAM, TANIA. "La mujer cubana y la participación social: educación y ciencia." M.Sc. diss., University of Havana, 1996.

―――. "La mujer cubana y la participación social: educación y ciencia. Un estudio de caso." *Revista de Ciencias Sociales*, (University of Costa Rica, San José), no. 80, 1998.

Cuba, transición de la fecundidad. Cambio social y conducta reproductiva. Havana: CEDEM, 1995.

CUBAN WOMEN'S FEDERATION. *Las cubanas: de Beijing al 2000.* Havana: Editorial de la Mujer, 1996.

————. *Mujer, economía y desarrollo sostenible.* Havana: Editorial de la Mujer, 1998.

————. *Participación política y acceso a la toma de decisiones.* Havana: Editorial de la Mujer, 1998.

DÍAZ, BEATRIZ. "Cuba: modelo de desarrollo equitativo." In *Sistemas políticos, poder y sociedad. Estudios de casos en América Latina,* edited by Latin American Society of Sociology (ALAS) and Center for Studies on America (CEA). Caracas: Editorial Nueva Sociedad, 1992.

————. "Desarrollo social y políticas públicas. El caso de Cuba." Study prepared for UNRISD, Geneva, at FLACSO, University of Havana, 1996. Typescript.

————. "Políticas sociales y justicia social: el caso de Cuba." Paper presented at the 21st LASA International Congress, Chicago, Illinois, 1998.

DÍAZ, ELENA. "Economic Crisis: Employment and Quality of Life in Cuba." In *Economic Reforms, Women's Employment, and Social Policies,* edited by Valentine M. Moghadam. Helsinski: World Institute for Development Economics Research (WIDER), The United Nations University, 1995.

DÍAZ, ELENA, TANIA CARAM and ESPERANZA FERNÁNDEZ. "Turismo y prostitución en Cuba." In "Cuba: impacto de la crisis en grupos vulnerables: mujer, familia e infancia," at FLACSO, University of Havana, 1997. Typescript.

DÍAZ, SOLEDAD, et al. "El caso de Cuba." Paper presented at the 4th World Conference on Women, Beijing, China, 1995.

ESPINOSA, EUGENIO. "La economía cubana en 1989-1995: crisis, reformas y relanzamiento, vulnerabilidades y perspectivas estratégicas" Working Document no. 7 at FLACSO, University of Havana, 1996. Typescript.

FERRIOL, ÁNGELA. "Política social cubana: situación y transformaciones. *Temas* journal, no. 11, July-September 1997.

LAGE, CARLOS. "Carlos Lage al resumir la Reunión Nacional de Presidentes Municipales del Poder Popular." *Granma* daily, 30 September 1999.

LÓPEZ, DELIA LUISA. "Período especial y democracia en Cuba." *Cuadernos de África y América Latina* journal (Madrid), no. 16 (1994).

MAJOLI, MARINA. "Ciencia, tecnología y desarrollo social. La industria biotecnológica cubana: una aproximación." Ph.D. diss., University of Havana, 1999.

Martín, Elvira. "El género y la gestión universitaria." CEPES, University of Havana, 1999. Typescript.

Martínez Puentes, Silvia. *Cuba Beyond Our Dreams*. Havana: Editorial José Martí, in press.

Más, Sara. "Crece empleo femenino." *Granma* daily, 16 September 2003.

Ministry of Health. *Anuario estadístico de salud, 2002*. Havana: MINSAP, 2003.

Ministry of Health, Pan-American Health Organization, World Health Organization, et al. *Annual Health Statistics Report, 2003*. Havana: MINSAP, 2004.

―――. *Health Care Situation in Cuba. Basic Indicators, 2003*. Havana: MINSAP, 2004.

Mayoral, María Julia and Sara Más. "Realidades para aquilatar la capacidad de nuestro pueblo." *Granma* daily, 22 December 1999.

Morales, Alfredo. "Batalla de ideas, empleo y seguridad social (I)." *Granma* daily, 5 March 2004.

National Office of Statistics. *Indicadores sociales y demográficos de Cuba por territorios*. Havana: n.p., 1997.

Núñez, Lilia. "Más allá del cuentapropismo en Cuba." *Temas* journal, no. 11, July-September 1997.

Osa, José de la. "En los últimos ocho años ascendió a 1 200 millones de dólares el costo del bloqueo a la salud pública." *Granma* daily, 7 January 1999.

―――. "Mortalidad infantil en Cuba." *Granma* daily, 4 January 2000.

Programa Nacional de Acción. Havana: Ediciones Pontón Caribe, S.A., 1997.

Rodríguez, José Luis. "Informe sobre los resultados económicos de 2003 y el Plan Económico Social para el 2004." *Granma* daily, 25 December 2003.

Rojas, Reynaldo. "Qué tipo de pareja queremos y para qué pareja nos preparamos?" In *Diversidad y complejidad familiar en Cuba*. Havana: Center for Demographic Studies (CEDEM), University of Havana, 1999.

UNDP. *Informe sobre el desarrollo humano*. Madrid: Ediciones Mundiprensa, 1999.

UNICEF. "El marco conceptual de igualdad y empoderamiento de las mujeres." In Magdalena León, *Poder y empoderamiento de mujeres*. Santa Fe de Bogota: T/M Editores, 1998.

―――. *Síntesis del informe anual de 1998*. Havana: n.p., 1999.

Valdés, Teresa and Enrique Gomáriz (Coordinators). *Mujeres latinoamericanas en cifras. Tomo comparativo*. Santiago: FLACSO, Instituto de la Mujer, Ministerio de Asuntos Sociales de España, 1995.

Zimbalist, Andrew and Claes Brundenius. "Crecimiento con equidad: el desarrollo humano en una perspectiva comparada. *Cuadernos de Nuestra América* journal (Havana), vol. 2, no. 13 (July-December, 1998).

The Hostile Tides of Cuban-U.S. Relations

Richard A. Dello Buono

Richard A. Dello Buono

Ph.D. in Social Economy and Social Policy. A sociology professor at Dominican University, his research areas include comparative social problems and Caribbean and Latin American studies. He is an invited professor at the University of Havana and was previously visiting professor at the National University of Colombia and the University of Panama.

Since 1959, Cuba has struggled to construct an egalitarian model of social and economic development in remedy to the long history of colonialism and capitalist dependency which preceded the revolutionary triumph. This momentous project of social transformation has from the onset had to coexist with a pervasive hostility on the part of United States. The unending engagement of U.S. interventionism aimed at Cuba has posed a continuous set of challenges for the island and its leadership, significantly intensifying the social and political pressures normally associated with development.

The initial unfolding of Cuba's revolution took place against the backdrop of the East-West superpower confrontation. As Cuba set out to construct Socialism within the Cold War context, decades of development assistance from the former Soviet Bloc provided a significant margin for maintaining Cuban sovereignty in the face of U.S. hostility. Cuba's alliance with the Socialist Bloc also proved vital in enabling it to support national liberation struggles throughout the world, a legacy that earned the island considerable respect and admiration around the developing world. As Nelson Mandela among others have consistently reminded the world, Cuba's military and political assistance was decisive in the struggle for liberation from apartheid in southern Africa, just as its principled stand on the developing world's foreign debt won great support from the movement of the non-aligned countries among which Cuba played a leading role. For its part, Washington relentlessly branded Cuban internationalism as "interventionism" and the work of "puppets of the Soviet Empire."

With the collapse of the Socialist Bloc at the end of the 1980s, Cuba was subjected to a brutal series of economic shocks resulting from the near total collapse of its principal trade and assistance agreements.[1] Inevitably, these shocks affected virtually all sectors of the Cuban economy, creating immense uncertainty in its import and export markets, and decimated in relatively short order the basis for maintaining a rationally planned economy. Above all, the severe contraction of its oil imports threatened the viability of an industrial infrastructure constructed largely under cooperative assistance agreements provided by the former Soviet Union, an oil-driven infrastructure characterized by technologies largely insensitive to efficient energy utilization. With this same process affecting Cuba's military cooperation with its former strategic partners, Cuban internationalism had to be immediately and drastically scaled back.

Alongside of these abrupt structural shocks, Cuba was almost immediately subjected to a wave of hostile measures on the part of the United States as Washington sought to exploit the opportunities afforded by the moment. Intense diplomatic pressure was placed on the tenuous Yeltsin regime, demanding that

Moscow cease all commerce with Cuba. Washington even succeeded in winning a series of sharp criticisms of the Cuban Government from its newfound Russian ally. Similar pressures were brought to bear upon most of Cuba's existing and potential trading partners, including Mexico, Canada and various European and Latin American nations.

The result was the Cuban declaration of the "Special Period in Time of Peace" in 1990. This signified that existing policies could no longer operate within a "business as usual" framework and immediate emergency measures would need to be enacted. The essential economic features of these measures at the onset included the curtailment of consumption and selective cutbacks in state spending, implementation of a food self-sufficiency program, prioritization of foreign exchange earning activities, a systematic search for new import and export markets, renewed emphasis upon increasing productivity through increased popular participation, and a new reliance upon foreign investment for driving the national economy.[2]

Despite all predictions to the contrary, the Cuban Revolution did not come to share the common fate of its former Eastern allies. Indeed, by the end of the 1990s, the Cuban economy was showing definitive signs of recovery in response to the strategic development measures implemented during the Special Period. The effective exercise of Cuban sovereignty now hinged upon its ability to achieve an optimal integration in the regional economy, conditioned more than ever by the historical accumulation of its productive structures. In this process, Cuba's prospects for further development have been limited considerably by a variety of U.S. policies, all of which are designed to punish the island for its continuing refusal to abide by the rules of a neoliberal hemispheric order in a unipolar geopolitical context.

The fact that the Cuban Revolution not only survived the crisis of the 1990s but re-emerged in the 21st century as a significant economic presence in the Caribbean region is nothing short of remarkable. Cuba demonstrated considerable success in rapidly mounting an expanding tourist industry capable of generating substantial hard currency earnings. At the same time, the island developed a variety of new exports in the high-value service sector, all of this in the face of widespread tensions associated with unending U.S. hostilities. An adequate understanding of Cuban development over recent years and a realistic sense of its short- and medium-term prospects will require consideration of the ways in which antagonistic U.S. policies case long shadows over the revolutionary process.

U.S. Policies of Interventionism in Latin America and the Caribbean

The contemporary record of Latin America and the Caribbean is replete with examples of how U.S. interventionism seeks to adversely shape the fortunes of those nations who embark on alternative paths to development. Historically, Washington has always sought to minimize the influence of external powers in the region, acting at the same time to ensure full U.S. access to the region's strategic resources. In recent decades, the countries of Latin America and the Caribbean have experienced especially dramatic challenges to its development. These challenges have been associated with a rapidly accelerating process of globalization that has imposed an array of external, structural pressures on the regional political economy. The resulting agenda has demanded a systematic conversion towards policies of trade liberalization, adoption of more innovative production technologies, and the progressive incorporation of national econo-mies into regional integration initiatives. Given the contradictions which such demands have created within the majority of existing regimes of development, the region has been acutely affected by new hegemonic policies being promoted by the United States which themselves are conditioned by increasing globaliza-tion and the evolving realignments of international capital.

In this broad context, U.S. interventionism is best thought of as a subset of a larger set of policies that include incentives for those nations who closely cooperate with Washington's designs as well as punishments for those who resist the "Washington Consensus." Since revolutionary countries such as Cuba have generally been exposed only to the coercive portion of U.S. policies, there is a need to focus in greater detail upon the various kinds of punitive policies that have been employed throughout the region.

By the term "punitive policies," I refer to the application of a package of measures designed to influence, pressure, and ultimately impose upon targeted nations, concrete social outcomes that usually consist of economic policy changes. There is a great variety among the types and magnitudes of possible outcomes desired by those who enact such punitive policies, ranging from minor adjust-ments in particular development policies all the way up to the destabilization and the complete overthrow of a regime. Some typical categories of punitive policies that have been employed by the United States in Latin America and the Caribbean include the following:

- Unilateral changes in the status of commercial treaties, including reduc-tions in importation quotas, modification of a previously favorable trading

237

RICHARD A. DELLO BUONO

status of a specific trading partner, the imposition of punitive tariffs, use of non-tariff trading barriers, etc.

- Reduction or blockage, either directly or indirectly, of bilateral and/or multilateral development assistance.
- Pressure placed upon international banks, lending agencies or private creditors.
- Pressure placed upon multinational corporations or private investment consortia to interrupt or modify their business practices to the detriment of the target nation.
- Changes in fiscal and regulatory policies where jurisdiction exists over U.S.-based capital invested in the region targeted for punishment.
- Interference of U.S. federal agencies in regional affairs, including the formation of regional policies designed to exclude targeted nations from regional integration initiatives and/or pressures placed upon regional integration negotiations which have adverse consequences for the prospects of targeted nations.
- Interference in elections and/or the electoral institutions of targeted nations.
- Use of diplomatic representation as a mechanism of direct interference and/or indirect interference, for example, through the manipulation of the mass media of targeted nations, with the aim of interceding in the internal affairs of the targeted country.
- Use of judicial institutions, policing agencies and/or federal regulatory agencies so as to pressure or interfere in the legal order or institutional affairs of the targeted nation; such as "certification of cooperation" with anti-narcotics operations, including demands for extradition treaties, etc.
- Commercial trade embargoes on the business of targeted nations.
- Military pressures, including direct interventions, invasions, covert actions, visible military exercises, unilateral changes in the level of military assistance, and similar practices, all as related to a punitive agenda.
- Manipulation of visa and/or legal immigration policies so as to pressure or punish targeted nations.

In the Western Hemisphere, Cuba has by far been the most extensive target of U.S. punitive policies. But in many cases, the application of such policies against other countries in the region constituted in part, the U.S. response to governments who decided to establish closer relations with Cuba. The reestablishment of relations between Jamaica and Cuba in the 1970s marked a defining moment in the stigmatization of the Michael Manley government by Washington. Manley's administration had pursued a democratic socialist program as it moved to impose a development tax on its bauxite exports; the aluminum transnationals went screaming to Washington, resulting in a stiff dose of punitive U.S. policies. Manley's decision to normalize relations with Cuba fueled an intense political reaction that included a general package of economic and political destabilization policies. Manley eventually went on to lose the 1980 elections to the U.S. backed candidate Edward Seaga who converted the island into a Caribbean cheerleader for the policies of structural adjustment, the price of which Jamaicans are still paying to this day.

In 1979, the revolutionary government of Grenada was advised very shortly after coming to power that the United States would view "with alarm" any tendency for developing closer ties with Cuba.[3] The People's Revolutionary Government of Maurice Bishop responded that their country was sovereign over its own affairs and would develop foreign relations in accordance with their own interests, irrespective of how Washington viewed it. In less than a year's time, the declarations on Grenada from Washington were identifying the island as an enemy state. An advisory from the Department of State was soon forthcoming which designated the country as dangerous for U.S. citizens, something which had an immediate effect upon the pivotal tourism industry. Indeed, from that point forward, Washington never ceased to accuse the Grenadian Government of being a subversive, terrorist state who worked in collaboration with "Cuban interventionism."

The U.S. campaign against revolutionary Grenada intensified still further when the Reagan administration accused the island nation of building a military airport with Cuban assistance, alleging that it destined for the eventual use of Cuban and Soviet military forces in the region. All of this took place despite the verifiable fact that the airport had a design solely useful for the tourist industry, i.e., one capable of receiving night landings of commercial tourist charter flights without having to make stopovers in neighboring islands. Washington's hostile actions against Grenada soon assumed a military character as the Pentagon ordered military exercises in the Caribbean in 1980, 1981 and 1982, including symbolic invasions of the island of Vieques, Puerto Rico which publicly using a codename of "Amber and the Amberdines" to signal its eventual target of Grenada and the Grenadines.[4] Even as Washington eventually took advantage of the assassination of Maurice Bishop and the internal collapse of the People's Revolutionary Government of Grenada in October 1983 so as to invade and occupy the island, U.S. authorities argued that it had evidence that the coup was the "product of Cuba interference" and that Havana now wished to depose the most moderate factions in Grenada with an even more radical regime.[5] The fact that Cuba immediately and harshly reacted to Bishop's murder was not widely reported, but attention during the invasion was instead focused on the unexpectedly fierce armed resistance mounted by Cuban construction workers at the unfinished site of the new airport.

In Nicaragua, extensive use of punitive economic measures were also invoked against the Sandinista revolutionary government during the 1980s, including the elimination of bilateral assistance, the reduction of the sugar quota, the blocking of loans on the part of international lending agencies, and the pressuring of U.S.-based multinationals such as Castle and Cook to pull out of the country. By mid-decade, the imposition of a complete U.S. trade embargo against the Central American country was enacted which included a prohibition on direct routes of shipping and aviation between the two countries. At the same time, political and military pressures were likewise intense, including the non-recognition of the electoral results of 1984 and the mining of the Port of Corinto as part of the support strategy for the U.S. financed, contra war against the revolutionary government. Cuban support of the regime was frequently cited as the main justification for Washington's policies, particularly emphasizing Nicaragua's complicity in channeling Cuban support to insurgent forces in El Salvador and Guatemala.

Similar patterns were observable in the punitive policies which prepared the terrain for the 1973 military coup in Chile against Salvador Allende's Popular Unity Government and in various other countries, the details of which are beyond the scope of the present study. In most of these cases, closer ties with Cuba were portrayed as adequate cause for intervention. But behind the anti-communist scapegoating of the Cold War lurked a more important doctrine for the long-term economic domination over the region. One important manifestation of this doctrine was the Caribbean Basin Initiative (CBI) created in 1982. The CBI provides an instructive example of the reactionary and interventionist reorientation of U.S. policy towards the region during the 1980s. Designed explicitly as a means to produce structural changes in countries throughout the region, the CBI was unsurprisingly touted as an urgent response to "Cuban expansionism" in the region and the growth of insurgencies throughout Central America, and with specific concern over revolutionary Nicaragua and Grenada.[6] Just as the Alliance for Progress of the 1960s sought to undermine the conditions that produce revolutionary insurgencies, the CBI represented a new kind of economic alignment strategy which would become a predecessor of the later emphasis of the 1990s on regional integration organized under the hegemonic auspices of Washington.

In complete harmony with this design is its exclusionary character. While Grenada under the revolutionary government was excluded from the initiative, it was later incorporated following the U.S. invasion.

The experience which countries like Jamaica, Grenada, and virtually all of Central America afterwards had with the CBI would serve as prelude to the hegemonic integration schemes later envisioned for the region by the United States, including NAFTA, the FTAA and the Plan Puebla-Panama. It is therefore worthy to note that years after the destabilization and electoral defeat of Manley, and a protracted period of preferential treatment and assistance from the United States, including all of the provisions of the CBI, the restructuring of its economy had very few positive effects in mitigating the devastating impact of structural adjustment upon the poor. Much of the impact of the CBI was based in industries such as textiles which by the 1990s displayed few prospects for a prosperous future. Many analysts had predicted that the structural adjustment programs in countries such as Jamaica would have a variety of long-lasting negative implications.[7] As in other cases, the price for a tighter integration with the regional superpower was a significant decline in the wages of the labor force, a dramatic increase in poverty, a significant increase in the fortunes of certain sectors of the island's elite, and a dramatic reduction in the capacity of the state to intervene in the national economy.[8]

Cuba: Perennial Target of U.S. Punitive Policies

There is no question that Cuba has been targeted more than any other country in the region by U.S. punitive policies. Following the Bay of Pigs debacle in 1961 and the crystallization of the Cold War standoff as symbolized by the *de-facto* resolution of the 1962 October Missile Crisis that effectively eliminated the possibility of a U.S. invasion of Cuba, the way was paved for the implementation of every other imaginable punitive policy. In this context, the very survival of Cuban Socialism constitutes a significant and enduring case study in the failure of U.S. interventionist policies to accomplish its goals.

As Elena Díaz explains, the 20th-century history of the Cuban socialist revolution can be chronologically broken down into four main phases, each of which developed against the backdrop of aggressive U.S. hostility towards the island. In the first phase (1960-70), Cuba defined its own authentic model of Socialism. Beginning in 1970, the second phase involved the assimilation of the logic of the Soviet socialist model, something which was only partially carried out in the period leading up to 1985. By that time, extensive debate and criticism within Cuba led to a third phase (1985-1990) where the island's leadership attempted to redefine the revolution and regain its authenticity based on particular demands that were arising out of its own accumulated social conditions. The fourth phase (1990-2000) began with the onset of the former Soviet Union's collapse and developed through the 1990s in what later became known as the Cuban Special Period.[9]

During the first phase, the United States initiated its pressure by way of the progressive reduction and ultimately the complete elimination of the sugar quota for Cuban imports. The "Sugar Act of 1948" was modified on 6 July 1960, giving the U.S. president discretionary power to modify the Cuban quota "as seen fit in accordance with national interests." The following day, the Eisenhower administration reduced the quota to 2.42 million tons, the amount corresponding to the quantity already imported by the United States that year.[10] As the Cuban revolutionary government responded by nationalizing U.S. enterprises in a "dollar for dollar" retaliation for its economic losses, the Eisenhower administration decided to cancel the quota altogether. By January 3, 1961, Washington broke diplomatic relations with Cuba and two weeks later enacted a prohibition on travel to the island on the part of U.S. citizens without explicit authorization.

The elimination of the Cuban sugar quota represented the complete rupture of the most important economic link existent between the two countries for well over a half-century. When the United States also opted to cut off its petroleum exports to the island, Cuba felt the consequences of its longstanding dependency as a monocrop, sugar export economy completely predicated upon the importation of foreign oil for its energy source. Alongside of these aggressive economic measures, Washington also applied a comprehensive of package of diplomatic, ideological and military measures including terrorist actions such as the various attempts to assassinate Fidel Castro as well as giving logistical support to the mercenary invasion that failed so spectacularly at the Bay of Pigs.

As is well established, Cuba initiated its relations with the Soviet Union in this highly charged context of U.S. aggression, with a desperate need to obtain petroleum as well as a large new market for its sugar exports. From that initial base of cooperation, Cuban-Soviet relations deepened in the Cold War context, providing the backdrop for an intense, bilateral collaboration in the political, economic, cultural and military spheres. The rapid transformations which Cuba subsequently experienced, in concert with the rise of revolutionary forces in diverse parts of the Third World, transformed the island into a "double menace" for the United States. Over above its strategic alliance with the former USSR, *it exemplified an alternative model of development.*

The regional remedy for the Cuban "threat of example" was the Alliance for Progress, an assistance program directed towards Latin America as an alternative to the revolutionary and pro-Soviet path taken by the Cubans. Excluded from that program, Cuba was instead treated to a total economic blockade, a measure which in the U.S. tradition is tantamount to a state of war. With the United States continuing to occupy a military base on Cuban territory at Guantánamo, considerable pressure was brought to bear upon the rest of Latin America and the Caribbean, using regional isolation as a primary instrument for containing Cuban influence in the hemisphere. As this had the effect of deepening Cuban dependence upon the Soviet Bloc, all of the elements were in place for the dynamics that emerged in the second phase of Cuban revolutionary development.

Cuban integration into the CMEA trade and cooperation agreement of the Soviet Bloc assumed the form of an exporting country of primary goods such as nickel and citric fruits along with sugar. Based on this international "real socialist" insertion, it managed to create an extensive industrial base fueled by the massive importation of Soviet capital goods, thanks to highly favorable terms of trade, as well as an impressive system of social services. This notwithstanding, Cuba was unable to transform its dependency upon sugar exports during this period, but on the contrary, its dependency probably deepened even further.

By the latter half of the 1970s, Cuba and the United States experienced a period of moderately improving relations, leading to the establishment of a low level of renewed diplomatic relations in the form of Interest Sections housed in the embassies of third countries (Switzerland and Czechoslovakia). For a brief period, it appeared that the prospects were emerging for a gradual normalization of U.S.-Cuban relations, but this quickly disintegrated amidst the contradictory impulses of the Carter administration, whose Defense Department could not accept the successes being registered by the Cuban military in its solidarity efforts with the frontline states of southern Africa. As Pentagon pressure increased for a halt to the normalization, Carter buckled and announced the "discovery" of Russian troops in Cuba, bringing an end to the rapprochement. The freezing of relations and the ensuing exchange of mutual accusations resulted in a chain of events that culminated in the debacle of the Mariel Exodus, where both parties became embroiled in a new era of highly politicized disputes over migration policies. The exodus proved costly to Carter's re-election bid as it was cited as evidence by Republican candidate Reagan of his mishandling of foreign policy.

During the 1980s, an upsurge of revolutionary activity in the hemisphere re-intensified the Cold War climate of hostility, dramatically escalating tensions under the incoming Reagan administration which attributed all insurgencies throughout the region to Cuban interference backed by Soviet support. Washington now sought not only to maintain the trade embargo against Cuba but to extend it further to third countries, beginning with a prohibition on the imports of goods made in countries that utilized Cuban products. The Reagan administration also tried to extend the blockade to include a complete prohibition against the entrance of Cuban publications, a measure which was short-lived as the U.S. Supreme Court ruled it to be an unconstitutional restriction on the flow of information.

It was during this period that Cuba entered into the third phase of the Revolution under the auspices of an internal debate that culminated in the Rectification Process. The Rectification referred to the Cuban Communist Party's recognition of its errors in over-assimilating the Soviet model and its declared intentions to renovate Cuban society in the spirit of its early years of revolutionary struggle. For its part, Washington tried to influence the debate with its own ideological campaign aimed at illegally penetrating its mass media with radio broadcasts from the United States under the name of Radio Martí and later with television transmissions dubbed Tele-Martí. As an additional form of pressure, Washington continued to deny most legal visas to Cubans while at the same time assuring that any Cuban who arrived illegally would be granted permanent residence, creating a dangerous, illegal immigration drama that would last until well into the 1990s when both countries finally recognized the need for an immigration accord.

The rapid collapse of the Socialist Bloc exposed Cuba to an economic crisis without precedent in the hemisphere, thus cutting short the Cuban period of rectification and paving the way for the fourth phase identified above as the Cuban Special Period. The incoming Bush (Sr.) administration (1989-1992) decided to apply a strategy of maximum pressure so as to provoke a rapid collapse of the Cuban Government. As one U.S. official after another in the Bush administration predicted the impending collapse of the Revolution, sthe Congress went to work in designing new legislation that would seek to block any attempt of the island to reinsert itself into the hemispheric economy. This policy of economic strangulation culminated in the Torricelli Act which was signed into the law in 1992. The new characteristics of U.S. punitive measures as embodied in the Torricelli Act consisted in the application of steep sanctions against third countries that established commercial relations with Cuba. This law additionally provided for a prohibition on the entry of ships into the United States which had passed through Cuban ports during the prior six months.

Despite the incoming Clinton administration's recycling of former Carter administration figures into his Department of State, normalization of U.S.-Cuban relations was never placed back on the agenda by the Democrats. The early lack of progress was cemented into place by a Republican Party victory in the 1994 congressional elections, where the resurgence of the most conservative forces in the U.S. establishment now wielded their influence over Clinton administration foreign policy. Despite a successful process of negotiations which yielded an immigration agreement in 1994, strong political pressure from an increasingly belligerent Cuban exile community made progress in bilateral relations too costly for the Democrats, particularly in terms of Florida's electoral votes. The result was a permanent commitment on the part of the Clinton administration to the politics of the status quo with respect to Cuba.

The status quo was not sufficient, of course, for the reckless fanaticism of the Miami-based Cuban exile community who now felt emboldened to carry out their own aggressive actions towards the island. Flotillas were organized which invaded the territorial waters of Cuba, and illegal small aircraft flights were dispatched with increasing frequency to pick up Cubans on the island seeking to emigrate. On several occasions, leaflets were dropped over Havana by small aircraft originating from the exile community, posing a hazard to aviation in one of the busiest airspaces of the world. Yet, the opportunistic policy of official tolerance from the Clinton administration served to embolden the exile community ever further, until finally in the presidential electoral year of 1996, Cuba responded forcefully to the provocations.

Despite the relative ease with which federal authorities could have acted to control the frequent and dangerous aerial provocations carried out by the exile group known as "Hermanos al Rescate," (Brothers to the Rescue), Washington persisted in allowing them to act with impunity, almost to the group's own disbelief. The culminating event occurred on February 24, 1996, which by no coincidence took place just a couple of weeks before the Florida presidential primary. Three small aircraft from the exile group invaded Cuban air space several times on the same day, ignoring calls from the island's air control authorities to abandon Cuban airspace. Cuban authorities, having stated on numerous occasions that the islands territorial integrity would be defended by force if necessary, decided on that day to intercept and shoot down two of three planes that had neared the capital city.

Just like in other decisions that reflected a kind of "functional incoherence" of the Clinton administration, something always more pronounced during campaign

season, Clinton reacted strongly and radically shifted course in his position towards Cuba in mitigation of Republicans who were seeking to gain political
capital through tougher anti-Cuba policies. In short, the aerial incident offered
the Cuban exile community of Miami an opportunity to influence U.S. policy
towards the island like never before and in a manner clearly contrary to the
interests of both contending governments.

The Clinton administration proceed to order the suspension of charter
flights between the two countries, offered compensation to the families of the
victims to be paid out of Cuban assets that were frozen in the United States,
promised to expand and extend the scope of Radio Marti so that it would reach
all parts of the island, tightening the restrictions on Cuban diplomatic representatives while in the United States and most importantly, reversing its position on
the proposed anti-Cuban legislation sponsored by Helms-Burton, signing it into
law as a punishment for the downing of the exile plane.

The signing into law of legislation whose original draft was put together by
lawyers of the Cuban exile community signified that the Clinton administration
had come to support the position of the most rightwing elements in the United
States, putting all forms of bilateral negotiation to rest, and frustrating the growing chorus of U.S. business interests who wished to do business with the island.
The Helms-Burton Act, in extending the logic of the Torricelli Act, stood out as
a punitive policy totally directed at third countries that have relations with Cuba,
seeking to criminalize their business relations under the label of "trafficking with
stolen U.S. properties" by way of reference to the nationalization of U.S. firms
that occurred more than three decades earlier. The law offered U.S. citizens the
right to enter into litigation against third party investors who do business in
Cuba while retaining assets based in the United States. Taking it a step even
further, the law provided for the possibility to reject or revoke U.S. visas issued
to foreign nationals and their families who are identified with such investments.

International reaction to the Helms-Burton Act was predictably strong and
highly unfavorable to Washington. Canada, Mexico and the European Union
reacted sharply and decisively against the law. Formal complaints were filed
before the grievance board of the WTO. Canada and Mexico asserted that it
violated the terms of NAFTA and filed formal complaints. Mexico held internal
discussions around the creation of legislation aimed at impeding any cooperation with the law on the part of Mexican investors, provoking an unusual consensus among all of the principle political parties of Mexico in opposition to the
U.S. law. For its part, Canada already had a law in effect, implemented in
response to the Torricelli Act that penalizes enterprises based in Canada that

comply with any foreign instructions to avoid doing business in Cuba, but proceeded to engage in discussions as to how to strengthen that existing Canadian law. The European Parliament likewise rejected the law and ordered a commission to set forth a prohibition against any compliance with the law. The OAS considered the law and voted overwhelmingly to denounce Helms-Burton Act and to take actions against compliance, with only Dominica choosing to remain absent for the vote, with the United States itself offering the lone vote against the initiative.[11]

The pressure mounted so quickly that the Clinton administration, having opposed the legislation initially, had to unilaterally suspend for six months the most important elements of the law so as to consider a strategy to cope with the international firestorm it had generated. While most provisions were eventually implemented, the Helms-Burton Act caused innumerable instances of friction with Washington's closest allies. But the 1990s did not come to end without producing one additional, defining moment in Cuban-U.S. relations came to have a decisive impact not only on the Cuban exile community in Miami but upon the U.S. presidential elections of 2000.

The Revenge of Elián

When little Elián González, a survivor of a broken raft that washed ashore in southern Florida after crossing the Florida Straits, was rescued in November, 1999, authorities were faced with the dilemma of what to do with the five year old boy. His mother had perished along with the other adults in the ill-fated attempt to immigrate illegally to the United States. His father who lived on the island had not been consulted by his estranged wife and was now insisting that that boy be returned to his custody. What on the surface was a straight-forward custody case became the object of an international dispute, with the rightwing Cuban exile community demanding that the child remain in the United States and be placed in the custody of extended family members. When the inevitable conclusion was reached over half a year later that Elián belonged in the custody of his father, who in fact was permitted to come to the United States to pick up his son, the Clinton administration had to mount an armed rescue operation of the boy, complete with a SWAT team in order to remove him at gunpoint from the exile community who chose to defy court orders to surrender the boy to his waiting father.

The highly publicized affair had three major impacts. First, it was a tremendous victory for the Cuban Government, since it demonstrated to the world that a brave and patriotic Cuban father would risk coming to the United States along with his family, despite threats that the U.S. Congress might prevent his departure, and recover his son's custody, remain unbroken by all of the efforts of the exile community to buy him off, and manage to completely convince even the U.S. District Attorney let alone world opinion that he wished for nothing more but to return home to raise his son in Cuba. The massive campaign which developed on the island for the repatriation of Elián was electrifying and unifying among the population, and resulted in a total and unconditional victory.

Second, it was a defeat that was disastrous for the Miami exile community. Although from the beginning, many Cuban-Americans felt queasy in supporting what amounted to a highly politicized kidnapping of the child in preventing his return home, the hard-line elements of the Miami exile leadership simply refused to put the boy's interests above their own self-interested political agenda. In the process, they managed to organize an unparalleled, fanatical resistance to the rule of family law and the federal government's decision to return the boy to the custody of his family, creating a public relations disaster of unprecedented proportions. Elián's return to Cuba was not simply a tactical defeat but rather a watershed in U.S. domestic opinion concerning the exile community leadership, revealing their limitless opportunism and contempt for domestic laws which had in fact had always characterized organizations such as the Cuban-American National Foundation (CANF). In the end, the Cuban-American community had reached a new level of soul-searching, feeling as though they had been coerced into fighting a losing battle. The fallout left the CANF in crisis and disarray, with increased divisions and defections from their ranks, first on the part of moderate elements, and later by even its most conservative, hard-line factions.

Thirdly, the Elián affair was badly managed by Janet Reno and the Clinton administration. In retrospect, it became obvious that the Justice Department's initial hesitancy to antagonize the exile community had managed to drag out the process just long enough to give hard-line exile elements time to make the boy's custodial transfer legally problematic. In the end, the quasi-military operation that was necessary to rescue the boy from his uncooperative extended family was universally abhorred, with an ugly show of force that filled newspapers worldwide, accompanied by the contrasting image of the smiling boy reunited with his father.

While Clinton and U.S. Attorney Reno had consistently indicated their belief that there was a legal obligation to return the boy to Cuba, with even many conservative Republicans in agreement, it should be noted that Vice-President (and Democratic Party presidential candidate for 2000) Al Gore took a divergent position, choosing this issue to distance himself from the administration as a "show of independence," opting to pander to the exile community for their crucial votes in the state of Florida.

The political miscalculation that presided over the whole affair backfired badly for the Clinton administration and Democratic candidate Gore since the hard-line Cuban Exile leadership had by then already sworn their allegiance to a "punishment vote." Their intense mobilization efforts in Florida helped reverse, albeit temporarily, the trend which had developed in the Cuban-American vote over recent elections in which there had been steadily increasing levels of support for the Democratic Party. In 1996, Clinton received around 35% of the Cuban-American vote in Florida while in 2000, Gore could not even muster 20%, leaving absolutely no doubt that the sharp drop-off was directly related to the political fallout from the Elián affair. The loss of Cuban-American votes tilted the balance in favor of Bush and the Republicans, with a little extra help from the Florida State Republican Party machinery that busily invalidated voter's ballots in heavily Democratic African-American precincts. By losing the state of Florida, the Democrats lost the controversial presidential election. Thus, the "revenge of Elián" was wrought upon the Democrats for their despicable pandering and mishandling of the situation. The state was now set for a new Republican administration, one that would turn out to be far more right wing than most voters could have ever imagined.

Fahrenheit 9/11 and the Bush Doctrine

As Cold War imagery faded over the course of the 1990s, the progressive liberalization of foreign trade and the "war on drugs" had emerged as the twin pillars of U.S. policies at the turn of the century.[12] U.S. policy towards illegal narcotics has generally been to condition its bilateral assistance in accord with the level of cooperation which each country offers in the war on drugs. But consistent with the preceding decades of the Cold War era, such policies inevitably became interwoven with military interventionism, with ever greater pressures for cooperation to assume a military character. By 2001, a regional anti-narcotics initiative aimed at the Andean region was firmly in place, initially enacted by the Clinton administration in 2000 under the auspices of Plan Colombia (in response to the Colombian conflict) and then expanded into a reconstituted Andean Regional Initiative by the incoming Bush administration. These initiatives formed part of a steady militarization of hemispheric relations in conjunction with an increasingly aggressive policy for protecting strategic interests such as oil, including increased moves towards intervention to quell insurgencies in Colombia,

Bolivia, and Ecuador as well as intensified threats of destabilization of "unfriendly" governments such as Venezuela and of course Cuba.

In abandoning the Clinton Era rhetoric of "grow the economy through productive investment," the aggressive conservatism and "free market" ideology guiding the Bush Republicans was quickly set into motion as one after another cabinet level appointee displayed their extreme rightwing credentials. Given lingering voter resentment over the highly controversial elections, the initially weak mandate of the Bush administration posed certain limits for the rightwing agenda. Those limits essentially went out the window following the September 11, 2001 attacks on the World Trade Center and the Pentagon. In the wake of the attacks, domestic opposition melted away as the acceleration towards a militarization of U.S. policy took place under the cover of the Bush team's promise to bring "justice to its enemies."

As suggested by a popular documentary film entitled *Fahrenheit 9/11* that was released in mid-2004, director Michael Moore characterized the Bush administration as a rightwing, dream team that effectively capitalized on the September 11 attacks to drag the country into war for their own set of narrow interests. More than simply settling a Bush family score with Saddam Hussein, the death and destruction wrought first upon Afghanistan and then culminating in the invasion and occupation of Iraq was the product of the interests of big oil and an alliance with the Saudi royal family, and a comprehensive plan to restructure the U.S. Government in and around massive deficit spending on the military. As further depicted in Moore's film, domestic opposition remained practically non-existent as the so-called "war against terror," driven with help from the corporate mass media, justified the hyper-militarization of U.S. foreign and domestic policy. The booty ranged from a new version of a "star wars" missile defense system to the conversion of wartime reconstruction contracts (including to the Halliburton Corporation and others) in Iraq and Afghanistan into a lucrative, high profile bidding process that had even the Europeans lining up for their share.

As this "Bush Doctrine" developed its rhetoric of openly endorsing the principles of "regime change" and "pre-emptive interventions," its combination of an unprecedented surge in military spending effectively removed the accumulated "restrictions" of recent years. Just to maintain the occupation of Afghanistan and Iraq, the Pentagon was spending more than 5 billion dollars per month in 2004 without any clear sense of when it would come to an end. This "military Keynesianism" led to increases on the military budget that passed $400 billion with an addition $40 billion in intelligence costs.

The transformed budgetary profile was likewise reflected in the organizational reformulation carried out by the Bush administration, in which the Department of State became completely subordinated to the Pentagon. In this arrangement, Secretary of Defense Rumsfeld was in complete control, with Vice-President Cheney overseeing the shadowing affairs of private sector and big business coordination, especially regarding petroleum interests, while Department of State Secretary Powell was relegated to "selling" the policy to publics both home and abroad. The intelligence apparatus was now fully consolidated under the Pentagon which controlled 90% of the intelligence personnel and budget. Rumsfeld personally created the post of Under Secretary of Defense for Intelligence without submitting the post for approval to the Senate Intelligence Committee. He also created the Office of Special Plans so as to better manage the manipulation of the mass media and the Congress. Meanwhile, ultraconservative Republican Tom Ridge was named to head the new Department of Homeland Security so as to neutralize the "enemy within."

International criticism of criminal war conduct and allegations of human rights violations were widely suppressed by the politics of pressure and intimidation of the Bush administration. In all of this, Cuba was one of the few voices to be heard in critique of the aggressive attitude to which Washington was assuming towards a variety of developing countries in the aftermath of the World Trade Center attack. While the Cuban Government clearly expressed its condolences for the innocent victims of the attacks, it also cited the longstanding U.S. record of terrorism against Cuba and other countries.

By May of 2002, the Bush administration by way of retaliation was once again engaged in incendiary rhetoric against Cuba. Ultraconservative John R. Bolton, named back in 2001 as Under Secretary of State for Arms Control and International Security, began to accuse Cuba in 2002 of being a producer of biological weapons. According to Bolton, "Cuba leads in the production of pharmaceuticals and vaccines that are sold worldwide."[13] This naturally meant that Cuba must have at least a "limited offensive biological warfare research and development effort." Numerous commentators, including U.S. officials were quick to point out that the theory of "dual use biotechnology" was an abstract allegation in the absence of any evidence.

Later the same month, the Department of State published its list of "terrorist states" with a renewed emphasis on the "threat" posed by Cuba. Even as the report recognized that Cuba was signatory to all 12 UN counter-terrorism conventions as well as the Ibero-American Declaration against Terrorism at the 2001 Summit, it lamely asserted that President Castro "has vacillated in his position on terrorism and has sharply criticized the 'U.S.-led War on Terrorism.'"[14]

In December, 2003, the Bush administration named a "Commission for Assistance to a Free Cuba" chaired by Secretary of State Colin Powel that was designed to draw up new measures to bring down the Cuban Government and to outline the process of "democratic transition." The move was almost universally understood as a campaign maneuver designed to shore up support from the Miami exile groups in strategic electoral battlegrounds such as Florida and New Jersey. On May 6, 2004, the White House announced that it would be adopting a new series of measures based on the Commission's recommendations. These measures included a commitment from the Bush administration to allocate up to $59 million over a two-year period to support additional new measures designed to help "hasten" the overthrow of the Cuban Government, including:

- $29 million in additional funding for assistance to Cuban opposition groups, in addition to the $7 million already allocated by USAID to this end.
- Up to $18 million to support new measures to overcome the Cuban jamming of the U.S. media broadcasts Radio Martí and Tele-Martí, using C-130 aircraft for more sophisticated aerial broadcasting.
- New measures designed to further restrict travel to Cuba and to tighten enforcement of existing Cuban travel restrictions.
- Up to $5 million to help to fund new measures designed to internationalize the economic blockade, including greater diplomatic pressure to adopt Washington's anti-Cuba policies; and channeling funding through U.S. embassies abroad for anti-Cuba conferences and grants for international groups opposed to the Cuban Government.

In announcing these extremely hostile measures, the obvious objective of the commission report was to appeal to the wealthiest and most powerful elements of the Miami based, Cuban-American Mafia. To this end, the report stated that the "post-Castro" regime can count on U.S. assistance to facilitate a quick resolution to the issue of confiscated productive and residential properties, "suggesting" certain guidelines that should not permit any discrimination or otherwise distinguish as to whether or not Cubans had remained on the island after the expropriation. U.S. assistance can also be counted on to "assist a free Cuba to develop a truly professional civilian police force" and to offer military assistance to "help transition authorities to prevent massive sea borne migration," although it is left largely unexplained as to why "recently liberated Cubans" would be trying to flee the island en masse.[15]

The Bush administration probably underestimated, however, the increasing differentiation of public opinion among Cuban-American exiles. As *The New York Times* asserted in its editorial of June 27, 2004: "The toughened policy, which cynically victimizes families, will backfire over time. Polls show that about half the Cuban-American community in Florida resents the intrusive new sanctions."[16]

At the end of April 2004, the Department of State once again reiterated in its Annual Terrorism Report "2003-Patterns of Global Terrorism" that "Cuba remained opposed to the U.S.-led Coalition prosecuting the global war on terrorism and actively condemned many associated U.S. policies and actions throughout 2003. . . . [Cuba was] consistently critical of the United States and frequently and baselessly alleged U.S. involvement in violations of human rights."[17] The report was understandably delayed from its original intended release date since the Department of State was reeling from the pictures being splattered across the global media, showing the systematic human rights violations practiced by U.S. occupation forces in Iraq. The scandal refused to quickly dissipate, however, and subsequent revelations further confirmed the systematic policy behind the violations, including in Afghanistan and in the detention facilities at Guantánamo.

Beyond the 2004 measures and the Commission Report, the widespread scandal concerning the human rights abuses of Iraqi and other prisoners, including those being held in Guantánamo, helped fuel growing support for the international movement to free the Cuban Five. This refers to the five Cubans who were working as counter-terrorist agents in Southern Florida until their arrest in 1998. The five managed to infiltrate several important exile organizations and pass on information about their operations. They were convicted of a variety of charges in 2001 while being subjected to a Miami venue. Despite admitting their information gathering actions while stressing they were working in defense of their country against terrorist groups being sheltered in South Florida, they were given draconian prison sentences that seemed to bear little resemblance to their convictions. Their case has resulted in appeals that stretched well into 2004 and an international campaign of solidarity that demanded the release of the Cuban Five.[18]

Another case on the diplomatic and intelligence front involved a senior analyst with the Defense Intelligence Agency who was arrested in September, 2001. Ana Belén Montes pled guilty of passing on information to the Cuban Government and was sentenced to twenty-five years imprisonment in October of 2002. At the time of her sentencing, she stated:

Your honor, I engaged in the activity that brought me before you because I obeyed my conscience rather than the law. I believe our government's policy towards Cuba is cruel and unfair, profoundly unneighborly, and I felt morally obligated to help the island defend itself from our efforts to impose our values and our political system on it. We have displayed intolerance and contempt towards Cuba for most of the last four decades. We have never respected Cuba's right to make its own journey towards its own ideals of equality and justice. I do not understand why we must continue to dictate how the Cubans should select their leaders, who their leaders cannot be, and what laws are appropriate in their land.[19]

Finally, the other important development in Cuban-U.S. relations has been the increasing amount of agricultural trade under the Trade Sanctions Reform and Export Enhancement Act signed into law by the Clinton administration in October, 2000. After hurricane Michele hit Cuba in November, 2001, conditional humanitarian aid was offered to Cuban NGOs but Cuba refused and instead indicated a willingness to purchase food products directly from U.S. suppliers.

With those first sales, Cuba went from being last on the global list of U.S. food purchasers in 2000 to 144th in 2001 and 46th in 2002. In 2003, Cuban purchases from the U.S. doubled again, reaching nearly $320 million, making it the 8th largest purchaser of chicken and 14th on the list of wheat purchasers.[20] This process has led to a sharp upsurge in demands on the part of U.S. farmers to fully normalize trade relations.

All of the geopolitical changes of the late 1980s notwithstanding, a hard line posture towards Cuba on the part of Washington prevailed throughout the 1990s. The heightened militarization of U.S. foreign policy which followed the 9/11 attacks reflected the intensification of an already established political shift towards the right in both the Democratic and Republican parties, a trend which has favored the increased use of interventionism and punitive policies designed to support U.S. hegemonic interests. This trend showed little sign of abatement by mid-2004 with the enactment of a new series of measures designed to provoke a collapse of the Cuban socialist system. The success of its survival strategy notwithstanding, Cuban development remains constrained by the expanding hegemonic logic of U.S. foreign policy.

The political influence of the Miami exile community continues to play a significant role in U.S. policy toward Cuba. In the wake of the Elián affair, there is a growing consensus that the Miami community no longer exhibits a unified position with respect to the most effective way of pressuring political change on the island. The Bush administration may have underestimated the resentment on the part of some Cuban-Americans due to the new measures enacted in mid-2004. At the same time, the U.S. agricultural lobby has become the unlikely new political force that is seeking the end of the economic embargo. Together, these developments may have the effect of undermining hard-line policies towards Cuba in the medium term.

Notes

1. Richard Dello Buono, "Introduction to the Cuban Special Period," in *CartaCuba*, 1-5. (The full facts of publication of all the sources are found in the Bibliography, at the end of the essay. *Ed.)*

2. Ibid.

3. Latin American Bureau, *Grenada: Whose Freedom?*, 46.

4. Anthony Payne, et al., *Grenada: Revolution and Invasion*, 65.

5. Ibid., 161-164.

6. Paul Sutton, "U.S. Intervention, Regional Security, and Militarization of the Caribbean," in Anthony Payne and Paul Sutton (eds.), *Modern Caribbean Politics*, 277-293.

7. Elsie Le Franc, *Consequences of Structural Adjustment: A Review of the Jamaican Experience.*

8. Patricia Anderson and Michael Witter, "Crisis, Adjustment and Social Change: A Case Study of Jamaica," and Lynette Brown, "Crisis, Adjustment and Social Change: The Middle Class under Adjustment," in Elsie Le Franc, op. cit.

9. Elena Díaz, "Cuban Socialism: Adjustments and Paradoxes," in José Bell Lara (Co-ordinator), *Cuba in the 1990s*, 56-57.

10. Michael Krinsky and David Golove (eds.), *United States Economic Measures against Cuba.*

11. Washington immediately indicated that it did not consider that the OAS had jurisdiction over the matter.

12. Petre Andreas, "Free Market Reform and Drug Market Prohibition: U.S. Policies at Cross-purposes in Latin America," in *Third World Quaterly* journal, vol. 16, no. 1, 75.

13. Anya Landau and Wayne S. Smith, "CIP Challenges Bolton on Cuban Bio-Terrorism Charges."

14. Wayne S. Smith, "CIP Challenges State Department's List of Terrorist States."

15. Colin L. Powell, "Commission for Assistance to a Free Cuba: A Report to the President," 158.

16. *The New York Times* Editorial Board, "Election-Year Cuba Policy."

17. Secretary of State and Coordinator for Counterterrorism, U.S. Department of State, "Patterns of Global Terrorism."

18. For further information about the Cuban Five, visit the web sites: www.freethefive.org/ and www.antiterroristas.cu/. ED.

19. Tim Johnson, "Spy for Cuba Gets a 25-Year Term."

20. Marelys Valencia, "Purchases from the United States Doubled in 2003."

Bibliography

ANDERSON PATRICIA and MICHAEL WITTER. "Crisis, Adjustment and Social Change: A Case Study of Jamaica." In Elsie Le Franc, *Consequences of Structural Adjustment: A Review of the Jamaican Experience*. Kingston: Canoe Press / University of West Indies, 1994.

ANDREAS, PETRE. "Free Market Reform and Drug Market Prohibition: U.S. Policies at Cross-purposes in Latin America." *Third World Quarterly* journal, vol. 16, no. 1 (1995).

BARRY, TOM, BETH WOOD and DEB PREUSCH. *The Other Side of Paradise: Foreign Control in the Caribbean*. New York: Grove Press, Inc., 1984.

BELL LARA, JOSÉ. *Cambios mundiales y perspectivas de la Revolución Cubana*. Havana: Editorial de Ciencias Sociales, 1999.

BELL LARA, JOSÉ and CLARA PULIDO ESCANDELL. *Visión desde Cuba*. Madrid: Sodepaz, 1996.

BEST, TONY. "Manley Got Screwed." *New York Carib News*, 24 April 1990. Cited in Ivelaw L. Griffith, "Caribbean Security: Retrospect and Prospect." *Latin American Research Review*, vol. 30, no. 2 (1995): 3-32.

BROWN, LYNETTE. "Crisis, Adjustment and Social Change: The Middle Class under Adjustment." In Elsie Le Franc, *Consequences of Structural Adjustment: A Review of the Jamaican Experience*. Kingston: Canoe Press / University of West Indies, 1994.

BURKI, SHAHID JAVED and SEBASTIÁN EDWARDS. "Consolidating Economic Reforms in Latin America and the Caribbean." *Finance and Development* (March, 1995).

BUSH, GEORGE W. "A Transcript of Bush's Address on the Decision to Use Force in Panama." *The New York Times*, 21 December 1989, A19, 29.

CANUTE, JAMES. "Caribbean Manufacturers Set Mission to Cuba for April." *Journal of Commerce*, 25 March 1996.

―――. "Cuba Partners Fear U.S. Hammer." *Financial Times*, 25 September 1995, 8.

CELIS ALBAN, FRANCISCO. "Hora cero para los Noal." *El Tiempo*, 15 October 1995, sec. A, p. 7a.

CHILD, JORGE. *Alternativas*. Bogota: Tercer Mundo Editorial, 1995.

"Cuba: nuevo régimen de inversiones." *Latin American Newsletters* (London), no. 36 (September 21, 1995).

DELLO BUONO, RICHARD. "Introduction to the Cuban Special Period." In *CartaCuba*. Havana: FLACSO, 1995.

DEPALMA, ANTHONY. "Tightened Embargo Threatens Foreign Investment in Cuba." *The New York Times*, 7 April 1995.

DÍAZ, ELENA. "Calidad de la vida en Cuba: Efectos de la política norteamericana." Working Document II at FLACSO, University of Havana, 1994.

―――. "Cuban Socialism: Adjustments and Paradoxes." In José Bell Lara (Coordinator), *Cuba in the 1990s*. Havana: Editorial José Martí, 1999.

DOS SANTOS, JOSÉ. "La utopía necesaria." *Cuba Internacional* magazine, vol. 32, no. 299 (1996): 6-9.

DUNCAN, NEVILLE C. "The Anglophone Caribbean and the Summit of the Americas." Paper presented at the 20th Annual Conference of the Caribbean Studies Association, Wilmenstaad, Curaçao, May 21-23, 1995.

THE ECONOMIST GROUP. "Big Government Is Back." *The Economist*, 29 September 2001.

THE EDITORIAL BOARD of THE NEW YORK TIMES. "Election-Year Cuba Policy." *The New York Times*, 27 June 2004.

FERNÁNDEZ, OLGA. "El 'efecto Elián': inédito acontecimiento de opinión pública." *Cuadernos de Nuestra América* journal, vol. 13/14, no. 26-27 (2001).

FIGUERAS, MIGUEL A. and SERGIO PLASENCIA VIDAL. "The Cuban Economy in the 1900s: Problems and Prospects." In *The Caribbean in the Global Political Economy*, edited by Hilbourne A. Watson. Boulder, Colorado and London: Lynne Rienner Publishers Inc., 1994.

GONZÁLEZ NÚÑEZ, GERARDO. "Cuba y el mercado mundial." In *Cuba en crisis: perspectivas económicas y políticas*, edited by Jorge Rodríguez Beruff. San Juan: Editorial Universidad de Puerto Rico, 1995.

GRIFFITH, IVELAW L. "Caribbean Security: Retrospect and Prospect." *Latin American Research Review*, vol. 30, no. 2 (1995): 3-32.

HARKER, TREVOR. "Caribbean Economic Performance in the 1909s: Implications for Future Policy." In *The Caribbean in the Global Political Economy*, edited by Hilbourne A. Watson. Boulder, Colorado and London: Lynne Rienner Publishers Inc., 1994.

HEMLOCK, DOREEN. "Puerto Rico's Cuba Worries." *CubaNews*, vol. 2, no. 6 (June 1994).

JOHNSON, TIM. "Spy for Cuba Gets a 25-Year Term." *The Miami Herald*, 17 October, 2002.

KRINSKY, MICHAEL and DAVID GOLOVE (eds.). *United States Economic Measures against Cuba.* Northampton, Massachusetts: Alethia Press, 1993.

LANDAU, ANYA and WAYNE S. SMITH. "CIP Challenges Bolton on Cuban Bio-Terrorism / Charges." *Center for International Policy's Cuba Program.* May 8, 2002. http:/ciponline.org/cuba/cubainthenews/newsarticles/ IP050802oltonreply.html. Accessed August 6, 2004.

LATIN AMERICAN BUREAU. *Grenada: Whose Freedom?* London: Latin American Bureau, 1984.

LE FRANC, ELSIE. *Consequences of Structural Adjustment: A Review of the Jamaican Experience.* Kingston: Canoe Press / University of West Indies, 1994.

LERDA, JUAN CARLOS. "Globalización y pérdida de autonomía de las autoridades fiscales, bancarias y monetarias." *Revista de la CEPAL* (April 1996): 63-75.

LÓPEZ, DELIA LUISA. "Crisis económica, ajustes y democracia en Cuba." Working Document no. 3 at FLACSO, University of Havana, 1994.

MARQUIS, CHRISTOPHER. "Republicans Put Cuba on Front Burner." *The Miami Herald*, 6 March 1995, 6A.

PAYNE, ANTHONY, PAUL SUTTON and TONY THORNDIKE. *Grenada: Revolution and Invasion.* New York: St. Martin's Press, 1984.

PERALES HERNÁNDEZ, JOSÉ RAÚL. "Systemic Perspectives on Regional Integration: Latin American and Caribbean Experiences." Paper presented at the 20th Annual Conference of the Caribbean Studies Association, Wilmenstaad, Curaçao, May 21-23, 1995.

POWELL, COLIN L. "Commission for Assistance to a Free Cuba: A Report to the President." *U.S. Department of State.* http://www.state.gov/p/wha/rt/cuba/commission/2004/c12237.html. Accessed August 6, 2004.

REYNOLDS, CLARK W., FRANCISCO ELÍAS THOUMI and RINHART WETTMANN. *A Case for Open Regionalism in the Andes: Policy Implications of Andean Integration in a Period of Hemispheric Liberalization and Structural Adjustment.* Washington, D.C.: U.S. Agency for International Development, 1993.

ROJAS ARAVENA, FRANCISCO. "América Latina: el difícil camino de la concertación y la integración." *Nueva Sociedad* journal, no. 125 (May-June 1993): 60-69.

SCHNEIDER, WILLIAM. "Elián González Defeated Al Gore." *National Journal*, 28 April 2001.

SECRETARY OF STATE and COORDINATOR FOR COUNTERTERRORISM, U.S. DEPARTMENT OF STATE. "Patterns of Global Terrorism 2003." *U.S. Department of State.* April 2004. http://www.state.gov/s/ct/rls/pgtrpt/2003/c12108.html. Accessed August 6, 2004.

SEIBEL, MARK. "No Change in Hiring." *CubaNews*, vol. 2, no. 10 (1995), 6.

SMITH, PETER H. (ed.). *The Challenge of Integration.* New Brunswick, New Jersey: Transaction Publishers, 1993.

SMITH, WAYNE S. "CIP Challenges State Department's List of Terrorist States." *No War on Cuba Movement.* http://www.nowaroncuba.org/Documentation/CIP_Terror.html. Accessed August 6, 2004.

STUBBS, JEAN. "Structural Re-insertion into the 1990s World Economy: The Case of Cuban Tobacco." Paper presented at the 20th Annual Conference of the Caribbean Studies Association, Wilmenstaad, Curaçao, May 21-23, 1995.

SUTTON, PAUL. "U.S. Intervention, Regional Security, and Militarization in the Caribbean." In *Modern Caribbean Politics*, edited by Anthony Payne and Paul Sutton. Baltimore, Maryland: The Johns Hopkins University Press, 1993.

TARG, HARRY R. *Cuba and the USA: A New World Order?* New York: International Publishers, 1992.

UNCTAD. *World Investment Report 1995: Transnational Corporations, and Competitiveness.* New York: United Nations Secretariat, TAD/INF/2620, 1995.

VALENCIA, MARELYS. "Purchases from the United States Doubled in 2003." *Granma Internacional.* http://www.granma.cu/ingles/2004/enero/mier7/2alimpor.html. Accessed August 7, 2004.

WATSON, HILBOURNE, ed. *The Caribbean in the Global Political Economy.* Boulder, Colorado and London: Lynne Rienner Publishers Inc., 1994.

Is the Socialist Model Still a Viable Alternative for Cuba?

ELENA DÍAZ GONZÁLEZ

ELENA DÍAZ GONZÁLEZ

Ph.D. in Economic Sciences. A specialist in issues of social development and gender and society. Her work has included studies of Cuban women and their social participation as well as more general socio-economic problems in Cuba and the rest of Latin America. She is a senior researcher and professor in the FLACSO-Cuba Program at the University of Havana.

The purpose of this essay is to reflect upon some of the processes that have unfolded in Cuban society during the last five years. My approach will be to comparatively analyze some of the most important characteristics that have arisen within the present context of increasing globalization. Specifically, I will seek to demonstrate how the ethical values that currently prevail in Cuban society contrast sharply with the ethics displayed by the neoliberal model. Cuba's social reality has fundamentally intersected with the dynamics of increasing globalization and has indeed suffered from the dramatic impact of this trend. I will show, however, that it is precisely Cuba's capacity to pursue a different model in the context of globalization that has permitted the continuity of the Cuban socialist project. To draw this into sharp relief, I will select four essential aspects that I consider to be characteristic of the neoliberal model and simultaneously present the contrasting dynamics found in Cuban society.

The current international context can be characterized by an extremely negative situation, marked by a generalized economic recession, the occurrence of horrendous acts of terrorism (such as the attacks of 9/11/01), and the proliferation of armed conflicts such as the horrific wars later unleashed upon Afghanistan and Iraq, atrocities that stand to exacerbate still further an already high level of violence across the world. This rather dark period in global history corresponds to growing debates concerning the prospects for survival of a world ever more unequal and at ever-greater risk of losing its sustainability. An explosive demographic growth (75 million people annually join the existing 6.06 billion population, 95% of whom live in the Third World[1]) and a deepening pattern of environmental degradation must indeed be understood as imminent signs of an urgent situation. It is in this turbulent social context that capitalist globalization must be considered.

Globalization, understood as an objective process of the increasing internationalization of the capitalist cycle, goes hand in hand with the neoliberal political project that serves to reproduce expanding capitalist accumulation and domination. Neoliberal globalization as a general pattern seems to display continuity in the tendency towards the internationalization of capital of which Karl Marx had warned back in the 19th century.

Various authors have sought to explain globalization as a multidimensional phenomenon, emphasizing aspects such as the growth in world trade, the leading role assumed by transnational enterprises, the expansion of market forces and the logic of private enterprise, the strengthening of the role of international financial institutions, the restructuration of the productive system and the global labor market, the consolidation of regional superpowers, the progressive weakening of national states (particularly those of the underdeveloped countries), and the freeing up of the circulation of capital and goods (in contrast to the global labor force) between countries. What is absolutely clear is that within all of these dynamics, certain basic contradictions remain such as the progressive tendency towards the privatization of capital versus the socialization of the relations of production, or the contradictory relations between the productive and financial spheres of the global economy.

Over the past fifteen years or so, the world experienced important changes beginning with the collapse of the former-Soviet Union and the Eastern European Socialist Bloc and the resulting disappearance of the bipolar global order. This in turn has served to accentuate the contradictions between the capitalist superpowers (United States of America, Europe and Japan), particularly as manifested in their competition for domination over the Third World (North vs South). In this setting, neoliberal globalization at the political level signifies the restructuration of a world order where the emphasis has become placed on the hegemonic control on the part of these superpowers, above all, on the part of the United States.

Divergent Approaches to Poverty

The process of neoliberal globalization moreover implies an anthropological paradigm in its creation of an ethical conception that prioritizes the operation of the market, something that when placed into practice generates widening inequalities and a generalized suppression of human rights. In short, neoliberalism results in the increase of poverty, a progressive social polarization and the process of social exclusion.

But here the question arises: What really distinguishes the neoliberal ethical model with respect to humanity's centuries-old coexistence with poverty and exploitation? In the first place, the new and highly dangerous aspects of the model reside in the magnitude and profound scope of prevailing poverty. Poverty essentially signifies under-consumption, usually associated with a deficient nutritional condition, increased vulnerability to diseases, shortages of essential goods, an unstable integration with the productive system, and uncertain levels of income that chronically fail to satisfy basic needs. Extreme poverty displays all of these aspects in an exaggerated form and kills people in the final instance. One-fourth of the 4.5 billion people who live in the underdeveloped countries cannot rely on acquiring the minimal necessities for life. For many of them, there is no expectation to survive beyond their 40th birthday which is roughly about half of the average life expectancy for the more developed countries. It has been established that over 1.3 billion individuals do not have access to clean water and a commensurate number live under the poverty line, with around 840 million suffering from malnourishment.

Poverty in underdevelopment signifies the degradation of the natural environment, not like in the more developed countries where pollution and environmental degradation is caused by excessive consumerism, but rather by a desperate struggle for survival. This kind of poverty is the manifestation of the increasing social polarization between rich and poor countries as well as within both rich countries and poor countries alike.

According to UN figures, 1 out of every 8 inhabitants of the industrialized countries suffers from poverty. UNDP data concerning the indices of social polarization show that 225 of the wealthiest people in the world possess a fortune equivalent to the annual income of 47% of the world's population or more than 2.5 billion people. The richest 20% of the world's population are responsible for 86% of global personal consumption, consuming 45% of the world's meat and fish, 58% of the world's energy, 74% of the world's telephone services, and 87% of the world's personal vehicles. Meanwhile, the poorest 20% of the world's population engages in only 1.3% of global economic consumption. The steady increase in this global inequality is likewise observable in the available statistics. The income difference between the richest and poorest one-fifth of the world population was 30 to 1 in 1960, 60 to 1 in 1990 and 74 to 1 in 1997.[2]

In Latin America where the economic and social successes of neoliberal policy should be most evident, we can instead observe its resolute failure both as a generator of economic growth and as a catalyst for social progress. In this regard, the macroeconomic data are impressive: average annual growth for the 1990s was at 3%, more than the 1% of the 1980s but far less than the 6% average figure for the 1960s and 1970s.[3] The foreign debt, which in 1985 was around U.S.$300 billion, came to exceed U.S.$800 billion by the end of the 1990s, devouring around 56% of export earnings generated from goods and services. During the 1992-1999 period alone, there were 913 billion dollars in total debt payments. This made the 1990s the second consecutive decade in which poverty had increased, rather than decreased, across the entirety of Latin America. In other words, the region was entering into the new century even poorer that what it was in 1980. At the same time, the distribution of wealth and income continues to systematically worsen throughout a region already known for its enormous inequalities.

In the region categorized as having the worst income distribution in the world, where the 20% richest sector of the population receives 19 times that of the 20% poorest, there are 224 million poor and 90 million indigent people.[4] In that sense, it was possible to speak of another "lost decade" for the region in the 1990s.[5] This persistence and intensification of poverty and inequality thus constitutes the first essential characteristic of the ethical model of neoliberal globalization.

In the face of this desolate international panorama, the Cuban socialist project has continued to develop, keeping its ethical parameters rooted in the dream of a more just and equitable society. But if in preceding decades, it was the capitalist market that served as the foreign contrast for this project, beginning with the 1990s, the market became an important social actor within Cuba as many authors have described. This made it an everyday reality for Cubans.

In the face of this challenge, the country would now have to heavily depend upon the accumulated cultural, political and human values of its people, values that were produced over years of engagement in an emancipatory project. According to sociologist Aurelio Alonso, the principal strength of the Cuban socialist process rests in its "nationalist foundation with popular roots."[6] The recent trajectory of this process, its vision and the continuity of its principles are strongly intertwined with the country's history.

Another sociologist, Juan Valdés, considers that the most recent era in Cuban society can be divided into three essential periods: survival (1987-93) which encompassed the shock of international dislocation; recovery (1994-2000) with a relatively favorable albeit gradual evolution in social and economic indicators; and the new phase of development (2000-) that is predicated upon the progressive consolidation of certain bases that together imply economic stability.[7] Throughout this evolution has been the ever-present conditioning factor of the aggressive policies of the U.S. Government. This aggression which intensified in the 1990s, first with the Torricelli Act and later with the Helms-Burton Act, together serves to aggravate still further the pressures associated with the economic blockade which that country has maintained against Cuba for well over forty years.

Returning to the first characteristic of the neoliberal project mentioned above, the expansion of poverty and inequality, it can be seen that this dynamic did not develop in the same way in Cuba during the final years of the 1990s. Although a decline in the Cuban standard of living was evident, relative to that which existed during the 1980s, the data allows us to observe more recently a relative improvement in social and economic terms. With respect to the economy, a recovery has materialized that is tending towards stabilization. The average rate of economic growth for the period 1995-2000 was 4.7%. Although an even higher rate of growth was initially forecasted for 2001, the economy ultimately grew at only 3% due to the combined effects of hurricane Michelle in October which ravaged parts of the island (thankfully with only 5 human casualties) and the decline of tourist revenues associated with the global slump in the aftermath of the September 11 terrorist attacks in the United States. One of the most pronounced aspects of economic growth during this period could be found in the increase of worker productivity (19%) which alone accounted for the 75% of actual growth registered during this period, attesting to the country's spirit during this period.

Also significant over recent years are the following aspects: tourism increased around 8 times its prior earnings and registered an increase of around 5 times the number of foreign visitors (1,304,597 visitors up through August of 2001). The production of petroleum which was at 500 thousand tons in 1980 increased to the equivalent of 3.6 million tons of petroleum and gas. The most recent figures available show that Cuban exports for 2001 grew around 10.7% and imports increased at 0.7% in comparison with the preceding year.

All of these favorable trends have induced a progressive recovery of the Cuban standard of living. For example, the average salary which was 185 Cuban pesos in 1994 ascended to 242 in 2001. Unemployment which reached an 8% level descended to 5.4% in 2000, and has continued to decline since. In 1994, the worst year of the crisis, there were 344 days affected by blackouts of electricity while in 2000, there were only 74. In terms of daily per capita caloric consumption, the figure of 1948 calories for 1994 increased to 2578 for the year 2000, with the corresponding increase in daily protein consumption from 47.7 to 68.3 grams.[8] This sphere, one of the most affected by the crisis of the 1990s, thus displays a relative improvement, although still insufficient if compared with the levels of quality, diversity and equity in food consumption achieved prior to the crisis.

Other aspects which confer an overall stability in the social policies directed towards the population include the continuing free access to high quality education, health and social security. The educational budget for the year 2001 grew by 270 million pesos relative to 2000. Health spending increased by 135 million pesos, 60 million for social security, and 78 million for culture.

In summary, poverty is not a characteristic which grew unchecked in Cuban society. Extreme poverty does not exist and even more importantly, the inequalities which became generalized in Cuban social relations during the worst of the crisis and which persist to the present have not significantly intensified. This has been the result of explicit policies designed to impede further polarization in the distribution of wealth. This has included the imposition of taxes for application to private work which establishes a relative margin or ceiling over profits.

For example, the limit of 12 seats per private restaurant and similar regulations in other fields of private services contribute to achieving the larger social objective. The progressive revaluation and relative stability of the Cuban peso in relation to the dollar also implies a relatively favorable albeit still insufficient situation (the rate of exchange which hit over 100 pesos per dollar in 1994 was at 26 pesos in 2004).

At the same time, there has been an increase in social assistance programs aimed at those sectors most disadvantaged. This includes the creation of four schools for the training of social workers beginning in 1999, designed to offer youths who were neither working or engaged in studies, the opportunity to enter into this new profession. These young professionals are learning how to work at the community level to assess the most urgent social problems of the population and to contribute to channeling resources towards their solution in conjunction with the work of the People's Councils.

Another important measure taken in this direction was a 30% salary increase for teachers, physicians, nurses, and police officers who together account for 82% of workers employed by the state for social service delivery. Likewise notable was the development of incentive systems which have been designed to attenuate the continuing shortages of certain goods in high demand. These consisted of a periodic distribution of desirable goods for those who fully complied with their individual plans of work as well as distributions of dollar-equivalent currency based on increased work productivity. An estimated 1,200,000 workers received some form of these incentives. This notwithstanding, social differentiation is a reality which strongly affects the population, particularly in terms of the inequality of access to dollar-equivalent currency. Although it is estimated that more than half of the population has some access to such currency, the overall amount in circulation is not nearly sufficient to satisfy existing needs and to substantially mollify the existing differences.

The shortages periodically experienced by the population are severe and the feelings of dissatisfaction caused by an everyday standard of living considerably more austere and comparatively more difficult than that lived in the 1980s remain ever present.

Reflecting back on the first ethical characteristic of the neoliberal model, the following can be said about the Cuban case. In spite of the persistence of social differences and the fact that such differences have broadened the complexity of the Cuban social structure, there is an evident continuity in overall social policies with a persistent intention to avoid extreme poverty and the increase of social polarization.

Contrasting Values of Social Exclusion and Solidarity

A second characteristic of the neoliberal model is the presence of social exclusion as a basic, underlying tendency of the model, rather than as something transient or conjunctural. According to the Spanish philosopher Manuel Monereo: "This phenomenon, ever more visible within the rich societies of Western capitalism, has at the world level become concretized in the global system's capacity to "disconnect" groups of countries or even entire continents such as sub-Saharan Africa which have ceased being of interest to the hegemonic core countries. . . ."[9]

"This characteristic of permanent exclusion becomes repeated as an internal mechanism within countries, with particular gravity for the impoverished majorities that are "disconnected from the social order." It produces a discriminatory rejection based on the inequalities of class, ethnicity, gender and other social asymmetries. This marginalization progressively afflicts more and more people and families who become excluded from essential social structures, from their communities and from their intimate social surroundings. This in turn generates a kind of alter-ego, affecting not only the functioning of mechanisms for establishing social position, but likewise favoring a particular form of rejection that erodes subjectivity and the internal self-esteem of the individual. Social exclusion effectively accentuates social asymmetries. According to ECLAC: "In the majority of countries in the region, more than half of older adult citizens do not have an elderly pension. In fact, in 10 countries in Latin America and the Caribbean . . . the system of pensions covers less than 25% of the 60 and over population."[10]

At the other end of the age spectrum, children generally suffer the worst from social exclusion. "Children have been shown to be the Achilles heel of Latin America: 52% of the region's poor are children and adolescents and close to 39 million of those living in poverty are between the ages of 0 and 5 with another 43 million consisting of those between the ages of 6 and 12."[11] Females have in particular suffered from the worst effects of this model with their presence over-represented in what has been often referred to as the "feminization of poverty."

In order to make social participation possible, a platform is required that offers access to work, skills and health. But it is precisely the core elements of neoliberalism that increase the obstacles to such a platform, relegating many to conditions of poverty and social exclusion whereupon they become "disconnected." Social exclusion implies the loss or absence of opportunities and access to education and knowledge. It intensifies the risk of losing ones cultural identity. In 1997, it was estimated that there were more than 850 million illiterate adults who with this level of ignorance would be denied any further possibility of skill training, thus becoming inexorably condemned to poverty, frustration and disorientation.

This aspect is particularly relevant in the current era of globalization where knowledge constitutes the crucial element for the possibility of gaining access to development. It is an era in which the rate of obsolescence in technologies accelerates and the time period between discoveries and applications are greatly reduced. The activity of research and development becomes integrated into the productive system in an accelerated manner and the technological application of knowledge is the decisive factor in production.[12] Opportunities for skills training and advanced learning are the strategic means for advancing the development of a country, in enhancing its international competitiveness, and at the personal level, it signified the means for advancing a life project. The progressive loss of traditional comparative advantages within the underdeveloped countries (i.e. cheap source of labor and natural resources) becomes displaced by more dynamic advantages where the incorporation of technological knowledge intervenes.

But in the situation of the underdeveloped countries, economic adjustment programs limited the possibilities of free access to education by privatizing their educational systems. Increased poverty exacerbated the little time available to the population for gaining access to knowledge, precisely because the priority of survival becomes paramount with them. The end result is a desperate search for supplemental income that includes young children, adolescents and particularly females.

This characteristic of neoliberalism that we have identified as social exclusion greatly contrasts with the principles governing Cuban development. In Cuba, the ethical values underlying social policy revolve around the principle that not one person can be left abandoned and that every individual must be afforded access to educational opportunities and health services. By maintaining the system of food rationing, a basic basket of foodstuffs at subsidized prices reaches every individual. This same principle is present in the health care system. Massive public health campaigns such as a vaccination program against 12 infant diseases that achieved 98% coverage of the nation's children work to overcome the possibility of social exclusion and are palpable examples of this underlying ethical characteristic of the Cuban model.

If there is one characteristic of Cuban revolutionary society that remains unshaken to the present, it is the guarantee of mass access to the overall platform of social assistance. Some social indicators can help to illustrate this situation such as in the area of infant mortality where the figure of 5.8 per thousand live births was registered in 2004, the lowest in the entire history of the nation. In addition, the number of inhabitants per physician was 165 in 2003 and maternal mortality was recorded at 3.95 per 10,000 live births. Pregnant women received an average of 13.6 prenatal medical consultations. In the field of education, there are 52 centers of higher education and 9487 primary schools operating as of 1997-98. As UNESCO recognized, Cuban obtained the highest of results in a survey concerning the quality of education at the primary level. Out of every 100 workers, 7 have completed university studies and 13 are technicians. In addition, there exist 444 schools dedicated to special education, the most recent of which was inaugurated for autistic children.

The Cuban Government protects the population through an overlapping series of social assistance and social security policies which offer support in the form of free services, free materials (school supplies, medications, prosthetics, etc.) and financial assistance. The costs of this regime of social security and assistance have increased in recent years, and in 1998 represented 6.5% of the Gross Domestic Product.[13] All of this had been designed to ensure that there exist no abandoned citizens. In particular, the attention offered to elderly individuals living alone has been reinforced and efforts have been made to identify each and every one so that their prioritized care can be guaranteed.

Some social groups traditionally discriminated against around the world, such as women, have been integrated within Cuban society in very dramatic ways. In Cuba, 66% of the technical labor force is female, as are 30% of the nation's scientists, 60% of the enrolled student population in higher education, and 35.96% of the parlamentarians. Although there substantial gender inequalities persist, particularly with respect to insufficient access to the highest levels of decision making as well as the persistence of the disproportionate weight of domestic family tasks charged to women, Cuban women are not socially discriminated against and the majority of Cuban women do not perceive the existence of such discrimination.[14]

In an integral sense, we can summarize by saying that social exclusion is not a structural phenomenon of Cuban society. Those sectors of the population which are socially disadvantaged (i.e. with lower average salaries, residents of precarious or overcrowded housing) enjoy unfettered access to the basic services of health and education.

Social Fragmentation versus Social Participation

The third ethical characteristic of the neoliberal model helps to serve as an instrument of its own extension. Here, I refer to the fragmentation or annulment of collective action and active social demands of the people. For the majority of poor countries, there exist no systemic possibilities for incorporating the people's existing knowledge access directly into their everyday work and productive relations. This serves as a brake upon the process of innovation.

Human capital requires a dynamic and specialized formative process in which training can be inserted into productive relations. Thus, there is a mechanism of incorporation, at the same time of a tendency to displace a significant portion of unskilled workers to poorly remunerated and highly exploited forms of work. With the progressive disappearance of stable work opportunities for the unskilled laborer, the traditional practice of Taylorism is displaced to the periphery of the global economy, in free trade zones and maquiladora plants, while more flexible and decentralized labor regimes begin to prevail, requiring more skilled laborers to be capable of adapting to rapid changes, to assume new functions or work highly irregular hours. A change in the previous pyramidal figure (highly skilled elite laborers, intermediate managers and the base labor force) is produced among the labor force, becoming replaced by a form more closely resembling an hourglass. Here, the intermediate portion tends to diminish, while the technically specialized portion of the labor force grows. The impoverished portion of the population is particularly affected by these trends, producing a spiraling downward process of lack of work and educational training with laborers trapped in poorly remunerated jobs with the poorest working conditions.

In this context, the informal economy surges as an alternative for survival and it is estimated that three-quarters of all new jobs in Latin America are located in this sector. There, the requirements for training are low or non-existent, productive technologies and organization are usually primitive, and the small scale of production strongly favors a familial and labor-intensive logic within the units of production. Likewise on the increase are jobs that satisfy subcontracted portions of the production process as counterparts for the increasingly flexible organization of work in the formal sectors. This is a structural consequence of the loosely articulated links in the production process of transnational enterprises that have increasingly become more decentralized and flexible, favoring the creation of new forms of heavily exploited labor.

Together, these processes result in a growing fragmentation of workers as well a massive de-skilling process. This in turn scales back the impulse for creating new educational opportunities. Over and above the scarce access to employment and skills training, elements which make greater social participation possible, the overall access to health services likewise contracts. Neoliberal globalization demands the privatization of essential health services as part of its overall logic. In the past decade, many countries reduced their public investments in primary health care as a proportion of government expenditures.

AIDS, the raging epidemic of the new millennium, is a principal cause of death in Africa and places fourth among the most common causes of mortality worldwide.[15] At the end of 1999, there were 34.3 million men, women and children living with HIV and 18.8 million had already died of the AIDS illness. In 1999, there were 5.4 million new infections of the disease worldwide, 4 million of which occurred in sub-Saharan Africa and approximately a million others in Southern and South-eastern Asia. AIDS is largely an illness of the poor and its devastating effects have reduced the life expectancy of various African countries, 9 of which have estimated that their average life expectancy will have fallen 17 years by 2010, representing a return to levels prevalent during the 1960s. The unchecked obsession to obtain the highest possible profits on the part of large pharmaceutical monopolies has done much to prevent the effective control of this epidemic as well as those involving other infectious diseases.

Of all research and development conducted in the area of health, only 0.2% is dedicated to pneumonia, diarrhea-related diseases and tuberculosis which together constitute 18% of the total of worldwide diseases. Privatization results in struggles dedicated to even greater enforcement of intellectual property rights in the field of medicine, symbolizing the relationship between the neoliberal model and its devastating effects upon the sphere of health.

The capacity to manipulate genetic resources offers another vast terrain for exploring the ethical content of neoliberalism. Extraordinary advances in new technologies such as cloning, which in principle could lend to tremendous new therapeutic possibilities, likewise stirs concern about the utilization of such powerful resources if left unregulated by fundamental human values.

This third ethical aspect of neoliberalism, the fragmentation and annulment of collective demands, becomes completely inverted in the Cuban model. In the area of work, it can be seen that private employment is restricted to specific occupations and is treated differently than in the majority of other countries. The informal sector did appear as an important alternative source of employment during the economic crisis of the 1990s, symbolized by its legalization in 1994. This is largely because such work can often generate greater earnings that those occupations requiring higher skill levels in the formal sector. While the transformations which take place in this sector do not generally imply the dispersion of the labor force from other sectors, it is true that the presence of new social actors does substantially complicate the scenario of service delivery and normative means of popular participation.

In the area of health, the favorable indicators referred to earlier are in large part due to the integral system of primary attention that covers 99.1% of the population with a preventive character, erected atop an axis of community action. This system guarantees the coherence of health services to the population, reinforced with high levels of scientific research in this area, such that all new medications which achieve successful results are distributed to the population at the same time as they are first placed on the commercial market abroad.[16] This permits the system to control chronic illnesses and tends to reduce the costly periods of hospitalization which might otherwise be required.

Widely available prenatal care dedicated to the prevention of births with congenital illness (parents retain the decision to abort a pregnancy in the case of diagnosed congenital illness), mass campaigns for the early detection of breast and uterine cancer as well as for the detection and prevention of HIV/AIDS, and an overall system of prioritized care gives this sphere its integral character.

During the second half of the 1990s, Cuban society witnessed a growing process of collective participation, where youths in particular have played an important role. The mass movement which developed in protest of the detention of the young Cuban Elián González, kidnapped in 1999 by the Cuban-American Mafia in Miami, pulled together various generations of Cubans. For many of the youngest sectors of Cuban society, this signified their first incorporation into this kind of collective participation. Other mass protests such as those in condemnation of the Cuban Adjustment Law designed to incite illegal immigration to the United States as well as more recent protests in defense of Cuban sovereignty provide additional examples of this kind of collective mobilization.

The implementation of the schools for social workers as mentioned earlier represents another form of increased participation, particularly for young people who emerge from their communities with strong aspirations to serve their municipality. This becomes important precisely because through collective social participation, the revolutionary process had at the very beginning achieved its deepest roots. For the generations that followed after the revolutionary vanguard, its combatants of the Rebel Army and the clandestine struggle, ideological identification came first with the formation of the National Revolutionary Militias and later with the National Literacy Campaign. These events formed a kind of national school in the ideological affirmation of sovereignty, opening up the access to knowledge and popular culture. At the same time, they constituted mechanisms of human transformation, favoring different forms of conduct

274

and establishing new human values and aspirations for social justice. In this light, it is important to appreciate the importance for continuity of this social process which proposes the elevation of the standard of living as integral to its objectives for greater knowledge, health and social assistance.

Towards the end of the 1990s, the Cuban population participated in multiple forms of political participation with a social and human character, reviving a style of mass participation that had become significantly weakened during the worst years of the economic crisis. This process of participation had been present in other forms, for example, when sociologist Rafael Hernández refers to the electoral processes of 1993 and 1998 as a kind of people's plebiscite.[17] All of the process surrounding the revision of the Cuban Constitution and the modification and decentralization of voting broadened the possibilities of participation in Cuban civil society. It implied a deepening of the democratic character of the Cuban system, the generation of polemical debates, expectations that are as of yet not fully satisfied.

All of this has been conditioned still further by the "besieged fortress" character of the revolutionary process that has unfolded in the context of the persistent U.S. blockade. In the most recent period, the mass campaign in protest of the unjust convictions of five Cuban patriots who worked to obtain information against terrorism being planned against Cuba by counterrevolutionary elements based in Florida, resulted in their being declared Heroes of the Republic with the year 2002 being dedicated in honor of these prisoners. Unity continues providing the principal aspect of the defense of the country's sovereignty and it is this objective that prevails above all others. These are the social parameters that strengthen the popular currents of social integration in opposition to the social fragmentation otherwise associated with increasing globalization and neoliberalism.

Ideology As a Commodity and As a Tool for Struggle

An important aspect of the neoliberal model is the ideological machinery necessary to legitimate its rule. This machinery is in fact more powerful than ever. This is not only because it is supported by the utilization of modern and ever more powerful means of communications but also by the perversity of its message that seeks to homogenize people, forcing them to retreat from the advances achieved in the consciousness of human rights. The neoliberal model coherently produces a process of ethical impoverishment under the most intense and powerful ideological campaign of cultural restructuration ever witnessed in human history. It is a reconstituted message of consumerism trans-ported to all corners of the globe via the export of media products, videos and commercial advertisement. The most important export industry of the United States is not arms or airplanes, but rather movies and videos. These messages which assault the cultural identity of entire peoples, seeks to homogenize not only behavior but also the dreams and aspirations of people, transmitting the ethical content of neoliberalism across all corners of the world. Not only do narrow and specific values become transformed into absolutes, but indeed the very worst aspects of humankind become turned into human "virtues": intoler-ance, violence, discrimination based on gender, race and social class, individu-alism and selfishness. Perhaps one of the factors that makes possible this ideological propagation is the so-called "crisis of paradigms" and the relative weakening of the body of social theory of development and its service as a strategic arm for popular struggles.

In diverse ways and thousands of times over, portrayed as if it were some-how a natural and irreversible phenomenon, the mass media presents a sweet-ened world of profound social inequality, framed against a backdrop of mass consumption that has always presented itself with exaggerated claims of acces-sibility. The aim is to drown out the highest expressions of human spirituality and the values of autochthonous cultures.

The impact of radio, television and Internet has resulted in an increasing deadening of people's consciousness. In the United States, for example, one study showed that young boys and girls have seen an average of 8 thousand murders and 100 thousand cases of other types of violence depicted on televi-sion before entering into the secondary level of education,[18] something which most certainly might help to explain the alarming levels of violence which tran-spires in that country's schools. As far as Internet use goes, the discriminatory tendencies are fairly easy to appreciate. According to the UNDP, the 20% rich-est portion of the world's population enjoys a 93% rate of access while the poorest 20% displays a 0.2% level of access.[19]

Perhaps it is with regard to this aspect of ideological and cultural transmis-sion of values that the Cuban social project displays its greatest contrast with the neoliberal model. Among the most genuine values of Socialism in Cuban society are those which ratify the solidarity among people. Over the final years of the 1990s, the system of socialist values became counter-posed by those en-gendered by the widening scope of market practices, i.e., competitiveness, con-sumerism, individualism, and selfishness. However, important experiences have tended to revitalize the values engendered by the Cuban socialist project.

For example, the Latin American School of Medical Sciences which is dedicated to the training of young physicians from all over Latin America who come to study through grants awarded by the Cuban Government has been a way of projecting Cuban solidarity throughout the region. Those students who come to study have made the commitment to return to their respective countries and practice medicine in the most remote and challenging zones. This is part of a larger tradition where Cuban physicians practice and teach medicine in other countries with a similar end in mind.

These positive cultural elements are further strengthened by the articulation of Cuban pop culture, elements that ratify Cuban identity through a multiplicity of compositions, particularly in music. A phenomenon of crucial importance is the so-called "Battle of Ideas" which has reigned over the Cuban political process during the second half of the 1990s. The cultural campaign has achieved great relevance as one of the most important pillars in this ideological process.

Another concrete expression of this popular culture can be found in the "Universidad para todos" [University for All] program. This program transmits specialized instruction in a wide variety of subjects including Art, Literary Appreciation, History, Languages (French, English, Spanish, Portuguese and Italian), Introduction to Scientific Knowledge, Ecology, Geography, Music, and Plastic Arts. The really amazing aspect of this program of broadcasted course instruction in sophisticated subjects has been the tremendous popular response it has enjoyed. This mass program has awakened a strong social demand for greater knowledge on the part of a population with an already high educational level (average of ninth grade level). The support materials for these classes that consist of simple pamphlets reproduced at very low prices are constantly sold out.

Yet another manifestation of this policy is the acquisition by the Cuban Government of thousands of Chinese-made, color televisions which are being sold to the population in Cuban pesos in conjunction with various credit and interest-free payment schemes. Also established has been a system of collective discussion at the workplace level and at the community level of the CDRs (Committees for the Defense of the Revolution) so as to select those individuals who deserve priority for acquiring these television sets. In a similar manner, the computer equipment destined for schools at all levels (including the primary schools) are being prioritized as is the progressive expansion of Internet access in centers of higher education and research.

In this sphere, it is also worthy to mention the presence of an important trend in the decentralization of organization and in the growth of pluralism in Cuban civil society. In 1998, for example, the Pope was invited to visit Cuba and a process unfolded which made possible the widespread presentation of

Catholic ideas and greater interaction with the Cuban people. Other measures have attempted to contain the negative effects associated with the rapid growth of tourism alongside of various material shortages, for example, through changes in the Penal Code which toughened the policies towards certain crimes such as the trafficking of persons, money laundering and pimping.

The coherence of the ideas in the practice of the Cuban revolutionary project is alive and well, rooted in the integration of permanent Cuban values of social justice, those that Cintio Vitier garnered from Cuban thought as "Sun of the Moral World." It is alive in the ideas of José Martí who exhorted "I cast my lot with the poor of the Earth" and who felt "struck on his own cheek by a blow to the cheek felt by any person." It is the ethical thought of Martí, rooted in the principles of independence and spiritual autonomy, that found its expression in his prophetic thought: "they cannot honorably believe that excessive individualism, the worship of wealth, and the prolonged jubilation of a terribly victory can be preparing the United States for becoming a nation which typifies freedom."[20] Che Guevara also expressed this kind of spirit in his revolutionary thought and action, governed by a triad of indissoluble ethical principles: social justice, dignity and solidarity.

Neoliberal globalization strengthens the formation and dissemination of this anthropological model that nurtures inequality, exclusion and discrimination. This notwithstanding, the neoliberal project is showing definite signs of exhaustion through its ever more frequent crises that have shaken the entire global system (stagnation in Japan, economic recession in the United States, economic meltdown in Argentina and elsewhere, etc.). The model likewise exhibits deep moral and ethical fissures as evidenced by the continuing string of revelations seen around the world involving unprecedented corruption. This is something which in my view amply demonstrates its true moral character of operation as compared to its lofty official discourse.

This hegemonic model does not reign with impunity. In the face of its aggression, there is another ethical project that has engaged it in sharp opposition, one which values equality, the respect of human dignity and solidarity. This project is alive in the clamor for social justice being mounted by indigenous peoples throughout the region. In the Zapatista movement where the reaffirmation of people's cultural identity and the demand for women's participation can be heard loud and clear, the clear sounds of resistance are ringing out. In 1994, the Zapatista Army for National Liberation (EZLN) threw out the gauntlet when it declared "we aren't asking for handouts or presents, we ask for the right to live in dignity as human beings like our ancient fathers and grandfathers, that is, with equality and justice."[21]

The ethical project of equality is also alive in the struggles of the landless in Brazil and in the demands of the Mothers of the Plaza de Mayo in Argentina. On a daily basis, the social movements of women, environmental rights groups, and the demands of those who oppose all forms of discrimination and exclusion can be heard around the world in a growing global resistance. It has been felt in the streets of Seattle, Prague, Quebec, Miami and elsewhere.

My preceding reflections have likewise made it clear that this ethical project is alive and well in the practice of Cuban internationalist physicians, in the offer that President Fidel Castro made to contribute to the health of African peoples and to the people of Haiti. It is alive in the Cuban solidarity project of the Latin American School of Medical Sciences. In short, it is alive and present in the permanent struggle of the Cuban people in defense of its sovereignty and its revolutionary principles.

Notes

1. UNFPA, *Vivir juntos en mundos separados* [Living Together in Separate Worlds]. (The full facts of publication of all the sources are found in the Bibliography, at the end of the essay. *Ed.*)

2. UNDP, *Informe sobre el desarrollo humano* [Report on Human Development], 3.

3. Osvaldo Martínez, *¿Sabrá el Banco Mundial lo que es un pobre?* [Does the World Bank Know What a Poor Person Is?].

4. Ibid.

5. Elena Díaz and José Bell, "Situación socioeconómica de América Latina en los noventa. ¿Otra década perdida?" [Socioeconomic Situation of Latin America in the 1990s. Another Lost Decade?].

6. Aurelio Alonso, "La sociedad cubana en los años noventa y los retos del comienzo del nuevo siglo" [Cuban Society during the 1990s and Challenges at the Beginning of the New Century], 7.

7. Juan Valdés, "El sistema político cubano de los años noventa, continuidad y cambio en Cuba construyendo el futuro" [The Cuban Political System of the 1990s, Continuity and Change in Building Cuba's Future], in *Cuba construyendo el futuro* [Cuba Building Future].

8. Fidel Castro, "Televised presentation by Commander in Chief Fidel Castro Ruz, President of the Republic of Cuba, on the present international situation, the economic and world crisis and its impact on Cuba. Havana, November 2, 2001."

9. Manuel Monereo and J. Valdés Paz, "Mundialización, reestructuración productiva y reorganización del poder a nivel internacional" [Globalization, Productive Restructuration and the Reorganization of Power at the International Level], 9.

10. ECLAC, *Panorama social de América Latina 1999-2000*, 6.

11. Ibid., 2.

12. Francisco Alburquerque, *Cambio tecnológico, reestructuración productiva y estrategia de desarrollo* [Technological Change, Productive Reorganization and Development Strategy].

13. ECLAC, op. cit.

14. Elena Díaz, "Desafíos de la mujer cubana ante el nuevo milenio" [Challenges of the Cuban Woman Facing the New Millennium], in *La mujer en la sociedad cubana, desafíos ante el nuevo milenio. Análisis de coyuntura* [Woman in Cuban Society, Challenges Facing the New Millennium. Conjucture Analysis].

15. UNFPA, op. cit., 14.

16. Marina Majoli, "Ciencia, tecnología y desarrollo. La industria biotecnológica cubana. Una aproximación" [Science, Technology and Development. Understanding the Cuban Biotechnology Industry].

17. Rafael Hernández. *Mirar a Cuba. Ensayos sobre cultura y sociedad civil* [Looking at Cuba: Essays on Cultura and Civil Society].

18. T. Van Osch, "Aspectos de género en el proceso de globalización" [Gender Aspects in the Globalization Process], in *Nuevos enfoques económicos* [New Economic Approaches], 15.

19. UNDP, op. cit., 2

20. Cintio Vitier, *Ese sol del mundo moral* [That Sun of the Moral World], 98.

21. Zapatista Army for Nacional Liberation, *Documentos y comunidades* [Documents and Communities], 179.

Bibliography

ALBURQUERQUE, FRANCISCO. Cambio tecnológico, reestructuración productiva y estrategia de desarrollo. Santiago de Chile: ECLAC, 1995.

ALONSO, AURELIO. "La sociedad cubana en los años noventa y los retos del comienzo del nuevo siglo." In *Iglesia, cultura y sociedad en la Cuba de hoy.* Havana: Centro de Estudios Arquidiocesanos de La Habana, Ediciones Vivarium, 2002.

CASTRO, FIDEL. "Televised presentation by Commander in Chief Fidel Castro Ruz, President of the Republic of Cuba, on the present international situation, the economic and world crisis and its impact on Cuba. Havana, November 2, 2001." Cuba.cu. http://www.cuba.cu/gobierno/discursos/2001/ing/f021101i.html. Accessed October 14, 2004.

DÍAZ, ELENA. "Desafíos de la mujer cubana ante el nuevo milenio." *Análisis de coyuntura* journal, no. 11 (December 2000).

DÍAZ, ELENA and JOSÉ BELL LARA. "Situación socioeconómica de América Latina en los noventa. ¿Otra década perdida?" FLACSO, University of Havana, 2001. Typescript.

ECLAC. *Panorama social de América Latina 1999-2000.* Santiago de Chile: ECLAC, 2000.

FERRARI, SERGIO. "Un año después de Seattle." *América Latina en movimiento* journal (Quito), no. 324 (2000).

HERNÁNDEZ, RAFAEL. *Mirar a Cuba. Ensayos sobre cultura y sociedad civil.* Havana: Editorial Letras Cubanas, 1999.

MAJOLI, MARINA. "Ciencia, tecnología y desarrollo social. La industria biotecnológica cubana: una aproximación." Ph.D. diss., University of Havana, 1999.

MARTÍNEZ, OSVALDO. *¿Sabrá el Banco Mundial lo que es un pobre?* Havana: Asociación Nacional de Economistas de Cuba (ANEC), 2001.

MONEREO, MANUEL and J. VALDÉS PAZ. "Mundialización, reestructuración productiva y reorganización del poder a nivel internacional." Paper presented at the Internacional Seminar Mundialization and Neoliberalism: The Strategy of the Left, Havana, July 7-10, 1998.

UNDP. *Informe sobre el desarrollo humano.* Madrid: Ediciones Mundiprensa, 1999.

UNFPA. *Vivir juntos en mundos separados.* New York: UNFPA, 2000.

UNRISD. *Estado de desorden: los efectos sociales de la globalización.* Geneva: UNRISD, 1996.

VALDÉS, JUAN. "El sistema político cubano de los años noventa, continuidad y cambio." In *Cuba construyendo el futuro.* Madrid: El Viejo Topo, 2000.

VAN OSCH, T. "Aspectos de género en el proceso de globalización." In *Nuevos enfoques económicos*. Poscae, Tegucigalpa: Universidad Nacional Autónoma de Honduras, 1995.

VITIER, CINTIO. *Ese sol del mundo moral*. Havana: Ediciones Unión, 2002.

ZAPATISTA ARMY FOR NACIONAL LIBERATION. *Documentos y comunidades*. Mexico City: Ediciones ERA, 1995.

Looking to the Future

José Bell Lara
Richard A. Dello Buono

José Bell Lara

Ph.D. in Philosophy. A sociologist, he is senior researcher in the FLACSO-Cuba Program and professor at the University of Havana. He has conducted various studies concerning development, social change and social policies in Cuba and Latin America. His numerous publications include *Globalization and the Cuban Revolution* and he was coordinator of *Cuba in the 1990s*.

Richard A. Dello Buono

Ph.D. in Social Economy and Social Policy. A sociology professor at Dominican University, his research areas include comparative social problems and Caribbean and Latin American studies. He is an invited professor at the University of Havana and was previously visiting professor at the National University of Colombia and the University of Panama.

Can Cuba maintain its social project in the globalized world of the 21st century? The response to this, in our opinion, hinges on the ability of the Cuban Revolution not only to maintain the political support of the majority of Cubans but also to carve out a path to development that guarantees the population's quality of life in a sustainable manner. The first step in this struggle for development implies a change in the country's insertion in the international economy.

In this final note, we propose to summarize the broad potential that Cuban society has for achieving a competitive position in the world economy along with all of the challenges which that implies. The first element in this synoptic argument is the fact that the Revolution proved capable of overcoming the worst of its crisis in the 1990s and did so while maintaining the social project of the Revolution. The essays presented earlier have explored many of the principal areas of this process and together, they describe the new circumstances in which Cuba must find its way.

We believe that this collection of studies has demonstrably reaffirmed that the overarching thrust of the policies enacted to confront the crisis articulated a logic which defends the interests of the majority, this notwithstanding the tensions and contradictions that they generated. It is this logic which has contributed in a variety of ways to maintaining a social accumulation in favor of Socialism:

FIRST: By containing the abrupt decline of the economy and then organizing a slow process of economic recovery which included a sustained growth of the Gross Domestic Product, reducing excess liquidity in the monetary system, bringing the budget deficit under control and witnessing a relative re-valuation of the Cuban peso as a result. At the same time, there has been a parallel process of technological reconversion, a modernization of enterprise management, and last, but not least, a reinsertion of the economy into the new global order. The latter has been accomplished despite all of the best efforts of the United States to isolate the island and wage an economic war of destabilization.

SECOND: By containing the deterioration of the population's standard of living, registering a modest improvement albeit with substantial tensions and the appearance of inequalities that did not previously exist. These negative aspects were the product of some of the necessary measures taken to overcome the economic crisis and they have in turn become the impetus for the development of a creative social policy designed to mitigate the impact on social development.

THIRD: By accomplishing all of the above without the application of neoliberal policies, or more precisely, by having found the formulas for not applying them, this achievement is something which in our judgment is of key importance for the future of the Revolution. Put simply, it constitutes the principal means of demonstrating the possibility of an alternative path to development in the context of increasing globalization.

In summary, Cuba has indeed carved out a space for survival in the global economy, although the situation is quite complex. There is no question that the economic measures that were adopted to detain the crisis contain the elements of serious challenges for the Cuban revolutionary project. As most of the studies in this book have demonstrated, some important and constituent parts of social accumulation have been eroded over the protracted period of crisis. But in the final analysis, the socialist paradigm remains in place in Cuba.

Cuba maintains the most important prerequisite for defending its project, namely, political power backed by popular participation. Cuba's political system proved capable of withstanding what amounted to the worst crisis since the triumph of the Revolution. The country has continuously confronted the pressures that are being generated both structurally by the process of capitalist globalization as well as geopolitically by the aggressive campaigns being waged by the United States in seeking to eliminate all forms of resistance to its global hegemony.

Capitalist globalization in its neoliberal form is not a uniform process nor is it free of contradictions. Rather, it is a social configuration that maintains all of the old contradictions while new ones continue to emerge. The contradictions between North and South persist as do the contradictions between the hegemonic economic powers of the global system as well as within each bloc and likewise between the countries of the South and within the interior of each.[1]

Cuba has demonstrated that a revolution in power has the potential to attenuate the negative tendencies of global capitalism as well as to exploit the contradictions within the system. In the area of external affairs, for example, a rapid and more balanced reconstitution of its portfolio of relations with various regions of the world has helped to diversify what was once a very different situation. By the end of the 1980s, the CMEA countries accounted for more than 80% of our external commerce. Now Cuba maintains a more proportionate distribution of relations across Europe, Latin America and other areas.

Alongside of this and forming part of the process is Cuba's insertion into diverse schemes of integration and regional blocs both in the North as well as in the South. By the nature and tendency of such processes, Cuba is in a position to maintain growing economic relations with each of them and with the constituent countries of these economic groupings.[2] Further illustrations of this can include the economic ties which the island has developed and maintained with Europe, MERCOSUR and CARICOM. Despite even the high profile bloc created by NAFTA, Cuba maintains sustained economic relations with Canada and Mexico, the U.S. blockade notwithstanding.

By virtue of the control it maintains over the national economy, the Cuban State retains the capacity to establish relations with global capital in accordance with Cuban national interests. Within this basic framework, it can reach agreements with elements or certain fractions of transnational capital in the form of direct foreign investments (DFI) without placing the future of the country up for sale.

The DFIs in Cuba operate in large part through Economic Associations with Foreign Capital (EAFC) in which the Cuban State maintains a percentage of the enterprise. The regulatory framework of these associations, Law No. 77 of 1995 permits enterprises with up to 100% foreign capital as deemed appropriate by the state. The development of these links with foreign capital has been rapid, with 50 EAFCs existing in 1990 while 374 were in existence at the close of 1999.

In some economic activities, the role played by joint ventures is quite significant, constituting 100% in oil exploration, protective lubricants, telephone service, soaps and perfumes, rum exports, while having a large part in citric fruits, nickel, and cement. The industrial sector at 37% and tourism with 18% collectively have the highest number of joint ventures.[3]

In spite of the economic war being waged by the United States, there is a tendency towards growth in the magnitude of Direct Foreign Investment in Cuba. We calculate that more than half of the joint ventures have been formed after the promulgation of the Helms-Burton Act. On the other hand, we should also point out that Cuba has established Direct Foreign Investment in capitalist countries as a means of gaining market access and capital and this also creates opportunities for Cuban managers to gain experience with the world of capital. Cuba now operates more than 100 entities as joint ventures or company branches in foreign countries.[4]

Social accumulation, we should remember, implies economic accumulation proper and of those aspects which have the most to do with the development of the human being: educational levels, standards of health, engendering new values, and various forms of participation in everyday political life. This social accumulation has given Cuba the potential associated with an extraordinary human capital, composed of thousands of scientists and technicians that form a valuable reserve for promoting development in technologically advanced areas. Perhaps it would be appropriate here to highlight this important aspect.

Cuba has 1.8 scientists for every 1000 inhabitants, one of the highest rates on the planet, with some 600,000 university graduates and 1 out of every 5 inhabitants of all ages matriculated at any given time in the national educational system. The system of higher education includes 52 centers in which 21,600 professors are employed. Scientific activity is developed all across the country and there exist research institutions in every province.[5]

This mass training system is accompanied by a systematic campaign designed to elevate the cultural and scientific level of the population by way of a series of programs that include the mass media. There exist two educational channels that are transmitted throughout the nation. This includes the "Universidad para todos" [University for All] program that broadcasts university level courses oriented towards the general population. Another example would be the instructional audiovisual program that reinforces the teaching activities in the schools. To these human resources we can add the material and organizational base of technical support which includes laboratories, production plants and more than 200 scientific research centers.

The scientific activities of the country are presided over by the Ministry of Science, Technology and Environment (CITMA) which is the core institution of a system of scientific and technological innovation composed of a "network of relations involving state as well as mixed and private entities, local and foreign, whose activities and interactions generate, import, modify and disseminate new technologies."[6] The system includes 218 centers, of which 115 are important research institutes while the remaining are research and development complexes. In Cuba, more than 64,000 workers are professionally engaged in science and technology, of which 52% are women. This amounts to a proportion of 13.4 per 1000 inhabitants economically engaged in this sphere. In 2001, there were 3087 active projects of research, development and innovation underway throughout the island.[7]

The system is not exclusively dedicated to the creation of new products and productive processes, but is also involved in organizational aspects and with the ways in which different entities relate to each other and to the market. Participation is an essential component of this alternative project of development and Cuba has sought out ways to articulate the mass character of scientific development with the search for a culture of innovation. One mechanism involved with this is the National Forum of Science and Technology, an annual event where hundreds of thousands of workers, technicians, professionals and scientists from the local on up to the national level come together with the aim of stimulating and socializing innovation. The National Association of Inventors and Innovators (ANIR) is close to 600,000 members and their work is centered on solving production problems.[8]

Of particular interest are the organizational forms that have been created in the Cuban science and production complexes known as the Scientific Poles. These are entities of coordination and cooperation that exist among the research and production centers, displaying a spatial distribution designed to create determined synergies between them. In addition, there is the development of the Research-Production Centers, i.e., institutions which not only research but which also have at their disposal the infrastructure necessary for reaching industrial level production of products emerging out of their research.

We observe that in the operation of these kinds of centers, there is an ongoing, small scale application of the principle of connection/disconnection. In our judgment, the centers display a contradictory mode of operation in that on the one hand, they seek to provide answers to the requirements of the health system where the market and the law of value are not the guiding logic, while on the other hand, they seek to achieve the capability of operating as internationally competitive enterprises. Moreover, these centers are oriented towards the creation and application of their own technologies rather than just being consumers and distributors of imported technologies.[9] In this regard, they have had notable results in the area of creating new products, processes and medications, such as:

- The first and only vaccination in the world against Group B meningitis, so successful that by mid-1999, the U.S. Department of Treasury approved a license for the English-U.S. firm SmithKline to form a joint venture with the Finlay Institute in Havana so as to commercialize the Cuban vaccine.
- A vaccination against the Hepatitis B disease (Herber-biovac HB) which eliminates the contagion risk against any infective agent originating from human blood.
- Hebermin, a skin tissue healing factor which not only promotes more rapid healing but increases the quality and pigmentation of human skin.

Perhaps we could contextualize this by saying that the third generation of global biotechnology has generated around 36 significant products for the international market, and Cuba has 13 of them, two of them with inventor's patents. Also, 24 bio-pharmaceutical products and vaccinations have been developed, 49 advanced genetic pharmaceuticals, 5 products dedicated to the treatment of AIDS and 15 new medical apparatuses and 24 diagnostic systems have been developed, including the SUMA, the AUDIX, the NEURONICA, and the equipment for Cerebral Electromagnetic Tomography. All of this serves as an indicator of the country's capacity to compete on this terrain. Cuba possesses an intellectual property base composed of more than 150 objects of investment and more than 500 patents registered abroad, with 4 of these having won medals from the World Organization of Intellectual Property.[10]

Globalization has created a world where information technologies increasingly permeate all of its structures and processes, and the use of such technologies becomes ever more intertwined with economic growth. As part of a process of improving the country's global competitiveness, Cuba's strategy for the informatization has contemplated the following objectives: the creation of an informational and informatic culture, the utilization of information technologies in all sectors of social life and the stimulation of information industries.[11] The strategy envisions the development of resources and informational services as an integral part of national development policy. Also notable was the creation of the University of Informational Sciences that began to operate in the 2003-2004 academic year, with more than 4000 students from all across the country enrolled.[12] Some concrete results in this area can already be observed, such as the incorporation of Cuba into the networks of electronic commerce through virtual shopping sites.[13]

These observations can simply help us to perceive Cuba's potential with respect to the cutting-edge branches of the global economy. While the relative presence of high-tech goods and services remain weak in the overall structures of exports as of yet, not the least of which is because these sectors are highly monopolized markets that are quite difficult to penetrate. Yet, it seems clear to us that the process of development is a slow and complex endeavor that cannot be based solely on high tech, state of the art sectors, as promising as they are, nor upon any other specific branch for that matter.

The struggle against underdevelopment is an integral process and for that reason, over and above the active pursuit of technological development, the traditional branches of production must be maintained and developed. This is particularly true in areas where there is an accumulated productive experience, with historically formed articulations within the national economy and ample knowledge of its markets. There must be an aggressive policy of exports in multiple directions, including products and services that have specific qualities which permit their insertion into lucrative niches in the global economy. Together, these policies yield an approach that can be thought of as the process of walking on two legs: one of development and the other of underdevelopment.

Among those transformations being carried out in the Cuban economy over recent years, some rather interesting elements can be found. In the first place, there is the prioritization of development in the tourist sector which has become converted into the leading sector of the economy, generating around 30% of goods and services exports and inducing earnings in other branches of the economy amounting to around 800 million dollars.[14]

Important efforts can likewise be observed in the area of non-traditional exports. These would include, for example:

- Exports of intellectual services which display a high aggregate value (physicians, professors, technicians, and others who become temporarily engaged in posts being contracted by other countries).
- Exports of goods and services with a cultural content (art, music and others).
- Development of specialized forms of tourism that have specific niche demands (ecological, facilities for scientific events, etc).
- Varieties of agro-exports that have a higher aggregate value because of their exceptional characteristics and which are directed to specific segments of the global market such as organically produced agricultural products or certain designer varieties of tobacco.
- Development of health tourism (which in the Cuban case builds upon one of its most competitive areas).

An economy cannot be globally competitive if the society in its totality does not reach certain determinant qualities. In the Cuban case, the development of competitiveness has to be accomplished by putting limits upon the rationality that prevails in the world economy, being a capitalist one. In other words, the challenge is to achieve a globally competitive society and to simultaneously defend the revolutionary project.

From this advantage point, we can visualize a Cuban policy which recognizes the fact that the search for global competitiveness does not nullify and certainly does not replace the search for a new way of life. This explains the prominent role that ideology plays in Cuban society and the various national campaigns that have been carried out with the aim of maintaining and promoting the socialist values underpinning the revolutionary project. The campaign known as the "Battle of Ideas" plays a central role at present in Cuba and it reminds us that a famous French philosopher once stated that ideology is the cement of society.

From the analysis of all of these elements, it can be deduced that Cuba possesses a competitive potential in cutting edge branches of the global economy and is currently immersed in a process of creating the platform by which it can enhance its socialist path to development. In theory, Cuba's capacity for a competitive insertion would be assured given its available human capital and its capacity to optimally articulate the process of generating, transferring, mobilizing and utilizing knowledge. In practice, however, the real existing global context introduces other elements such as the monopolization of the circuits of commercialization by transnational enterprises, extra-economic barriers to trade, and the diverse forms of U.S. aggression.

This vision of the totality of the problem nonetheless permits us to affirm our long-term perspective that the Cuban Revolution will continue moving forward in the 21st century, this notwithstanding the short term challenges which will require serious attention, including the aggressive policy put forward by the United States. The extreme rightwing fundamentalism driving the Bush administration produced an extremely aggressive campaign against Cuba, keeping the window open for an eventual justification of a military operation against the island. Wrapped up in the ideological cellophane of a "struggle for democracy," the administration created the so-called "Commission for Assistance to a Free Cuba" towards the end of 2003, co-presided by the Secretary of State Colin Powel and then Secretary of Housing and Urban Development Mel Martínez. The idea behind the "Commission" was to create a series of recommendations, some public, others secret, that could "hasten" the overthrow of the Revolution.

The Bush administration initiated new measures in 2004 that would further restrict the contact between Cuban émigrés that reside in the United States and their families on the island. This meant that they would only be allowed to visit once every three years and spend only a very limited amount of money in Cuba, with their ability to send remittances to their family likewise limited. Meanwhile, Washington has dedicated tens of millions of dollars to support domestic subversion, further widen the field of operations geared towards invading Cuba's radio and television airwaves, and a concerted international effort to turn international opinion against the Cuban Government. These measures were all added on top of the prior existing economic blockade against Cuba, the pressures mounted against other countries engaged in business in Cuba, the continuing obstacles imposed on transportation and communications, and longstanding prohibition of ordinary U.S. citizens from visiting the island. More than just voicing the intention to impose by force what Washington calls a "political transition" in Cuba, the real objective is one of recolonization, the conversion of the island into a U.S. protectorate like in the days of the Platt Amendment.

Cuba is the only political process in the hemisphere that has managed to resist and overcome for more than forty-five years, the aggressive policies of ten different U.S. administrations. For that reason, we can speak of the "Cuba Syndrome" which represents a thorn in the side of the ruling class of the United States. Having spared no expense, their objective has not been realized and the Cuban Revolution continues to represent the haunting presence of an alternative to neoliberalism. The consistent response to all of the aggression over the year has clearly demonstrated that the Revolution remains firmly rooted in its people, making its internal dynamic irreversible. It is for this reason that the Bush administration has placed its sights more on a solution by force. A U.S. invasion will confront a resistance that will make an occupation of the country unsustainable. The neutralization of the real prospects of a U.S. military aggression is sa paramount issue for Cubans and for the international movement in solidarity with the island.

Although the decisive elements for maintaining the Cuban social project are internal ones, the Cuban Revolution maintains a high international profile in which it combines the continuity of its principles with a substantial dose of political realism. Cuba maintains relations with 171 countries and maintains a systematic policy of dialogue, at times a complicated process, with states and governments of Latin America and the Third World, always in defense of the interests of the underdeveloped countries. It participates in the Movement of the Non-Aligned Countries, the Group of 77, and it seeks the best possible interactions with distinct schemes of integration and the international forums that exist in Latin America and the Caribbean as well as in the Third World in general. As such, its participation in international organisms has had a strong projection in Third World causes. Alongside of this, it maintains relations of cooperation and solidarity with the popular and revolutionary movements around the world.

The international prestige of Cuba is evidenced by the high number of posts that the country has been elected to in international forums, for example, in the Presidency of the Movement of the Non-Aligned Countries and as a member of the UN Security Council. Cuba has likewise played host to numerous international events such as the 9th Ibero-American Summit and the South Summit. In summary, the Cuban Revolution maintains a high profile in the 21st century, inserted in the global framework with a sense of permanence.

Notes

1. Silvio Baró, *Globalización y desarrollo mundial* [Globalization and World Development], 32. (The full facts of publication of all the sources are found in the Bibliography, at the end of the essay. *Ed.)*

2. Eugenio Espinosa, "Globalización solidaria y procesos de integración" [Solidarity in Globalization and Processes of Integration], 9.

3. E. Pérez, *La evolución económica de Cuba: una valoración en América Latina y el Caribe. Realidades sociopolíticas e identidad cultural* [The Economic Evolution in Cuba: An Appraisal in Latin America and the Caribbean. Sociopolitical Realities and Cultural Identity].

4. E. Pérez, "Inversión extranjera directa en Cuba" [Direct Foreign Investment in Cuba], 27.

5. Silvia Martínez, *Cuba Beyond Our Dreams.*

6. E. García, "El sistema de ciencia e innovación. Conceptos, antecedentes y perspectivas" [Science and Innovation System. Concepts, Antecedents and Prospects], in *Análisis de Coyuntura* journal, year 2, no. 7, 19.

7. Silvia Martínez, *Cuba Beyond Our Dreams,* 123.

8. Ibid., 126.

9. Marina Majoli, "Ciencia, tecnología y desarrollo social. La industria biotecnológica cubana: una aproximación" [Science, Technology and Social Development. Understanding the Cuban Biotechnology Industry], 9.

10. Silvia Martínez, op. cit.

11. A. Olivé, "La información en el desarrollo nacional: desafío y alternativa para las economías emergentes" [Information in National Development: Challenge and Alternative for the Emerging Economies], in *Análisis de Coyuntura* journal, year 2, no. 3.

12. MINREX, "Informe del Ministerio de Relaciones Exteriores de Cuba. Programa de informatización de la sociedad cubana" [Report of the Cuban Ministry of Foreign Affairs. Program of Informatization of the Cuban Society].

13. M. Gil and Fernández, "Evolución internacional del comercio electrónico y situación actual de Cuba" [Internacional Evolution of the Electronic Trade and its Current Situation in Cuba], in *Análisis de Coyuntura* journal, year 2, no. 6.

14. H. Marquetti, "¿Por qué el turismo constituye la locomotora de la economía?" [Why Is Tourism the Locomotive of the Economy?].

Bibliography

Baró Herrera, Silvio. *Globalización y desarrollo mundial.* Havana: Editorial de Ciencias Sociales, 1998.

Espina, Mayra. "Panorama de los efectos de la reforma sobre la estructura social cubana: grupos tradicionales y emergentes." Paper presented at the 21st LASA International Congress, Chicago, 1998.

Espinosa, Eugenio. "Globalización solidaria y procesos de integración." *Análisis de Coyuntura* journal, year 2, no. 9 (October 1998).

García, E. "El sistema de ciencia e innovación. Conceptos, antecedentes y perspectivas." *Análisis de Coyuntura* journal, year 2, no. 7 (March 1998).

Gil, Melchor and Juan Fernández. "Evolución internacional del comercio electrónico y situación actual de Cuba." *Análisis de Coyuntura* journal, year 2, no. 6 (October 1998).

Majoli, Marina. "Ciencia, tecnología y desarrollo social. La industria biotecnológica cubana: una aproximación." Ph.D. diss., University of Havana, 1999.

Marquetti, H. ¿Por qué el turismo constituye la locomotora de la economía? *World Data Research Centre.* http://www.wdrc.info. Accessed April 15, 2002.

Martínez Puentes, Silvia. *Cuba Beyond Our Dreams.* Havana: Editorial José Martí, in press.

MINREX. "Informe del Ministerio de Relaciones Exteriores de Cuba. Programa de informatización de la sociedad cubana." *Rebelión,* March 1, 2004. http://www.rebelion.org/cuba/040301informat.htm. Accessed September 15, 2004.

National Office of Statistics. *Cuba en cifras, 1999.* Havana: n.p., 2000.

Olivé, A. "La información en el desarrollo nacional: desafío y alternativa para las economías emergentes." *Análisis de Coyuntura* journal, year 2, no. 3 (1998).

Pérez, E. *La evolución económica de Cuba: una valoración en América Latina y el Caribe. Realidades sociopolíticas e identidad cultural.* El Salvador: Ediciones Heinrich Boll, 2002.

———. "Inversión extranjera directa en Cuba." Ph.D. diss., University of Havana, 1998.